MW01620990

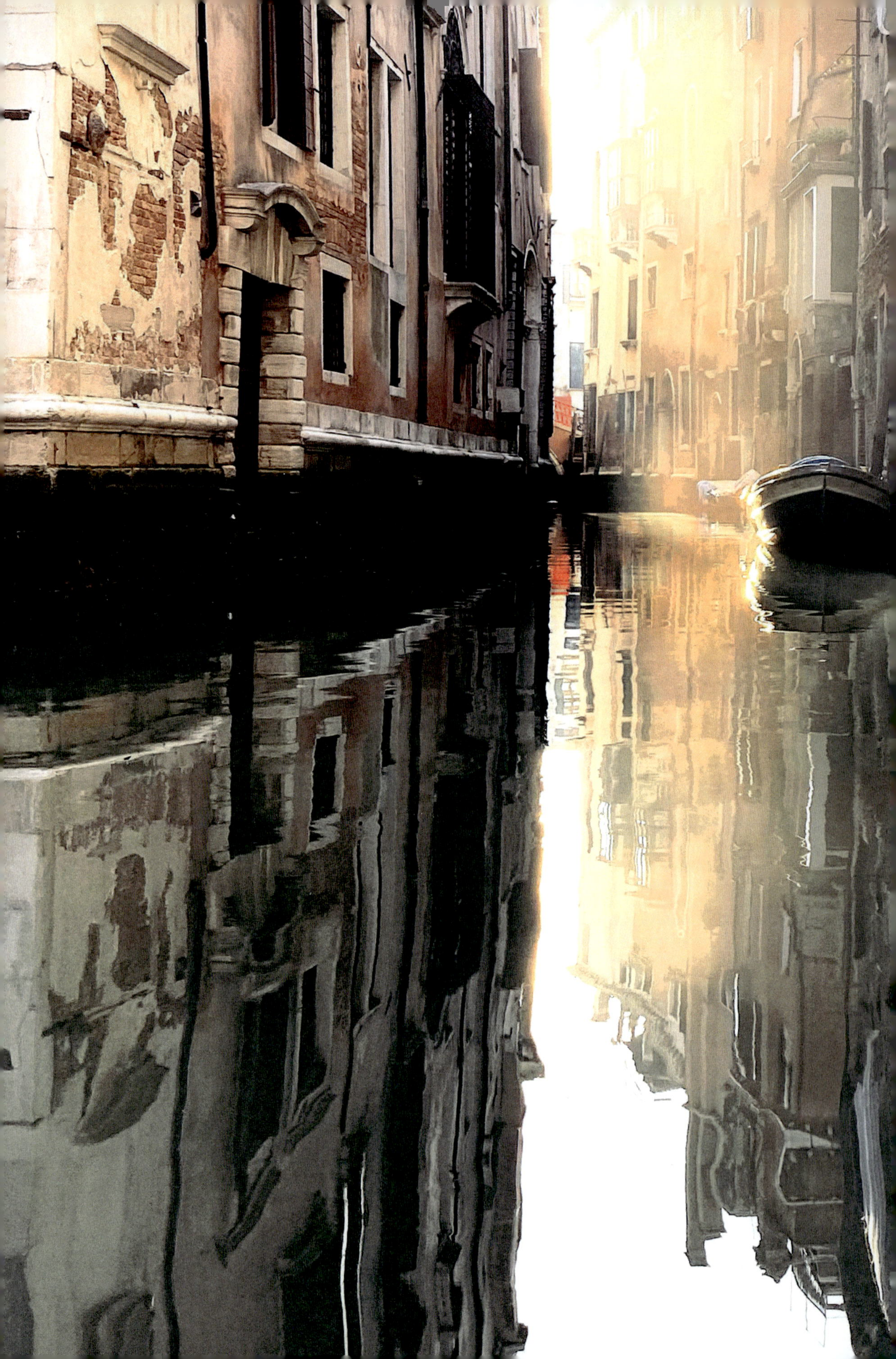

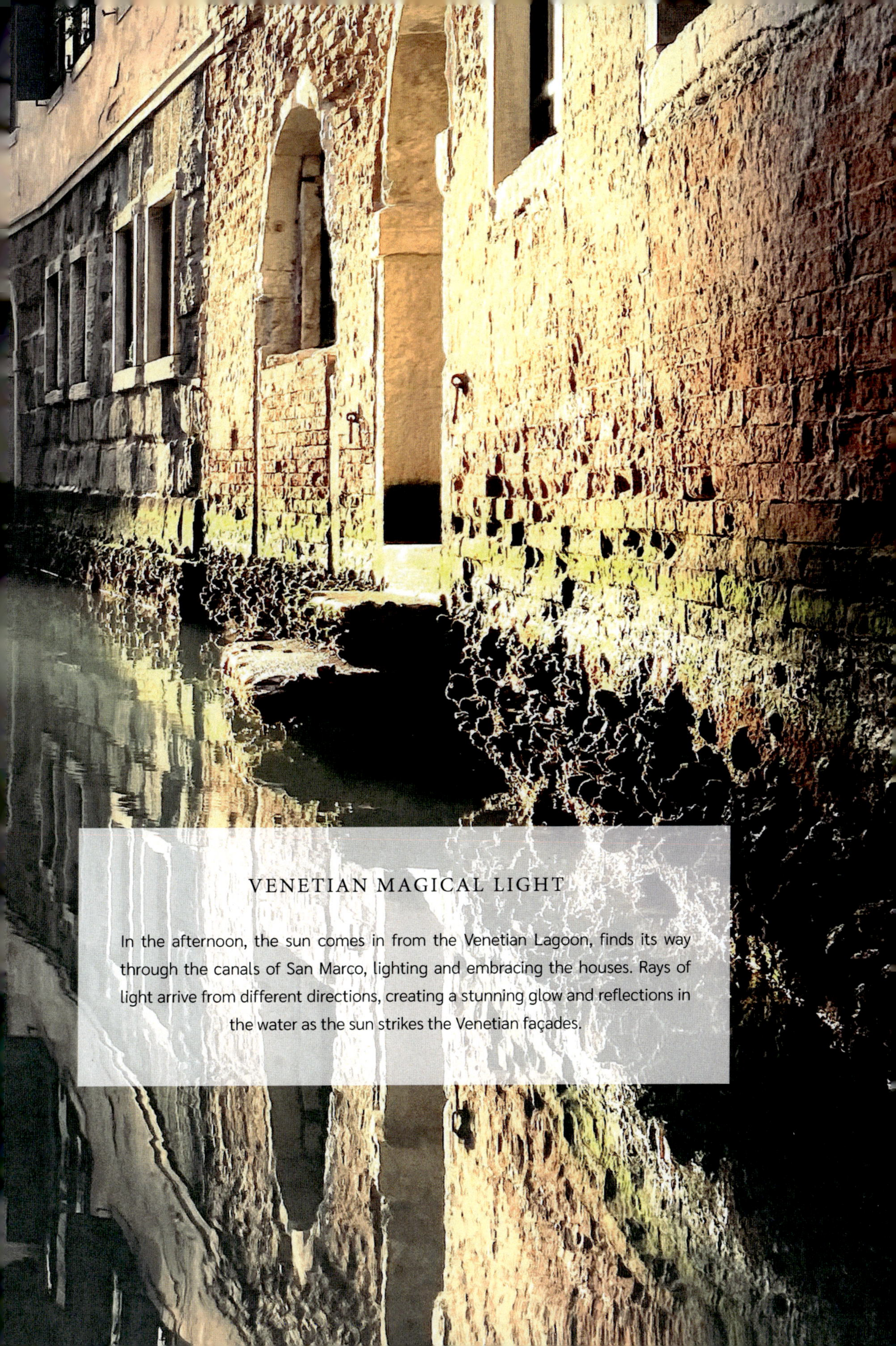

VENETIAN MAGICAL LIGHT

In the afternoon, the sun comes in from the Venetian Lagoon, finds its way through the canals of San Marco, lighting and embracing the houses. Rays of light arrive from different directions, creating a stunning glow and reflections in the water as the sun strikes the Venetian façades.

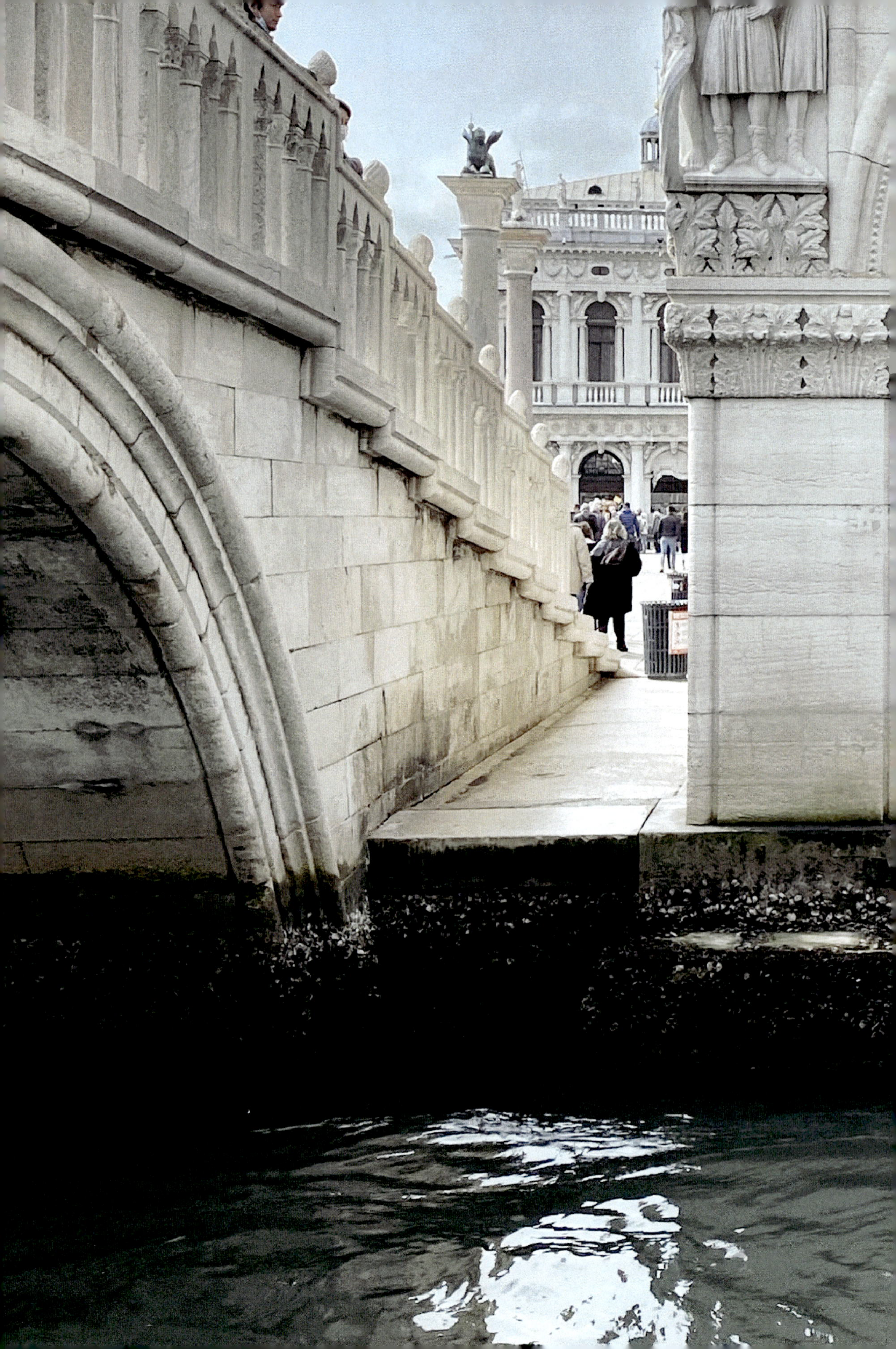

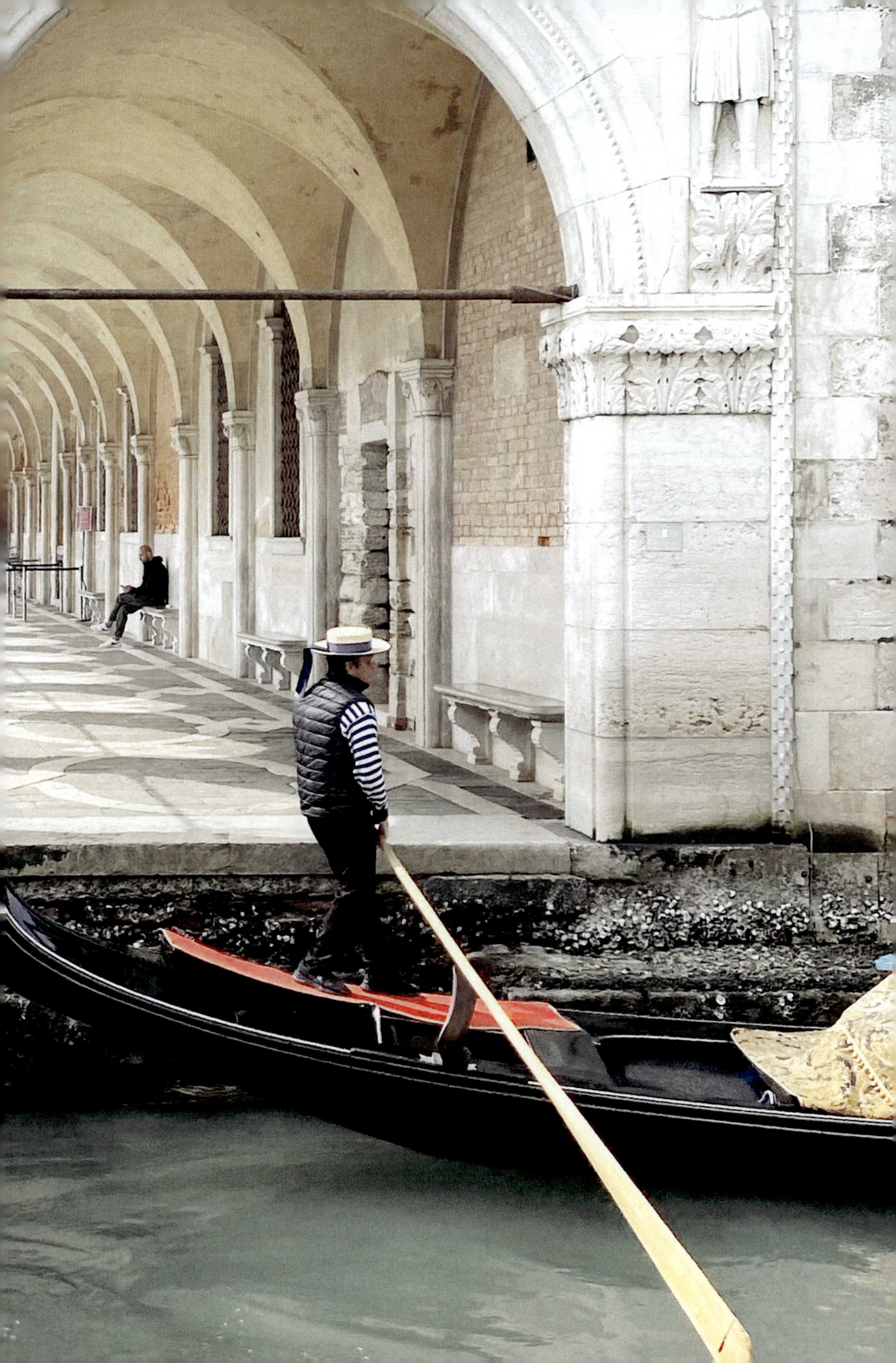

VENICE

IMPRESSIONS OF TIMELESS BEAUTY

This book is a pictorial journey through the timeless beauty of Venice. Celebrating the light, art, history and city's uniqueness, both in perspective and close up. Every alley and every corner has a story to tell, with stunning details and light that cut through the camera's lens. It is an imposing city in many ways. Venice's fantastic waterways and inviting glow inspire artists and loving couples from all over the world. Who can resist the beauty of the marble work of Basilica di San Marco? The beautiful architecture of Ponte di Rialto? Venice is art, love, tradition, drama, power, and more. It illuminates the soul and triggers curiosity. Please take a deep breath and come with me to Venice, and let's explore one thousand years together.

Lina Nicander
Photographer & Author

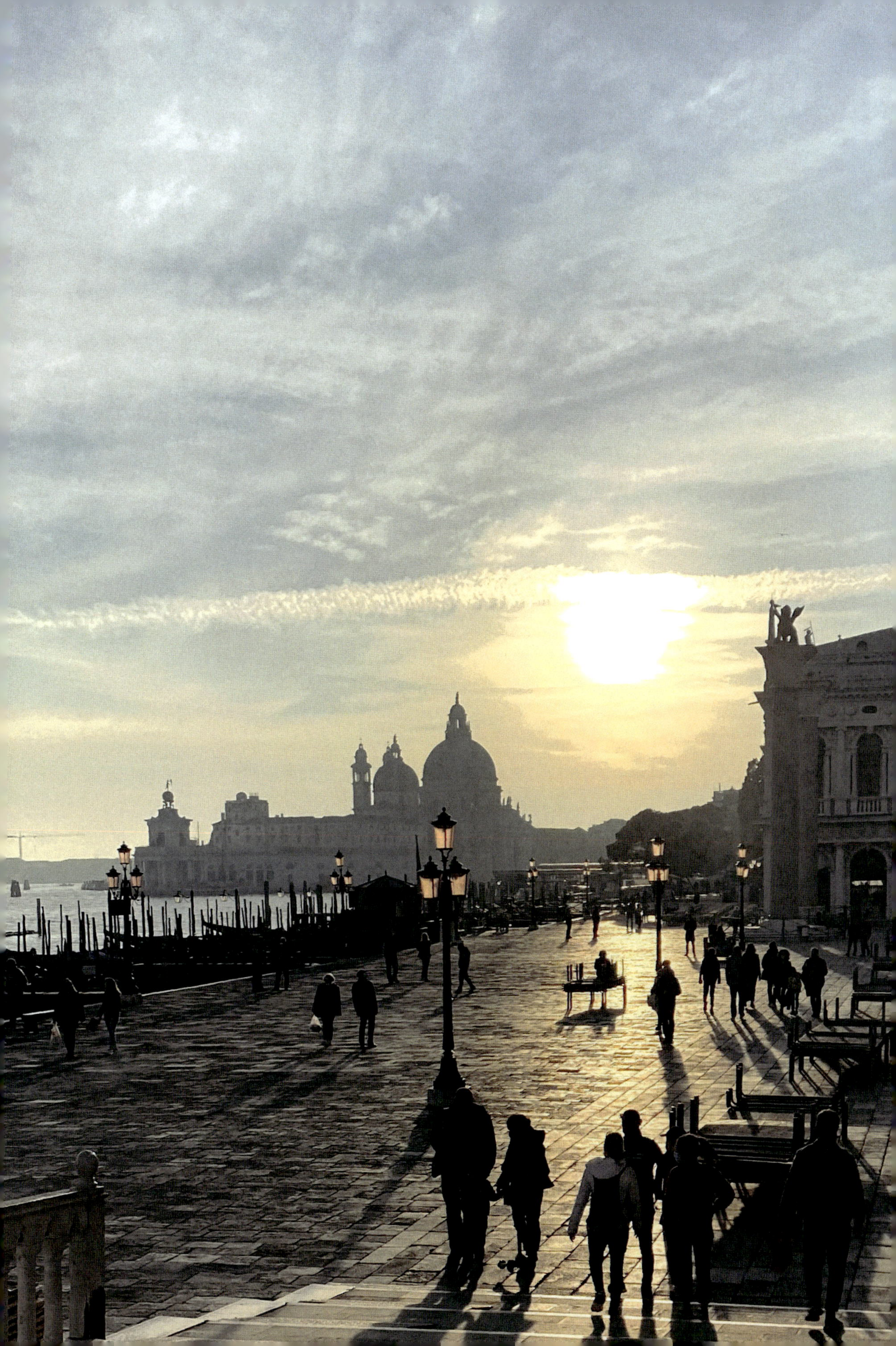

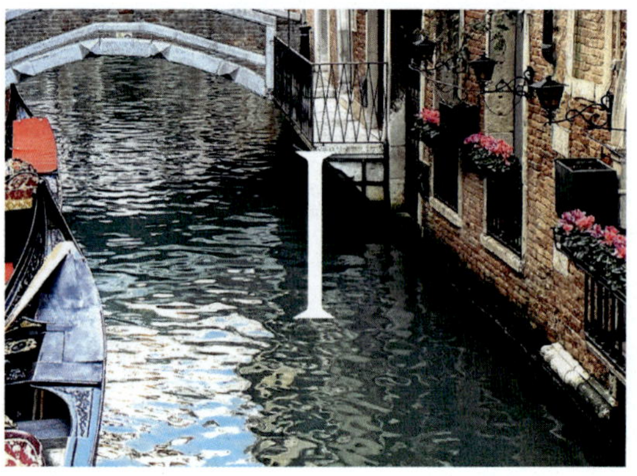

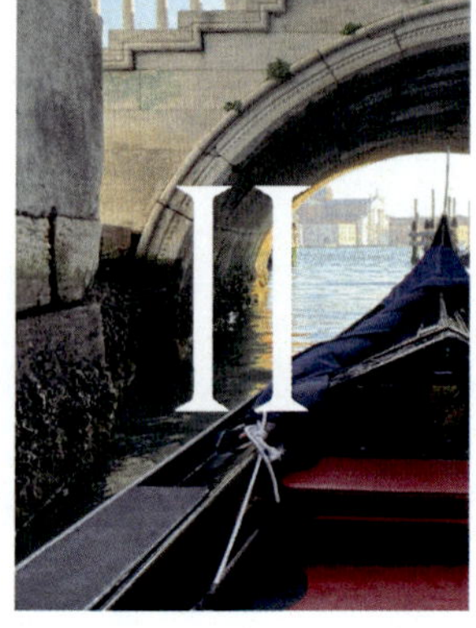

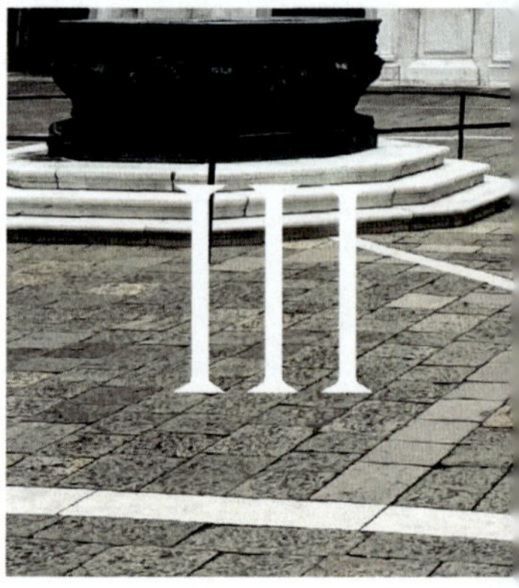

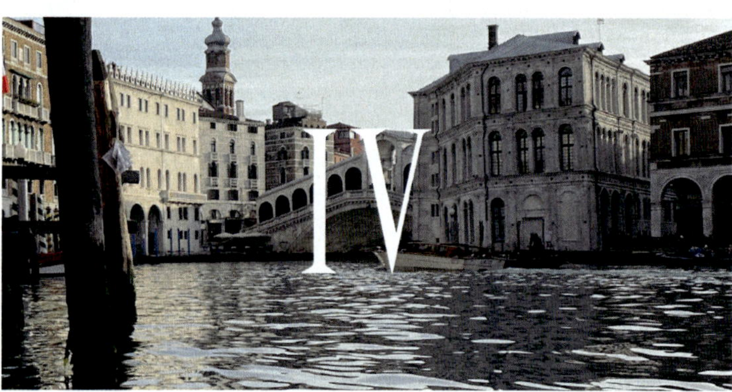

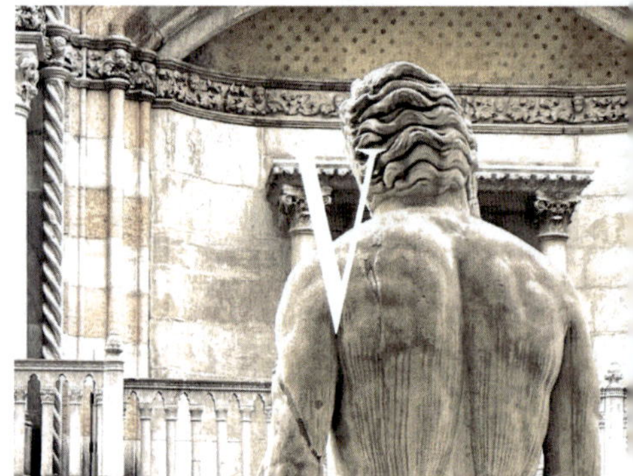

CONTENTS

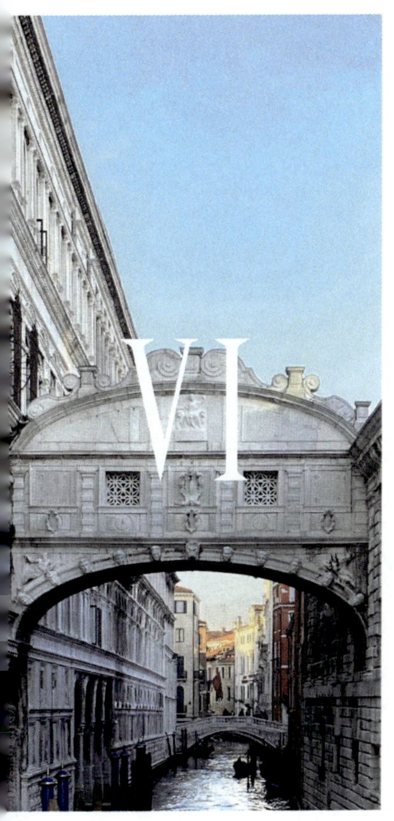
VI

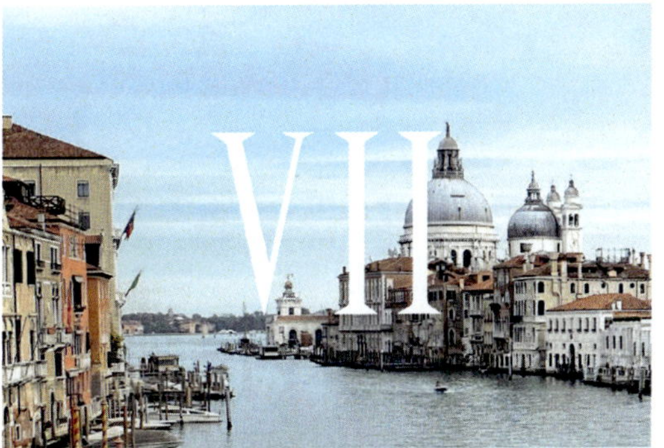
VII

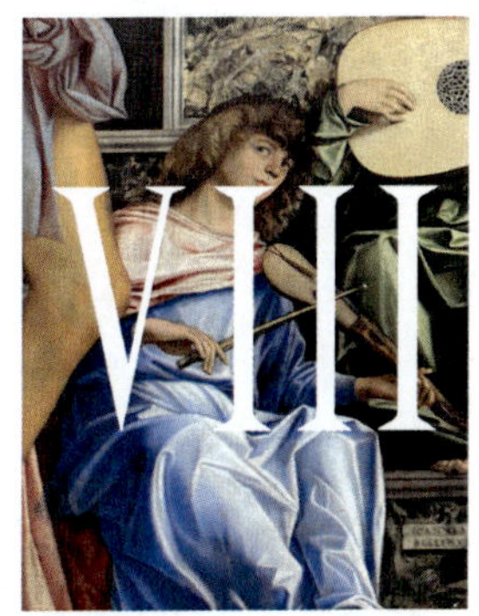
VIII

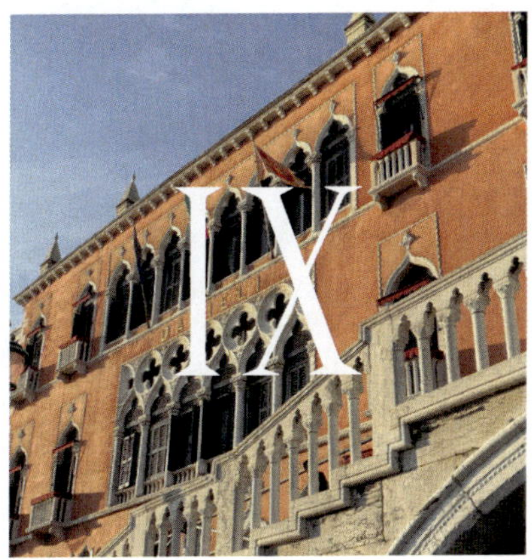
IX

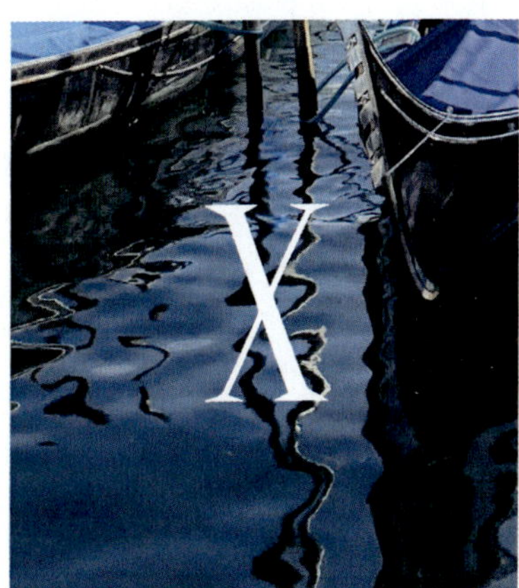
X

I

THE CANALS

ROMANTIC CANALS AND ICONIC BRIDGES

Venice has the most unique streets in the world – the canals. Venice is a collection of small islands where 150 canals and over 400 beautiful bridges, often with unique designs, connect the different islands creating the magnificent city of Venice. The city is built on several small, marshy, sandy islands in the Venetian Lagoon, separated by natural canals made deeper and broader over time. Venice has a solid construction underneath the water with a foundation of wooden logs – some of which are over a thousand years old. The Venetian light that runs through the canals creates a magical lustre where the light from the Adriatic Sea and the water in the canals reflect on the buildings along the canals. The canals and the Venetian light have inspired artists worldwide to express Venice through their art.

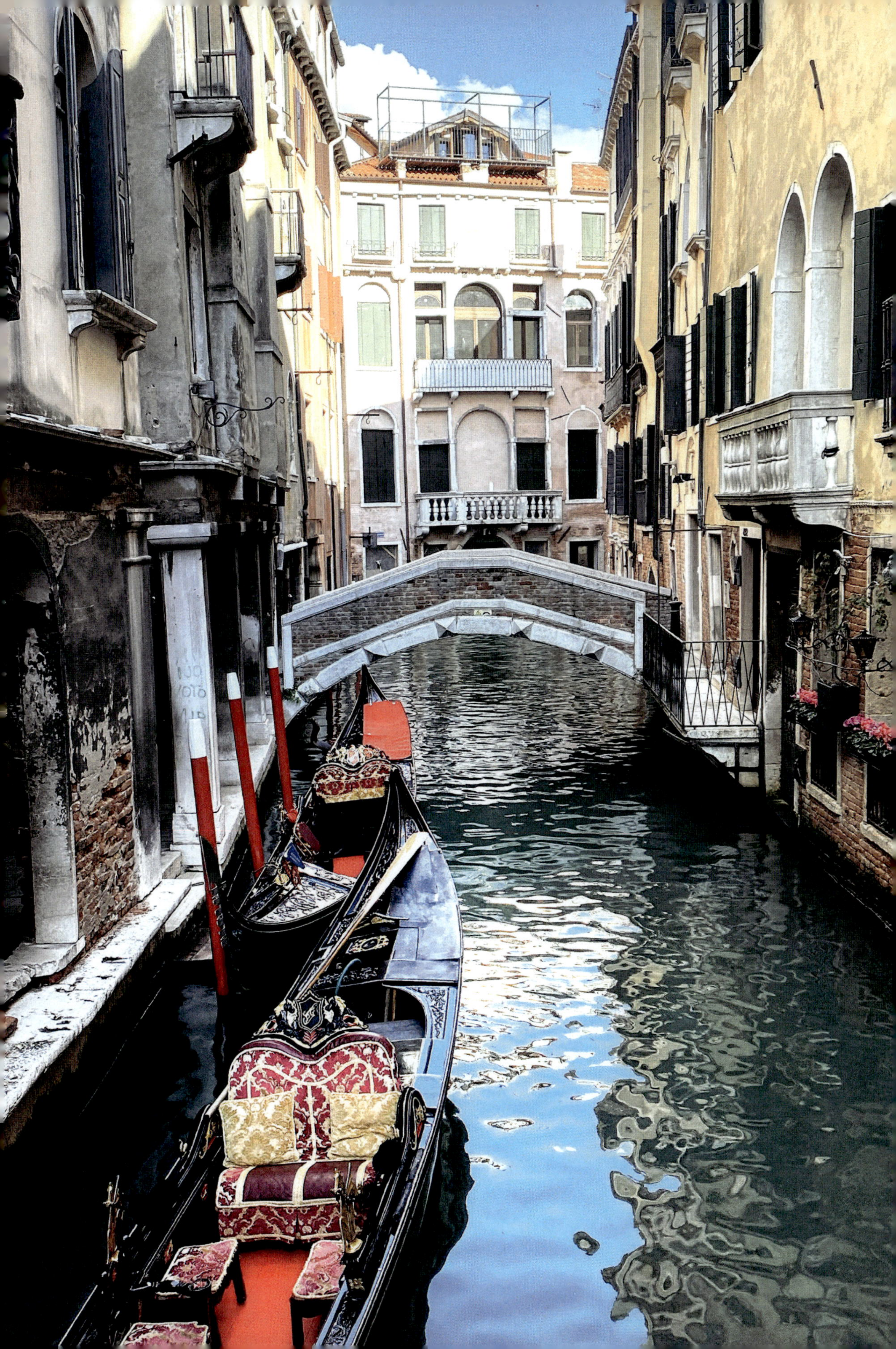

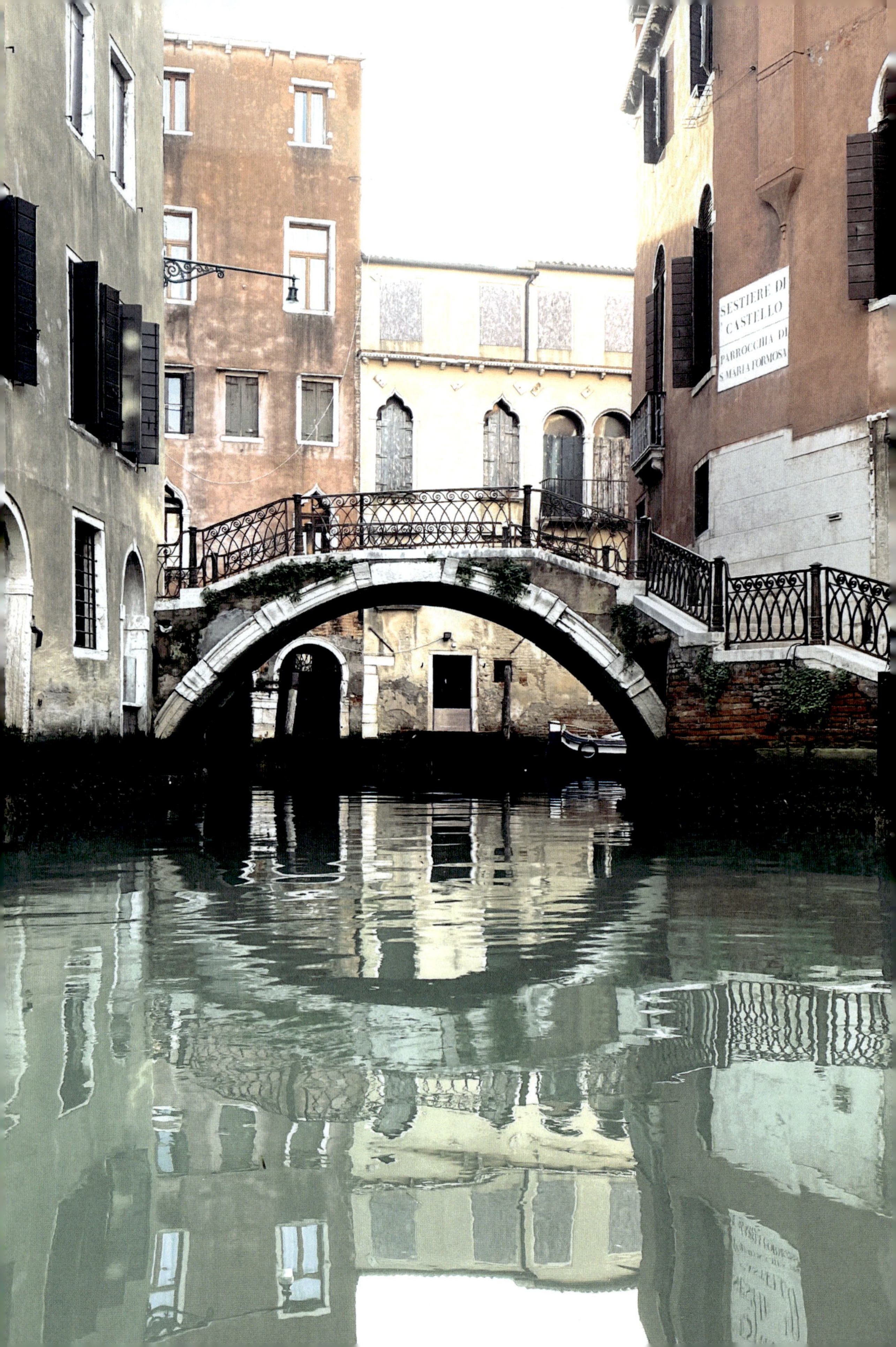
SESTIERE DI
CASTELLO
PARROCCHIA DI
S.MARIA FORMOSA

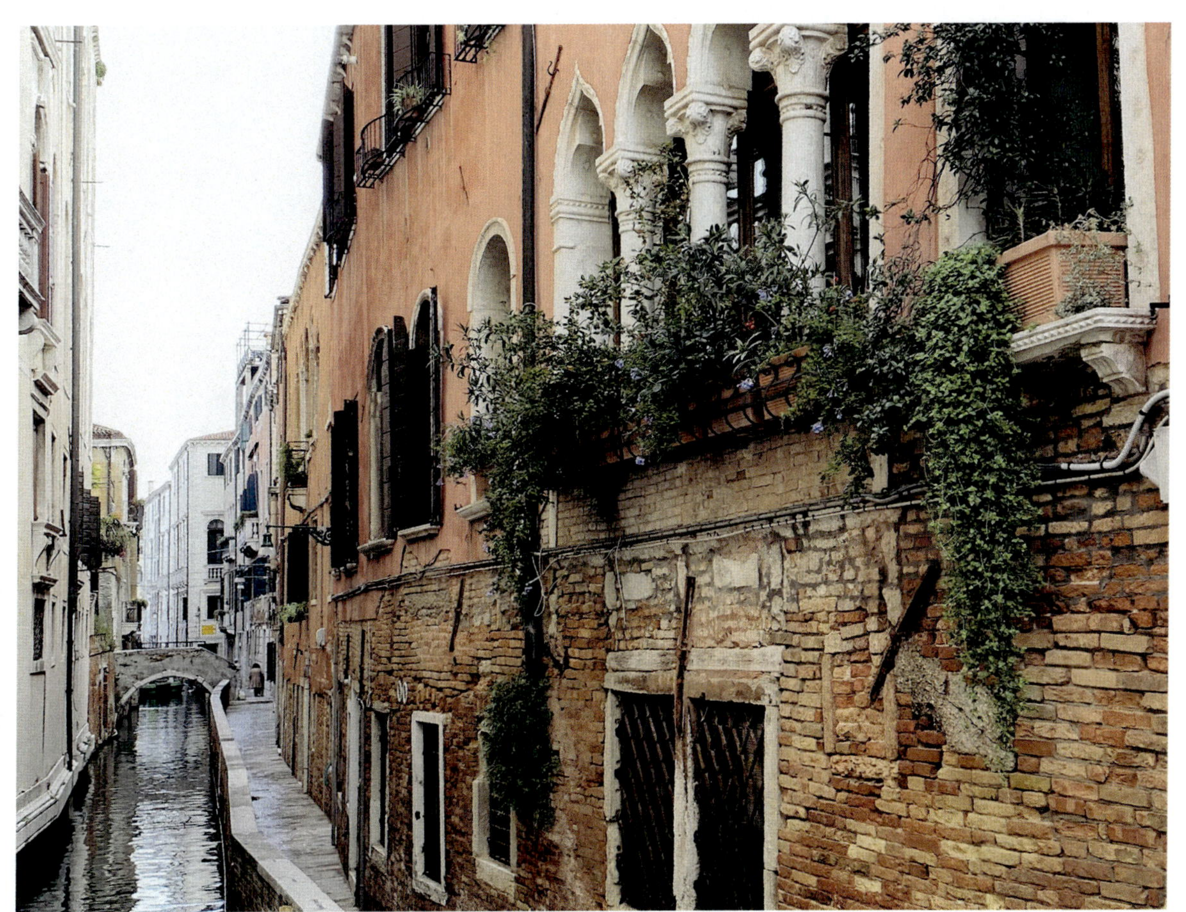

ROMANTIC CANALS AND ICONIC BRIDGES

Venice is a collection of small Islands where 150 canals and over 400 beautiful bridges, often with unique designs, connect the islands that create the magnificent city of Venice. Some bridges, like the Rialto Bridge (Ponte di Rialto) and the Bridge of Sighs (Ponte dei Sospiri), are iconic and world-famous.

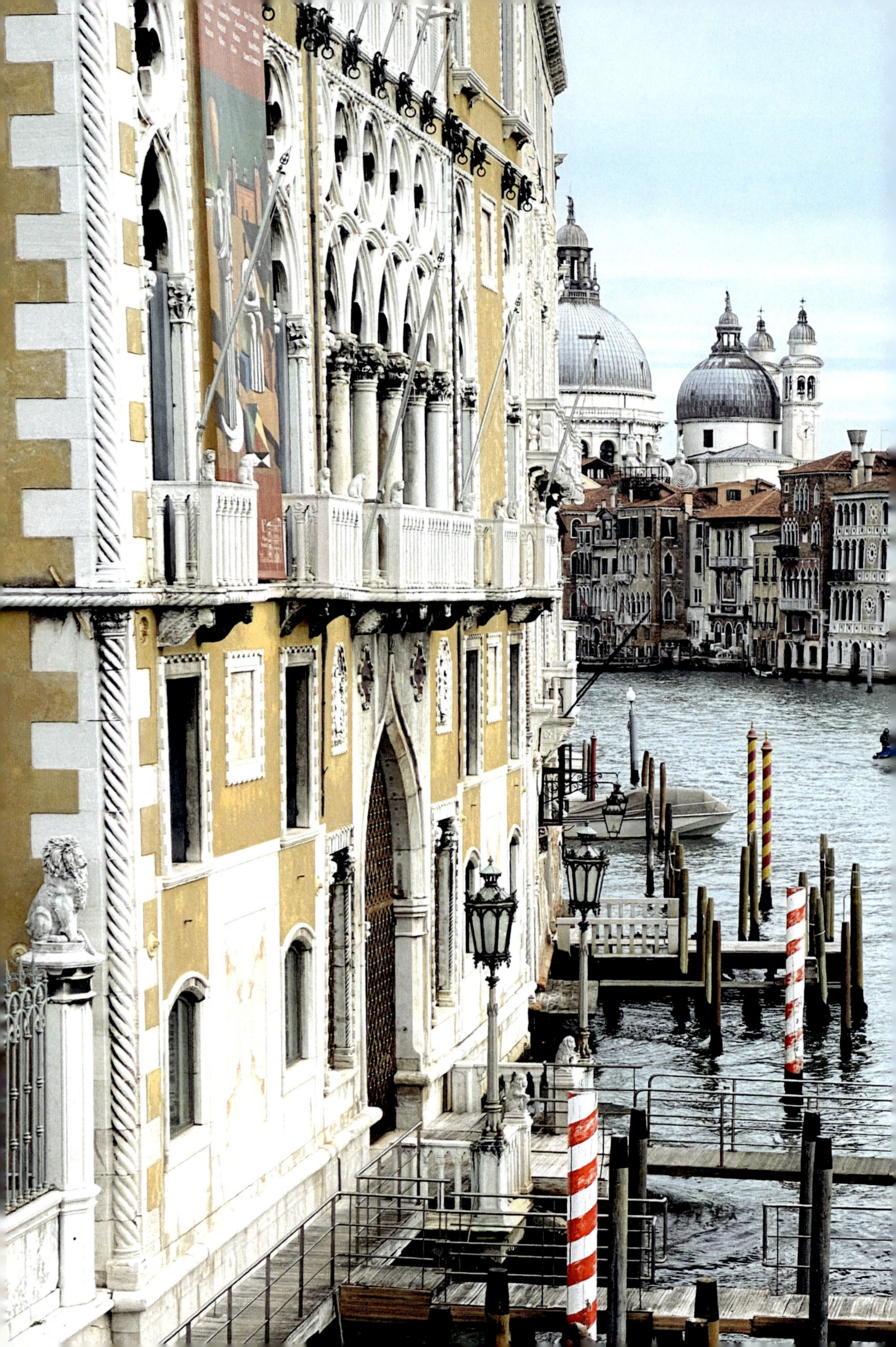

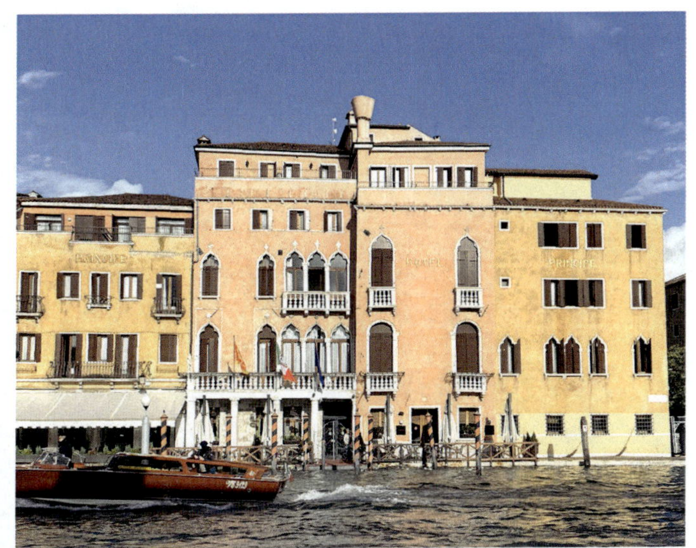

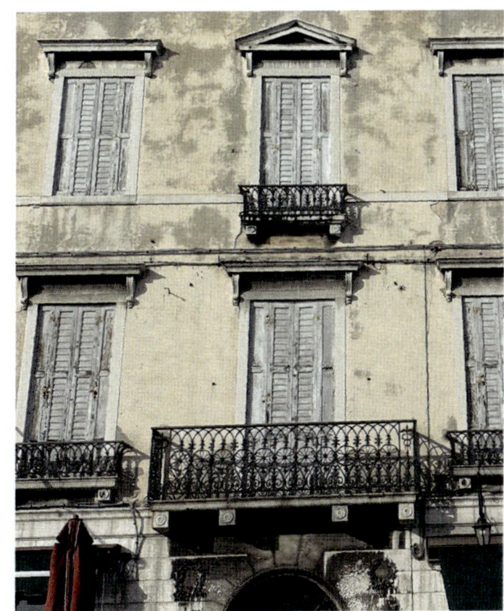

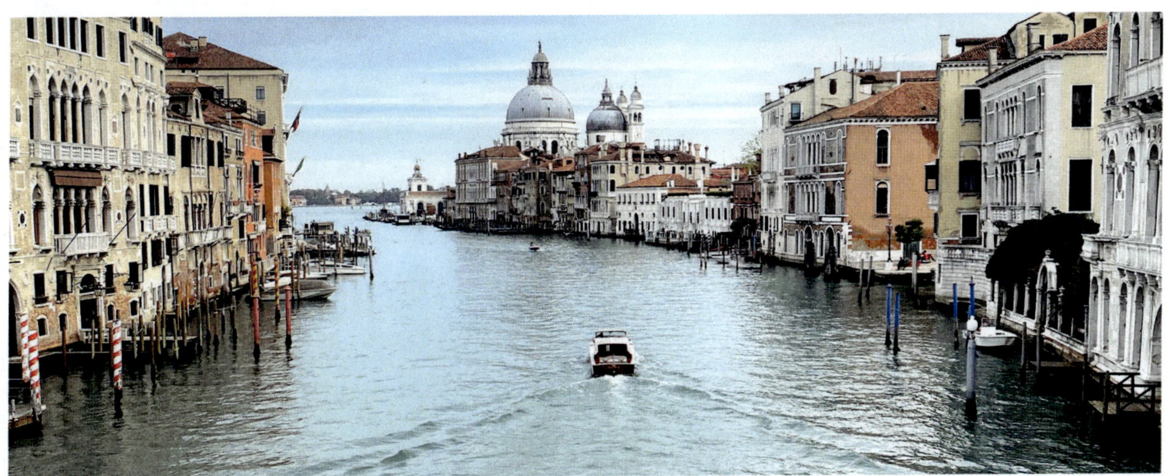

CANAL GRANDE – THE MOST BEAUTIFUL STREET IN THE WORLD

Canal Grande is the main waterway in Venice. As early as 1495, the French Ambassador stated it was "the most beautiful street in the world". Along the Canal Grande, the most prominent Venetian families built their private palaces in grand style. Living by Canal Grande's waterfront was the ultimate sign of success and prosperity, where it is much brighter than in the narrow canals. Here reflections of grandeur shimmer on the canal's surface.

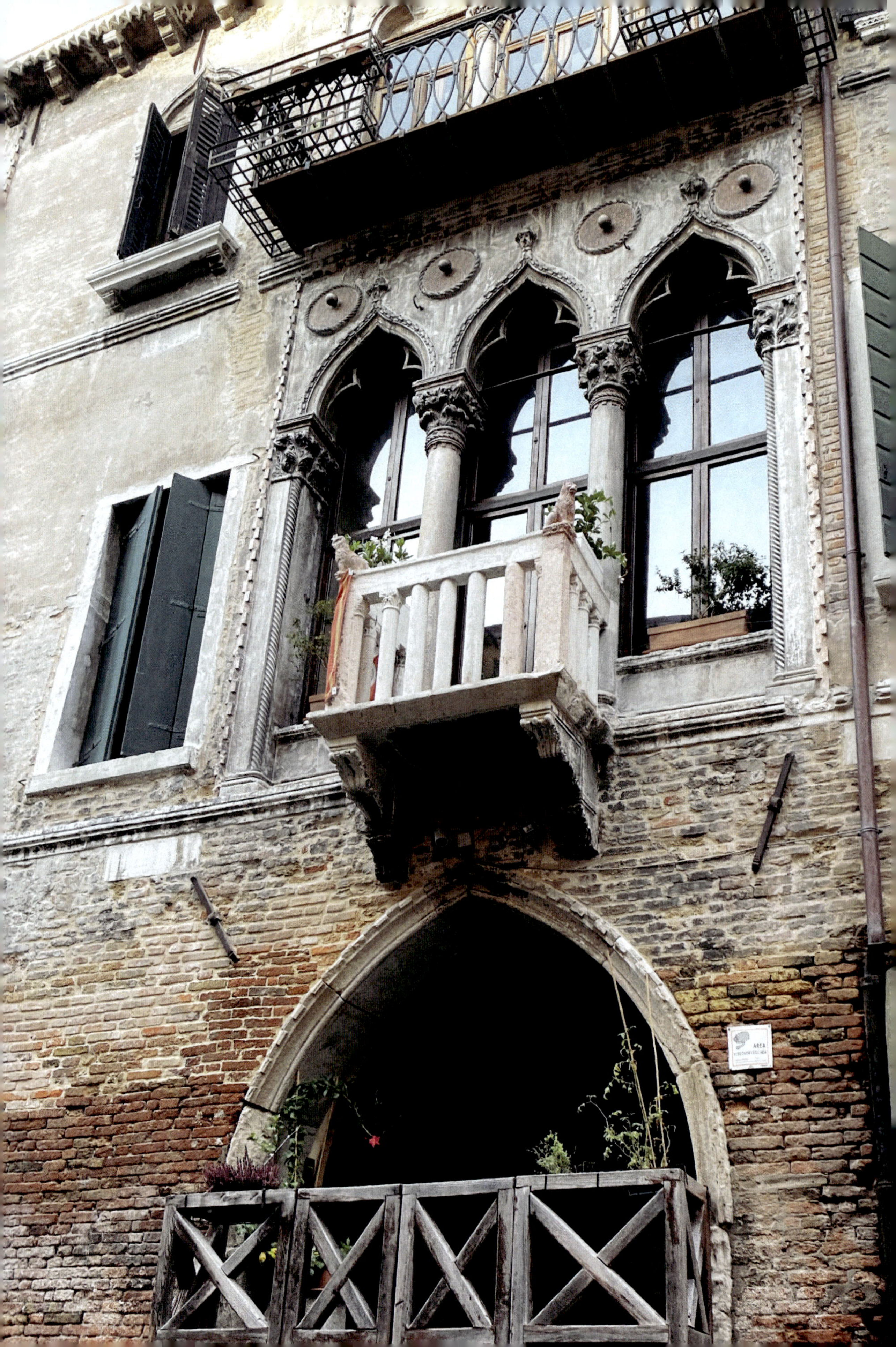
AREA

A HOME IN THE CANAL – IN VENETIAN GOTHIC STYLE

The small palaces and houses along the canals are in the traditional Venetian Gothic style. In the old town of Venice, it is mainly the windows and balconies that catch your eye. They elevate the impression of the house – standing out on the old and often worn façades.

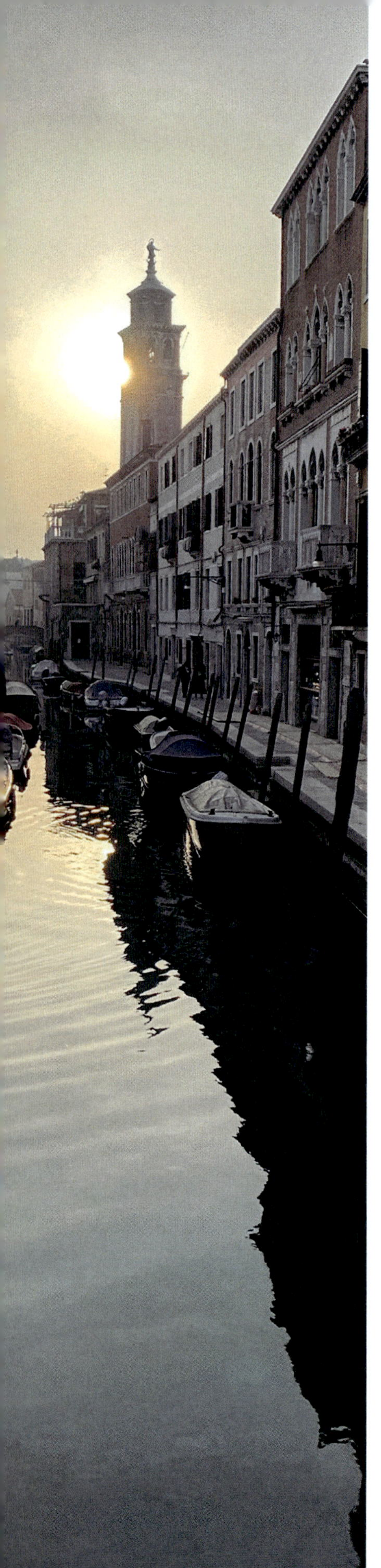

SUNSETS IN THE CANALS

The light softens at sunset in the narrow Venetian canals. The façades of the houses, bridges, and gondolas are romantically mirrored and reflected in the canal water. The golden light shifts to pink before dusk, taking us to the dark Venetian night.

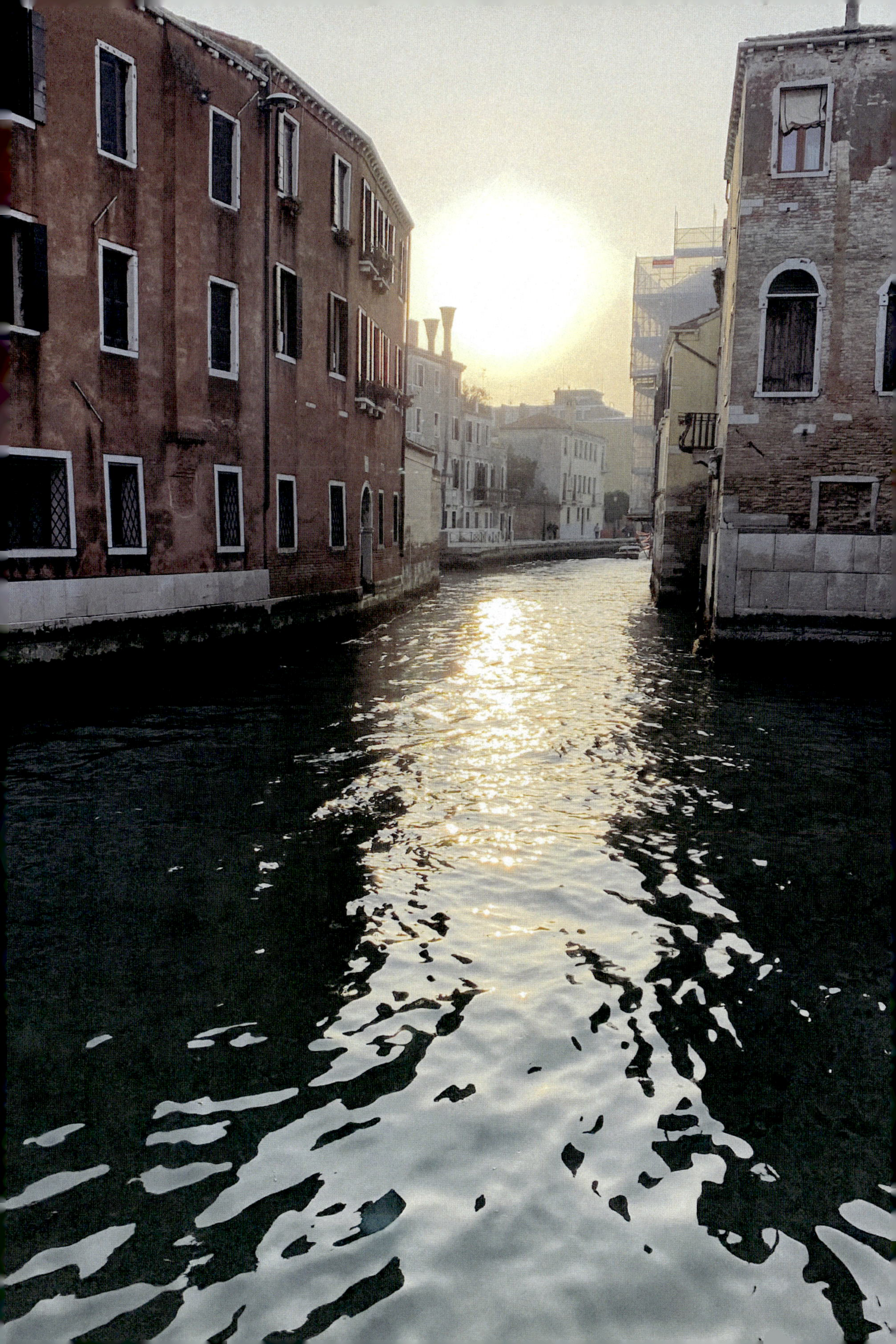

II

THE GONDOLA AND THE GONDOLIER

THE HERITAGE OF VENICE

The gondola and the gondolier play an essential role in Venice. Their smooth navigation in the canals provides a romantic shimmer over Venice and connects us back to history. Becoming a gondolier is inherited within families and is a thousand-year-old guild. It requires excellent skills and practice to manoeuvre the gondola through the canals, which involves considerable training, balance, and strength. The features of the gondola are well established and built following strict guidelines. Comprising of eight different kinds of wood, with decorative metal works and a sign with the gondolier's name placed in the front. It is a proud guild that navigates the canals of Venice.

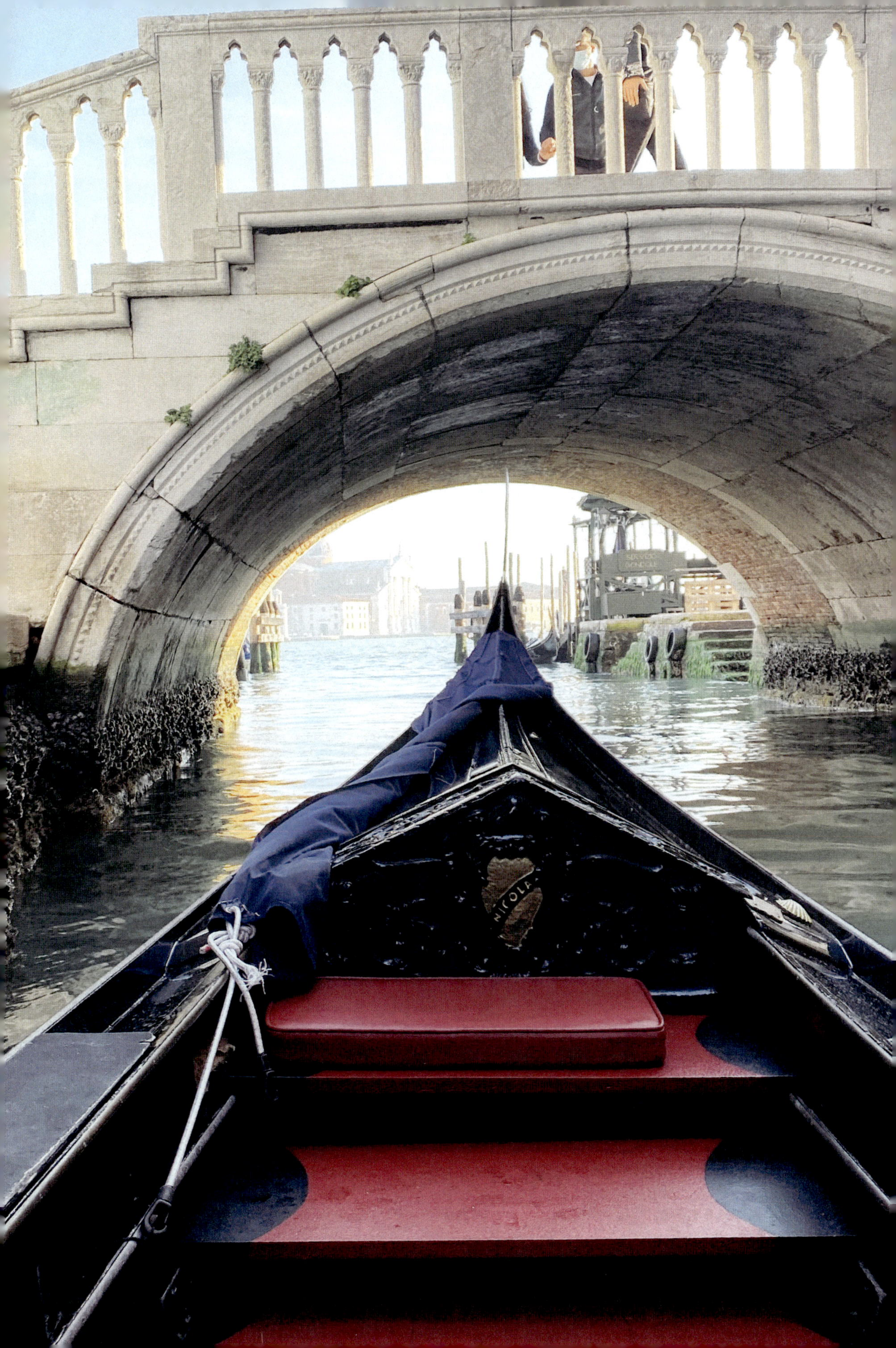
NICOLA

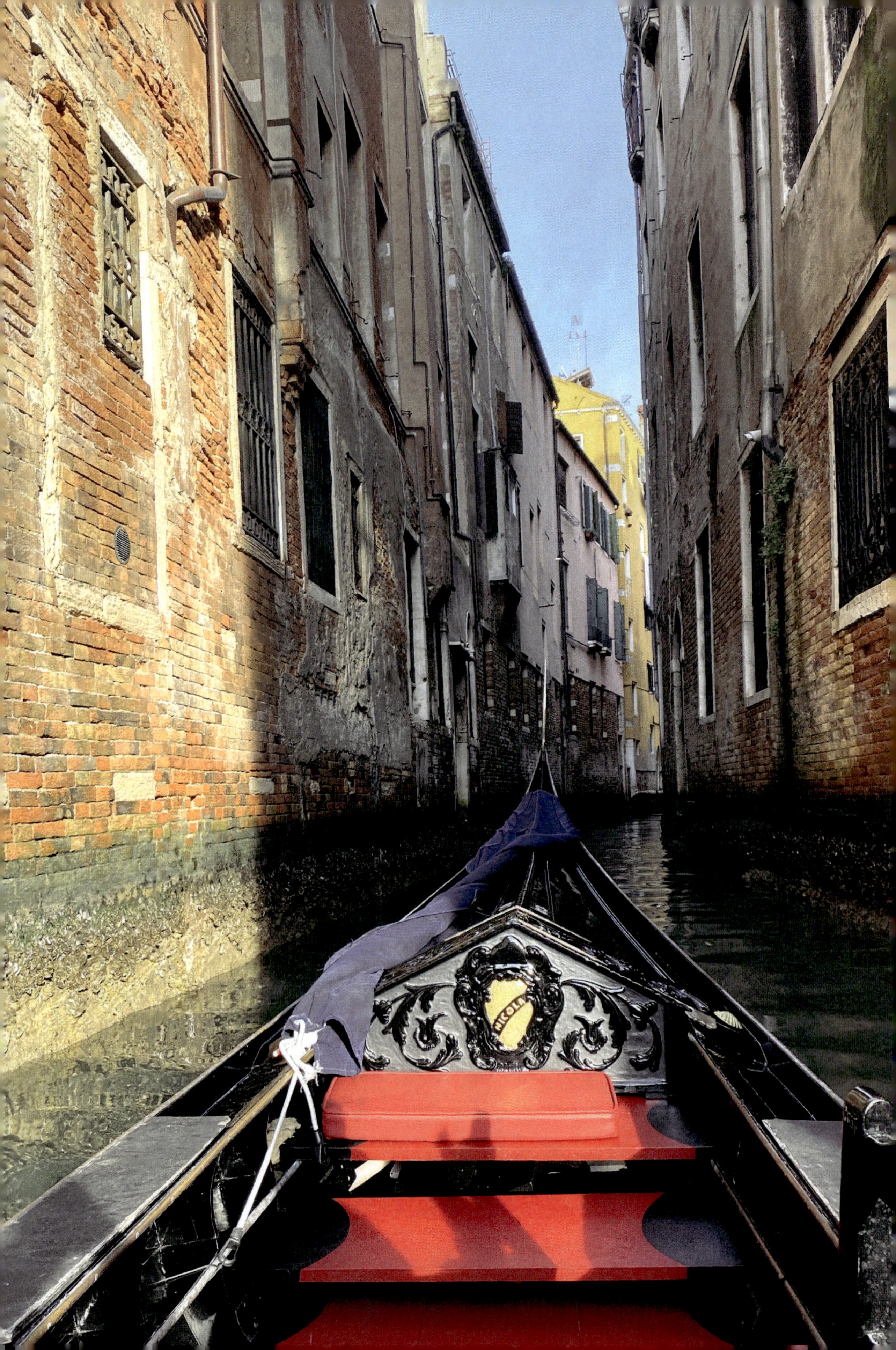
NICOLA

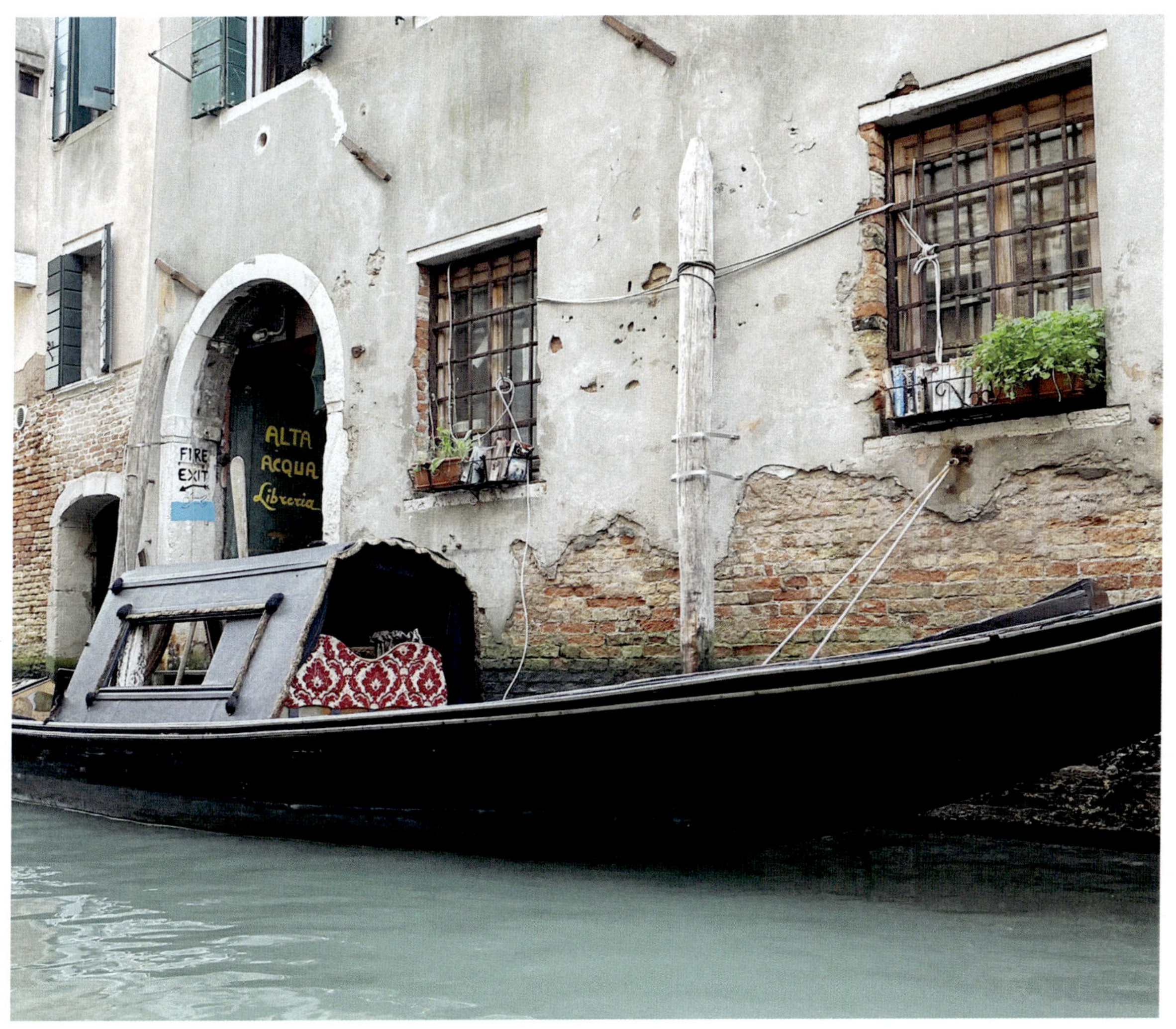

THE GONDOLA – HERITAGE OF VENICE

Historians have traced the first gondolas in Venice to 1094, when the Venice ruler and Doge, Vitale Faliero, mentioned the gondolas in a letter to the people. In art, the first paintings with gondolas were painted by Bellini during the 1500s.

A TRUE MASTERPIECE OF CRAFTSMANSHIP

The gondola is made of eight different kinds of wood – elm, mahogany, birch, oak, lime, cherry, walnut, and larch. Essential features are the decorative metalwork, the gondolier's sign, and the red pompoms.

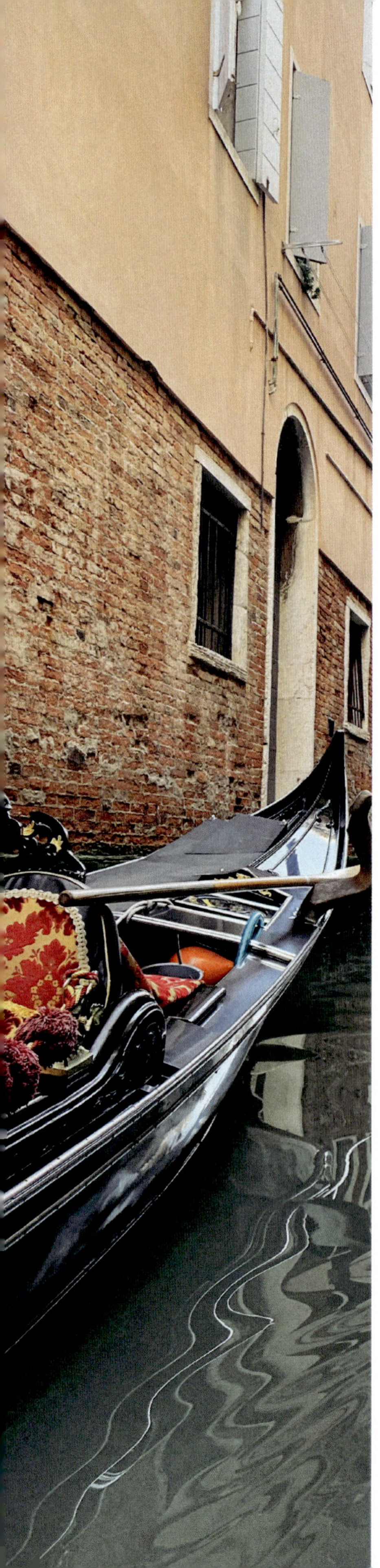

DECORATED WITH GOLD, RED AND METAL

Tradition and guidelines direct the adornment of the gondola. The ferro at the front of the gondola is created by a blacksmith. This decorative metalwork is made by hand, and the characteristic iron bow is shaped with unique tools from an iron sheet. Inside the gondola, the interior is often decorated in gold and red, influenced by the Baroque period.

RED POMPOMS AND A PERSONAL SIGN

The gondola's red yarn pompoms mark a soft contrast between the gondola and the greenish tinge of the canal. Each gondola holds the personal sign of its proud owner and gondolier.

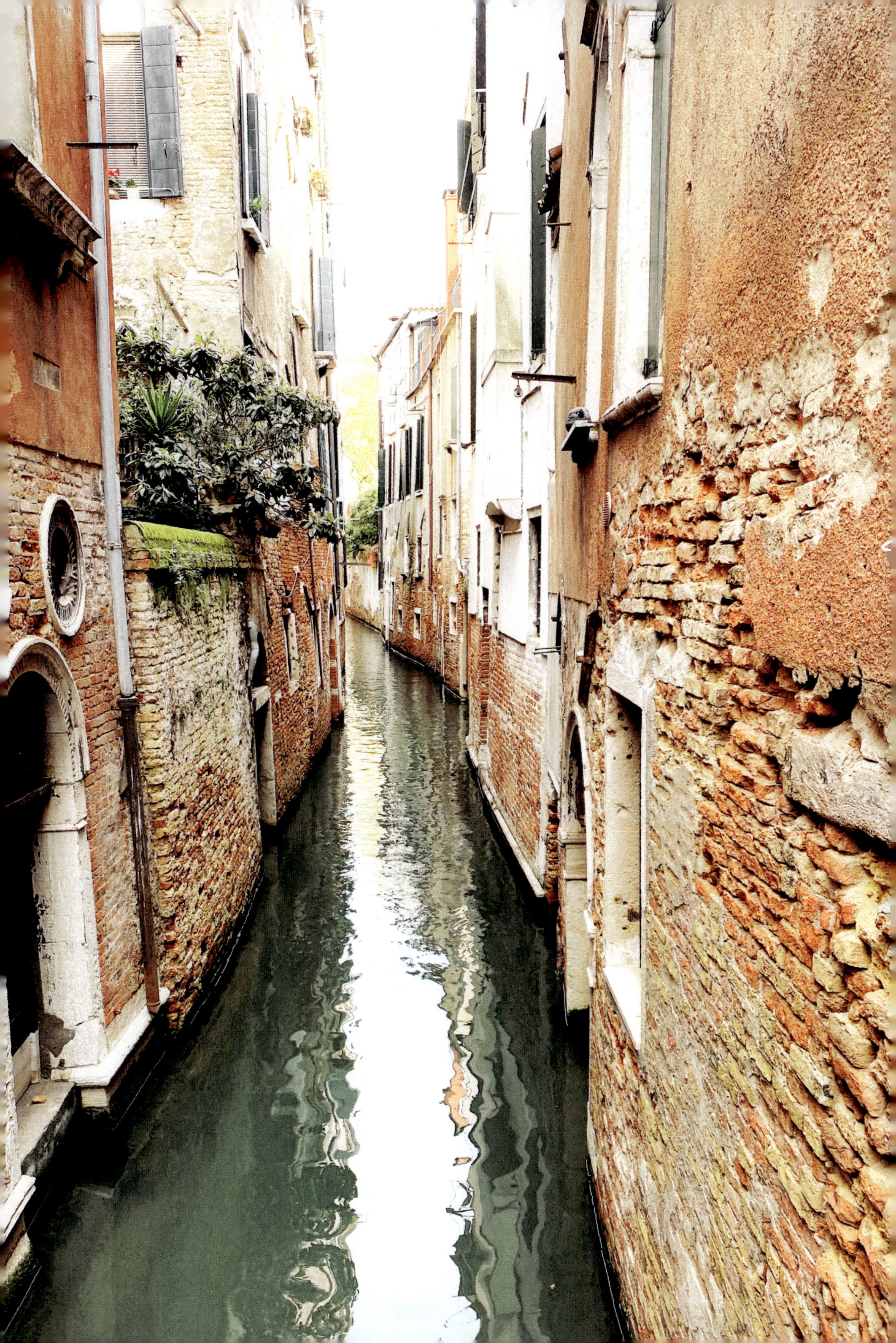

GONDOLIER – A THOUSAND-YEAR-OLD GUILD

With a proud, upright posture at the back of the gondola, dressed in stripes and a straw hat – the gondolier masters this beautifully asymmetrical vessel. The gondola and the gondolier are essential for bringing out and maintaining the romantic shimmer of Venice. It is a thousand-year-old guild, and you must pass several complex tests to become a gondolier. It is also a Venetian family affair. The profession has gone from father to son, for almost one thousand years. In 2010, Giorgia Boscolo passed the tests and became the first female gondolier. She followed in the footsteps of her father, Dante.

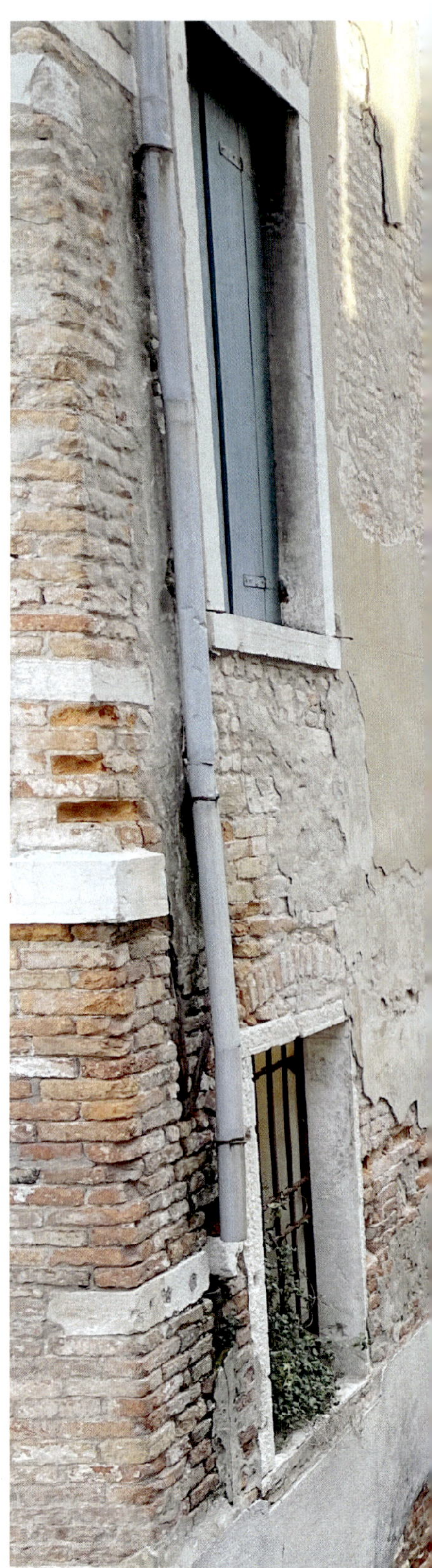

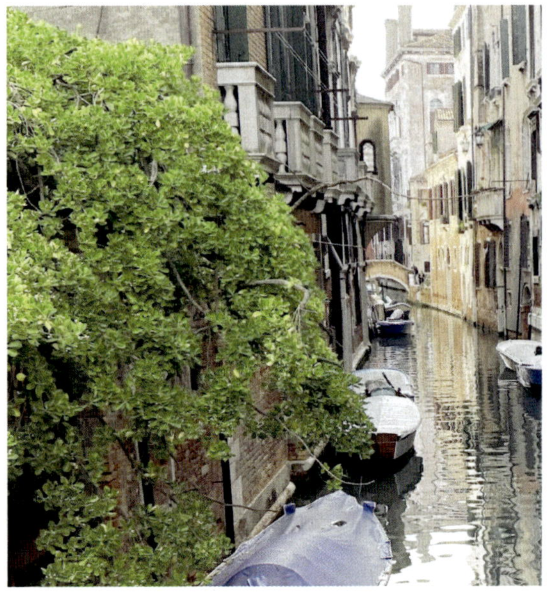

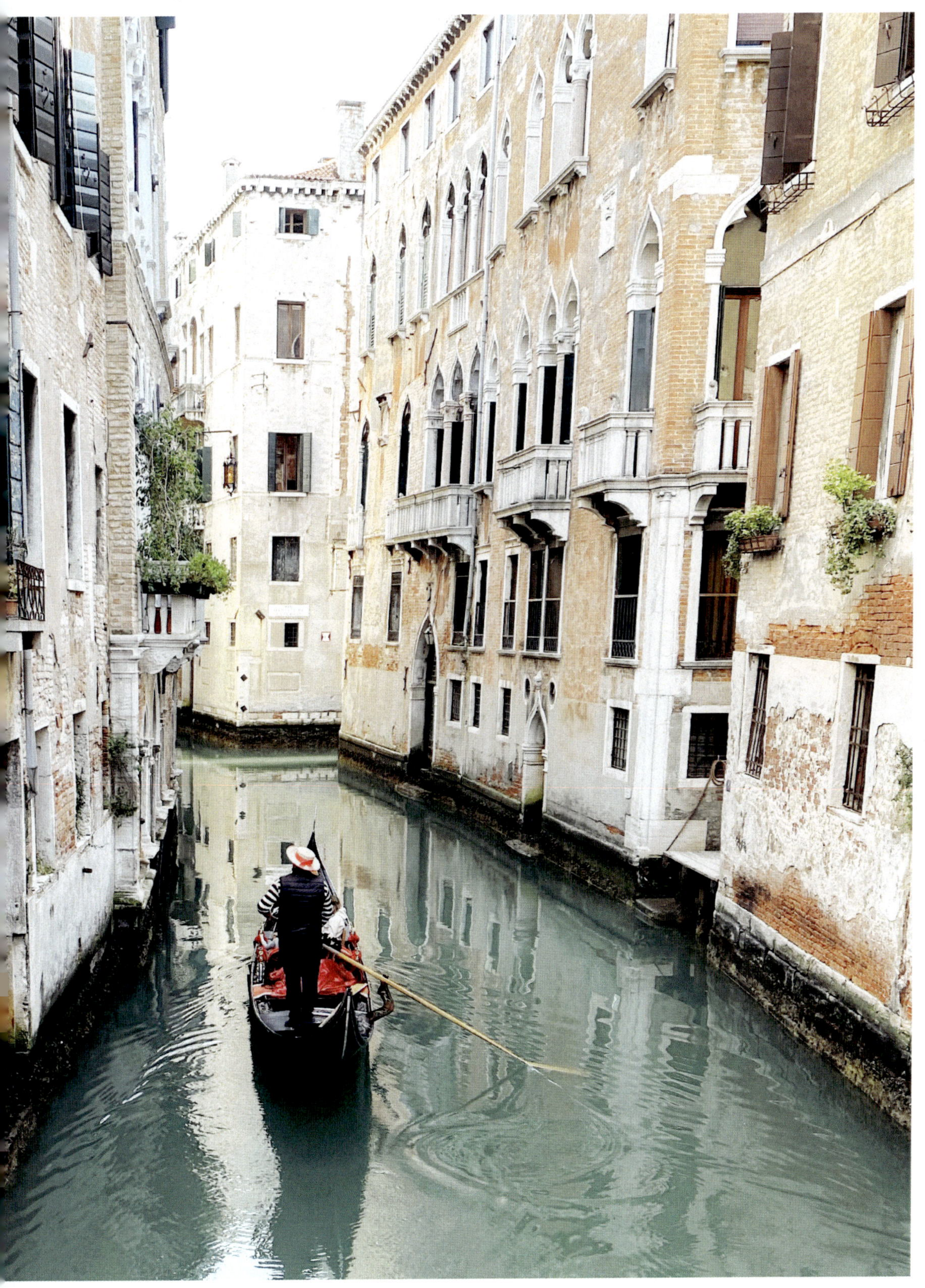

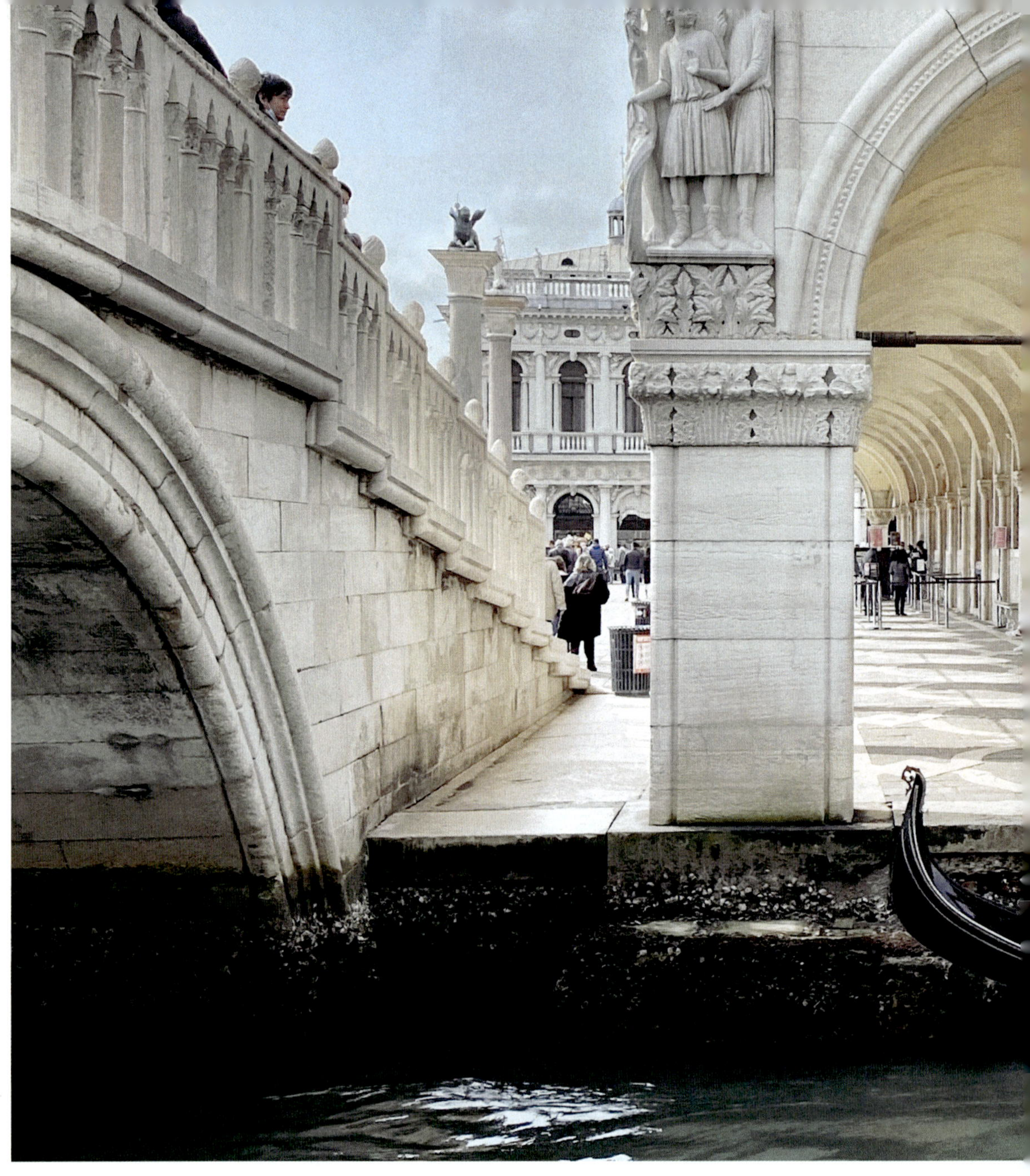

A CURVED BEAUTY

The gondolas navigate through the narrow canals of Venice. Stable but swift. The gondolier's job is to safely manoeuvre the gondola through the channels, requiring a lot of practice, balance, and strength. The gondola weighs 500 kg and is 11 metres long.

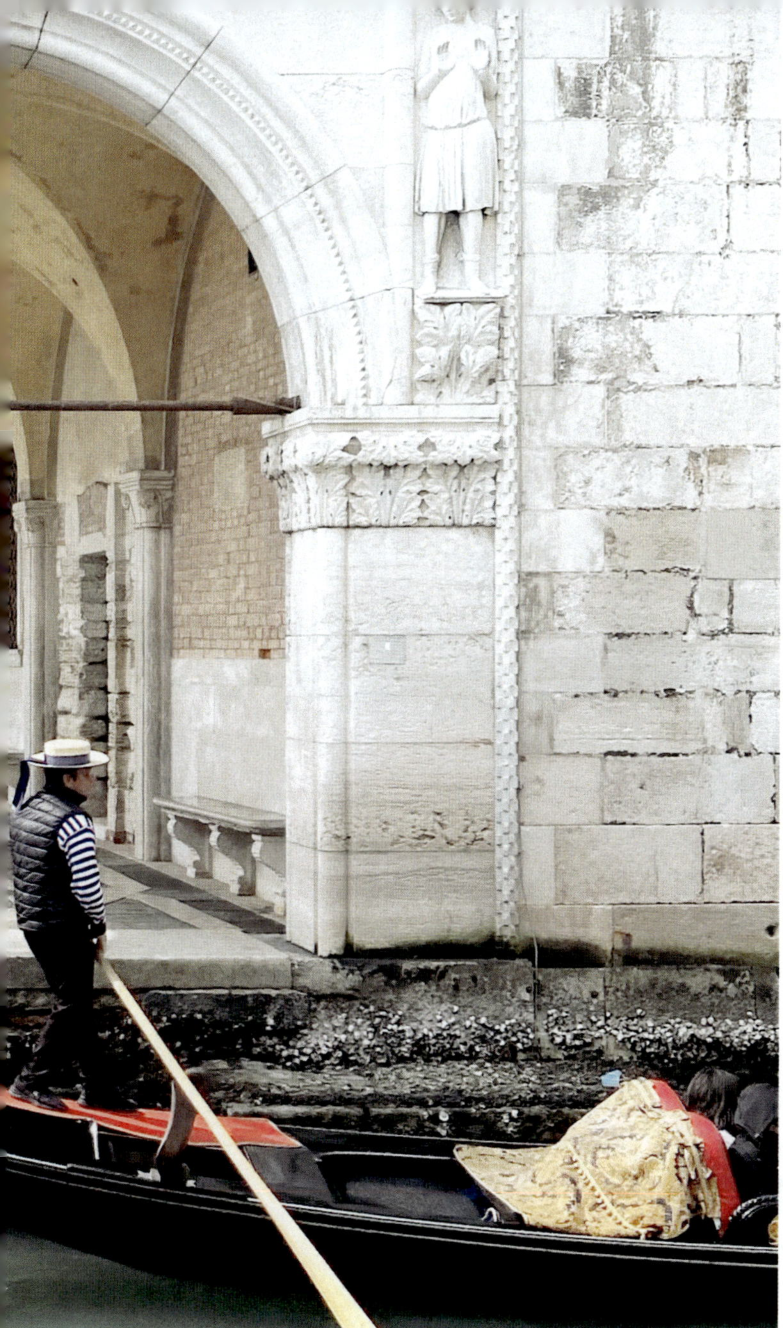

VOGA ALLA VENETA

Voga alla Veneta is the Venetian style of rowing. The gondolier stands up in a firm position facing forward. Steering the asymmetrical vessel through the canals takes many years of training.

III

SAN MARCO

HERITAGE FROM THE EASTERN ROMAN EMPIRE

The marble of the Basilica has an exciting story to tell with its unique heritage from the Eastern Roman Empire and Constantinople. Red porphyry is one of the most precious marbles and was used to symbolise imperial purple. It was the colour of the Roman Empire for royal and divine greatness. We can still enjoy the beautiful marble with our eyes and touch the Roman Empire with our fingertips. The ambience of Piazza San Marco is famous. From glory days to darker times, the square has conquered time with its beauty. Since the medieval ages, it has been a bustling place in the centre of Venice.

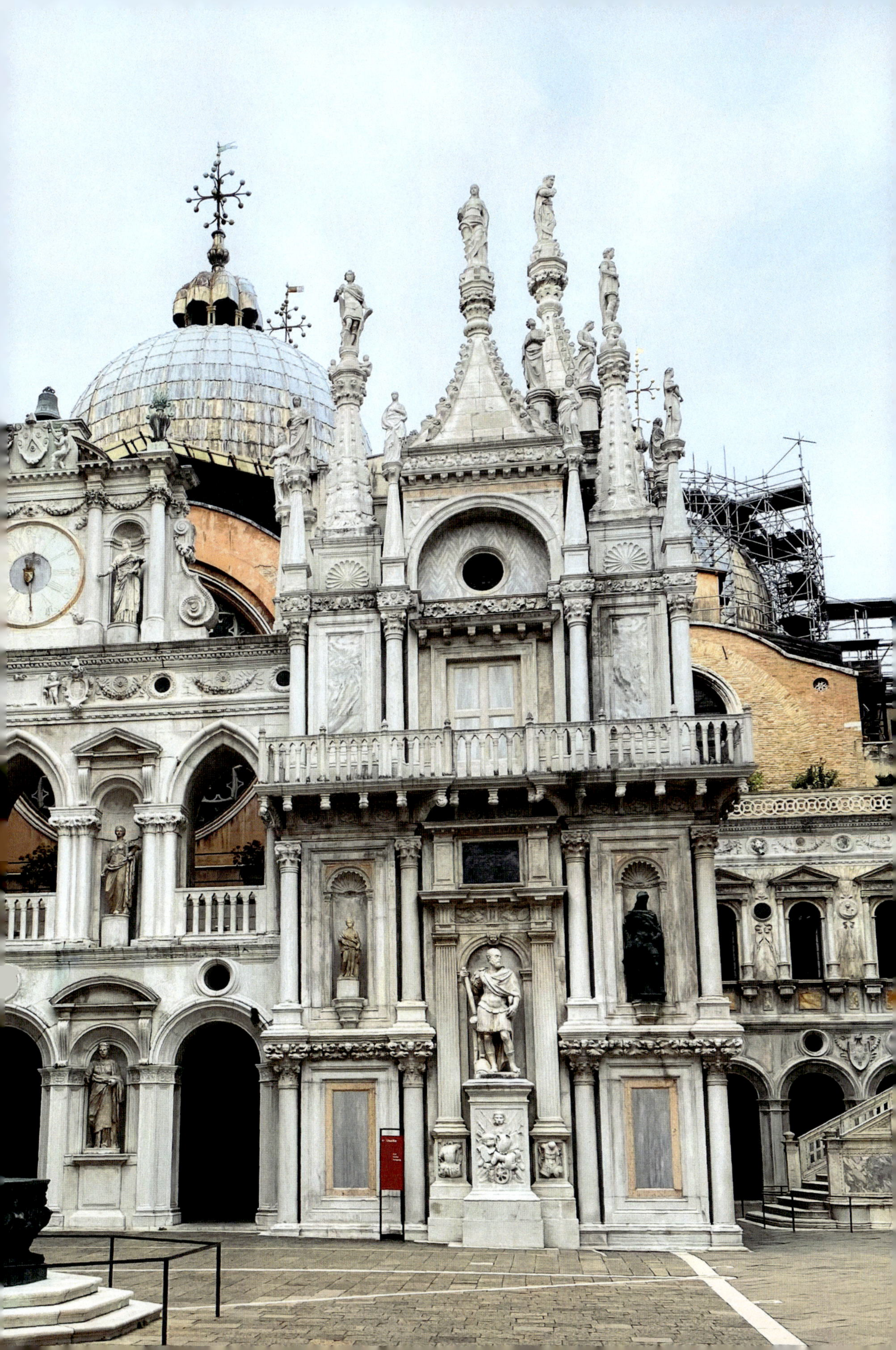

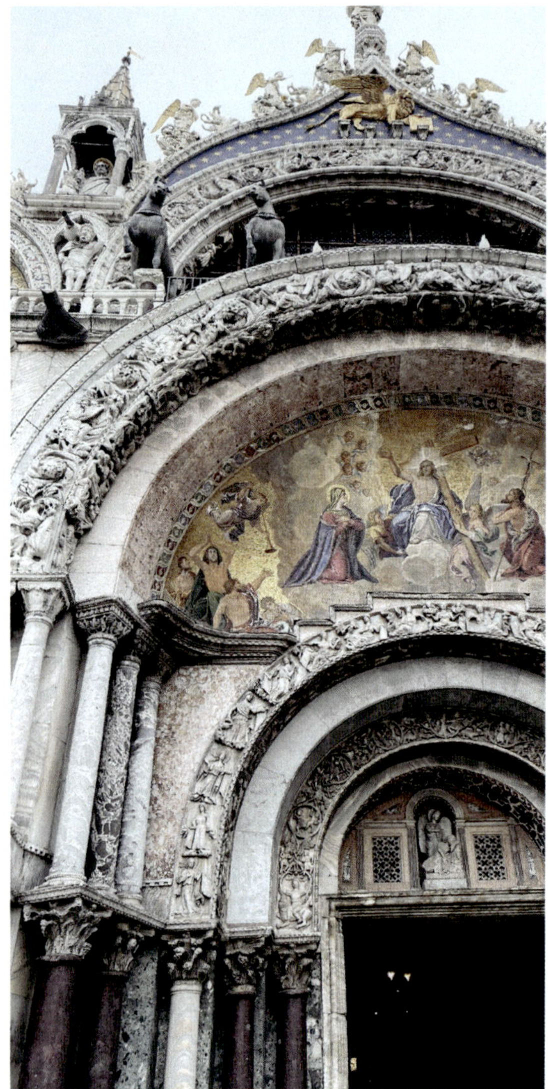

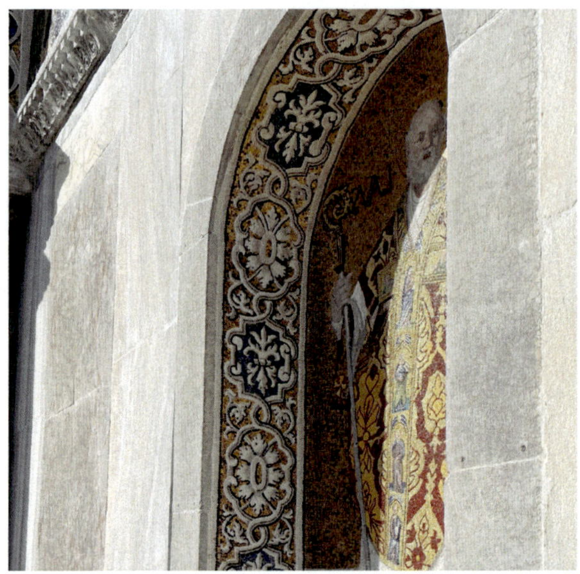

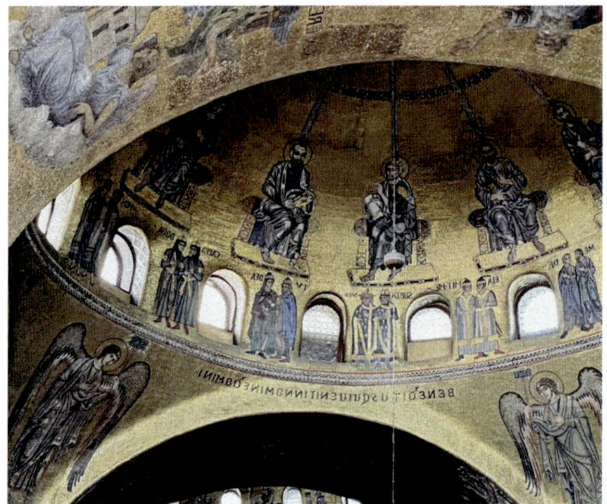

BASILICA DI SAN MARCO

Marble euphoria! The columns decorating St. Mark's Basilica's (Basilica di San Marco) magnificent entrance are rich and varied in colour. Stunning marble in soft pink, green and grey to deeper imperial purple captures the eye. It is a fantastic palette of opulent colours. The marble on St. Mark's Basilica in Venice has an exciting story with a unique heritage from the Eastern Roman Empire. This marble is a conquest from Constantinople and the Eastern Roman Empire was brought to Venice. It explains the rich variations on the marble of St. Mark's Basilica as it is reused marble taken from sacred and civic buildings in Constantinople during the Crusade in 1204.

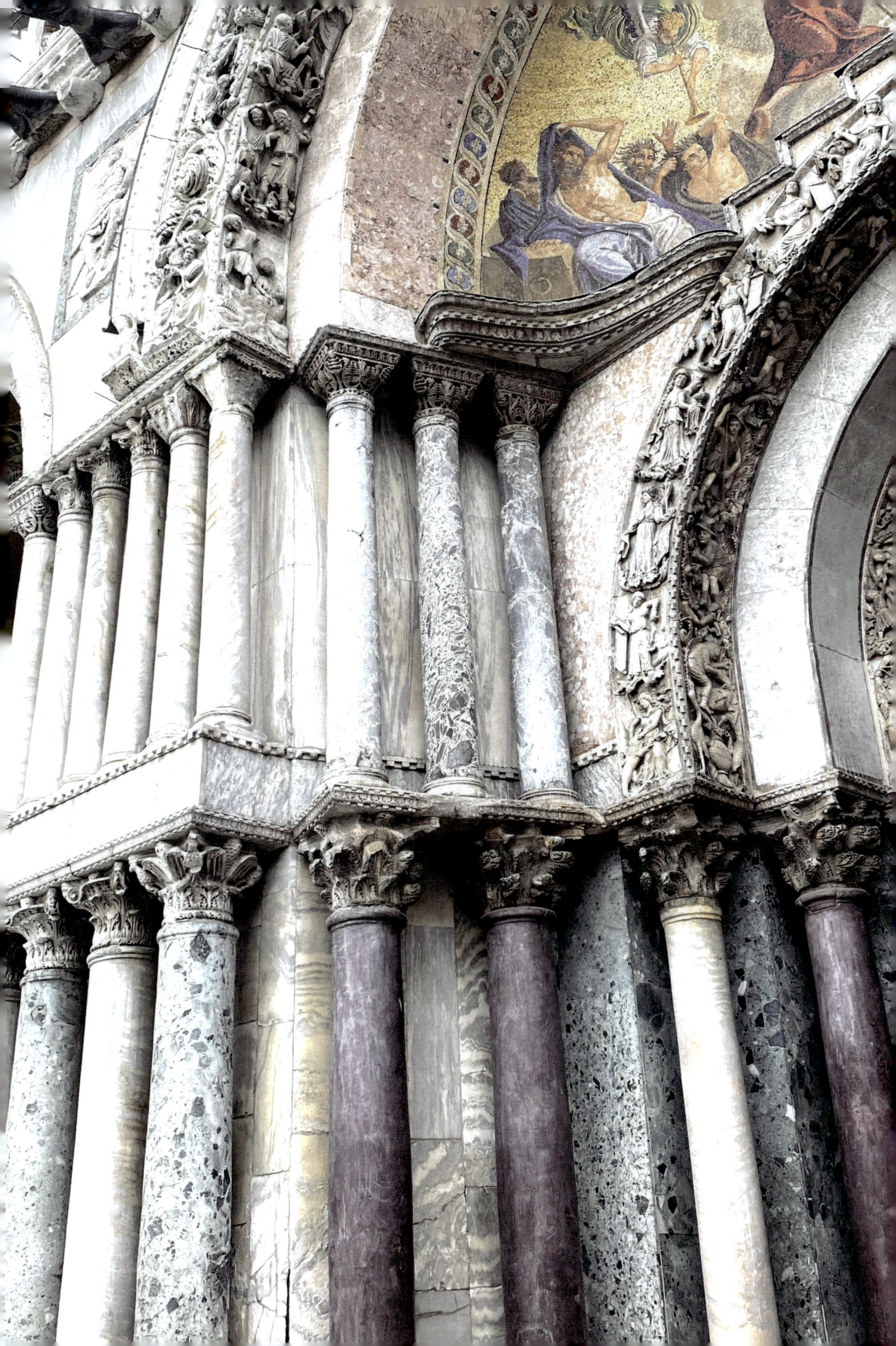

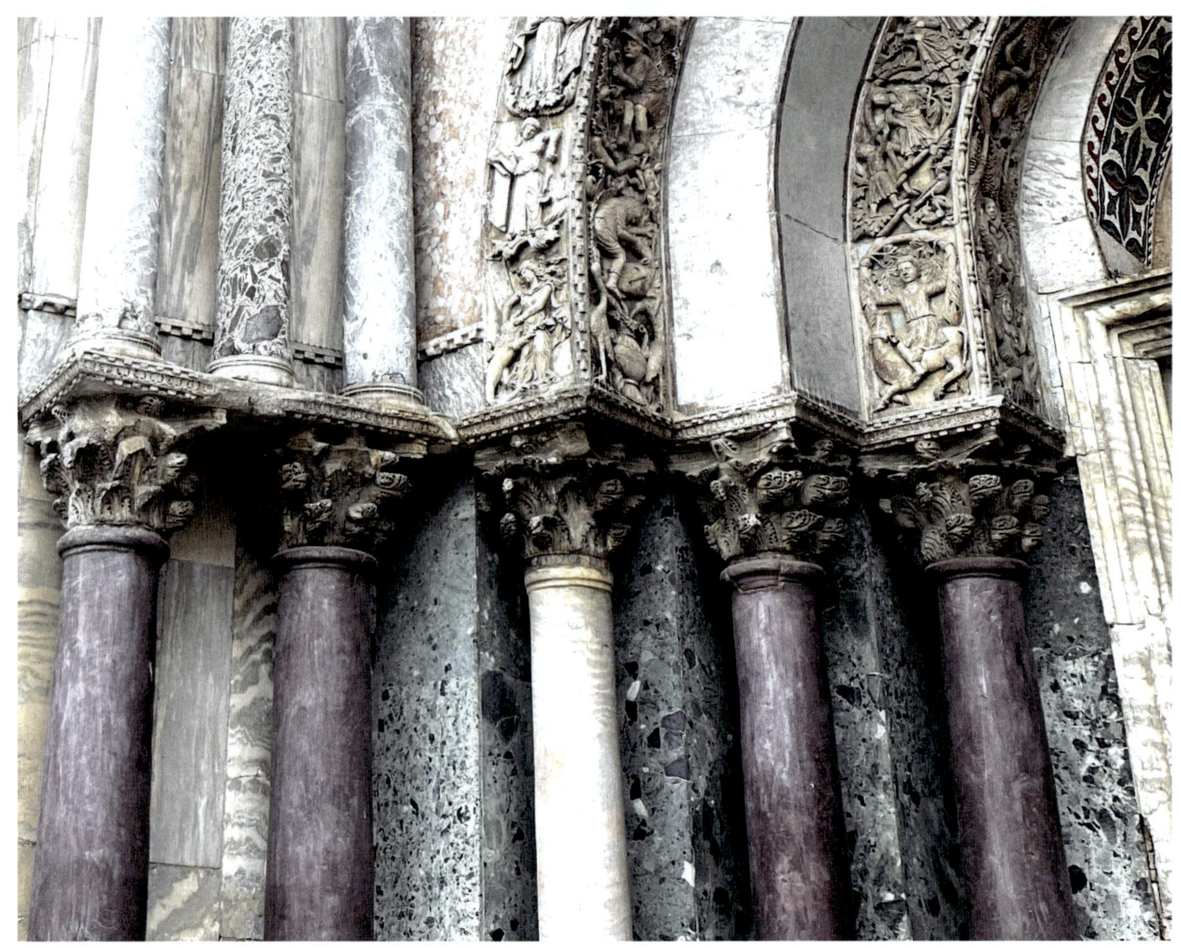

PRECIOUS RED PORPHYRY – IMPERIAL PURPLE

Red porphyry is one of the most precious marbles and was used to symbolise imperial purple. Imperial purple was the colour of the Roman Empire, expressing royal and divine greatness. The red, imperial porphyry came from ancient quarries – the Mons Porphyrites – in the Eastern Desert of Egypt. During the Roman Empire, they were the only known source of this specific imperial porphyry and, therefore, very precious for the Romans. Now, we can enjoy this beautiful marble with our eyes and touch the Roman Empire with our fingertips.

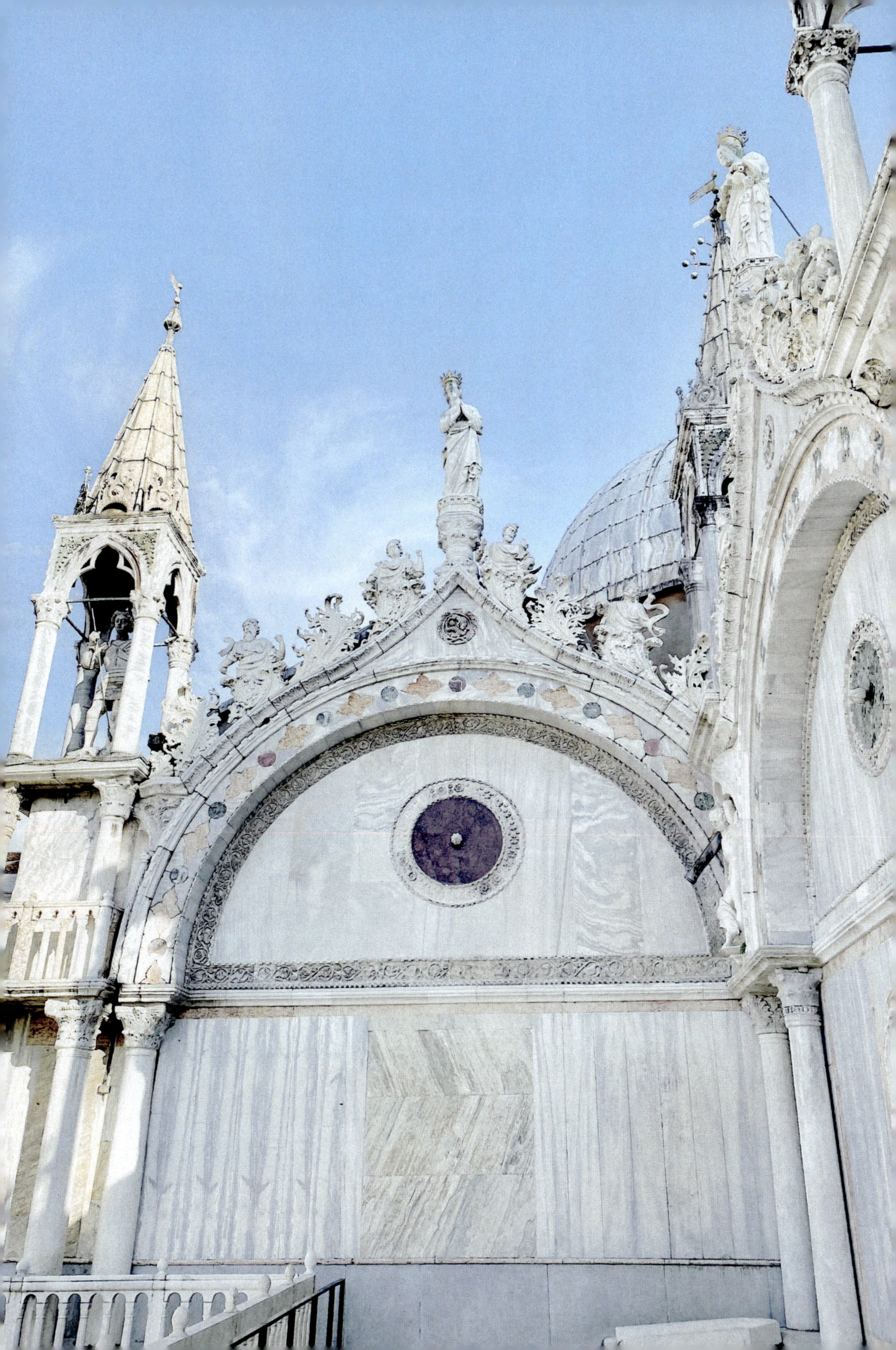

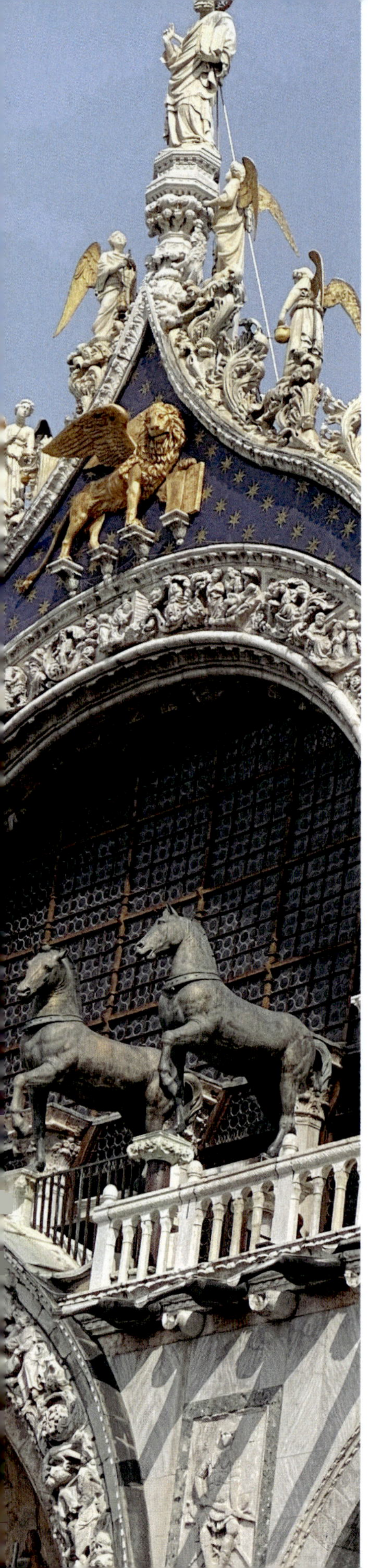

THE WINGED LION – THE SYMBOL OF VENICE

The winged lion of St. Mark's Basilica is the symbol of Venice. St. Mark is the city's patron saint, and the lion is the guardian of peace and power. Everywhere in Venice, the lion of St. Mark is visible.

SAINT MARK – THE MARTYR FROM ALEXANDRIA

Saint Mark was martyred in Alexandria and buried by Christian followers in the 1st century AD. In 828, the prestigious relic of St. Mark was brought to Venice and buried in the Basilica built to honour his memory. The Venetian lion holds a book in his hands where it says in Latin: "Pax tibi, Marce, Evangelista meus" – "Peace to you, Mark, my evangelist."

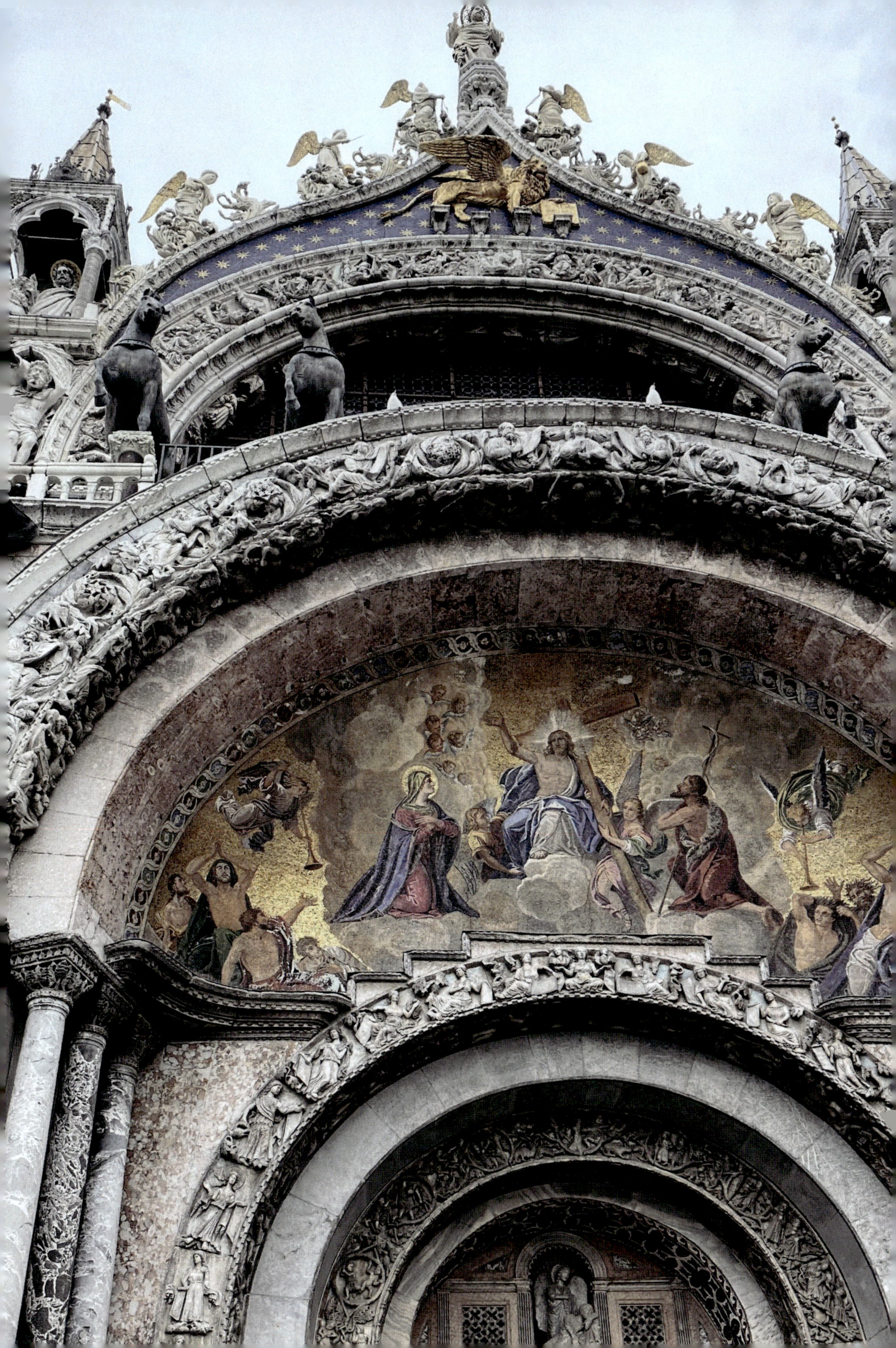

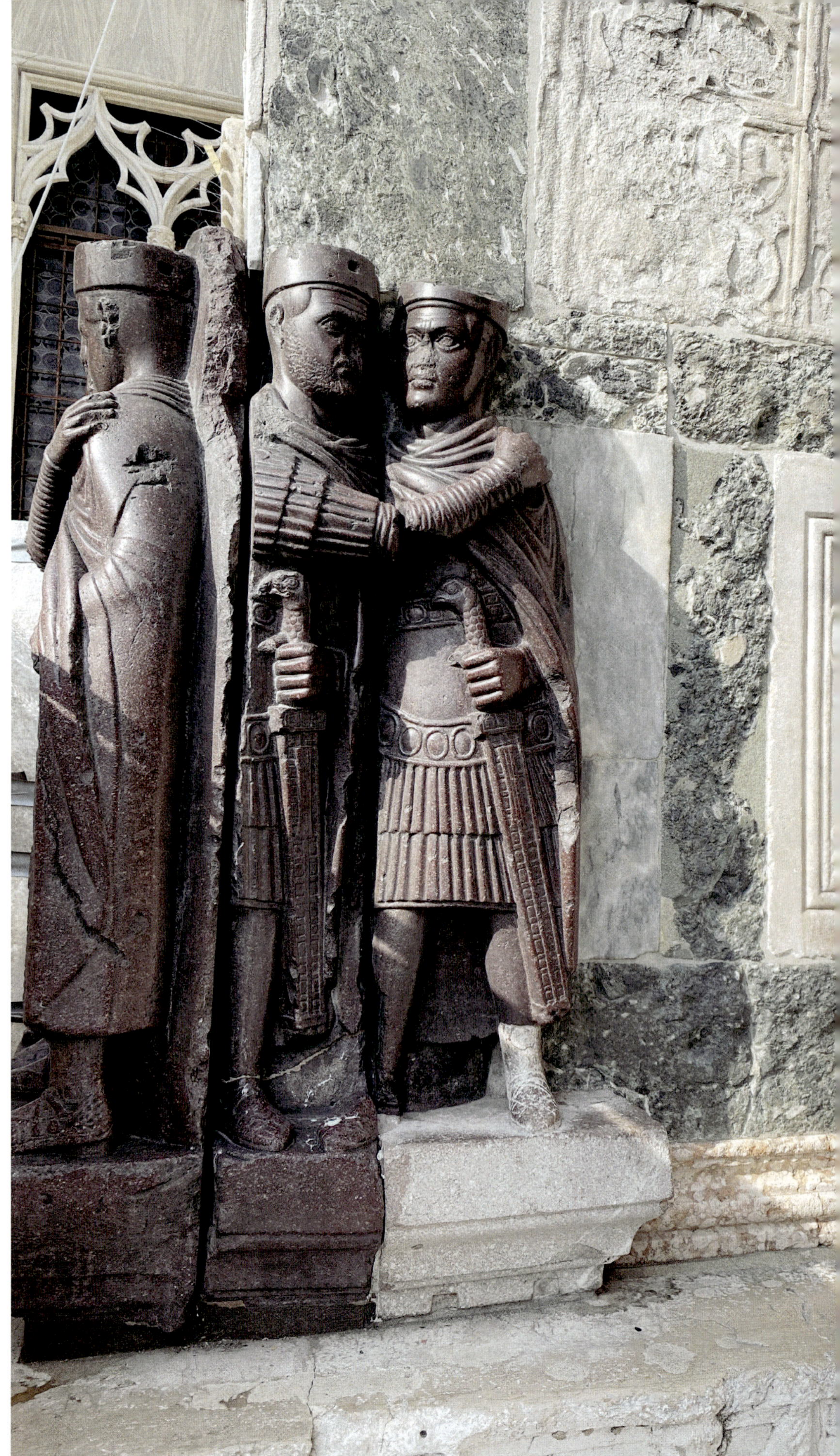

THE FOUR TETRARCHS – A WARM HUG AT THE CORNER

Warm hugs that have lasted for almost 2,000 years. It looks like four close friends guarding St. Mark's Basilica, but the four were Emperors of the Roman Empire. They were sculpted with red porphyry marble from Egypt as early as 300 AD and brought to Venice from Constantinople. The sculptures are to be found on one of the corners of St. Mark's Basilica. The four Tetrarchs were plundered and brought to Venice from Constantinople in the Middle Ages. It was two separate sculptures that were once fixed to two individual pillars. At St. Mark's Basilica, they are set at one of the corners. The warm hugs create a feeling of togetherness at the corner of St. Mark's Basilica.

CAVALLI DI SAN MARCO – A TOKEN OF VICTORY

Cavalli di San Marco or The Triumphal Quadriga of St. Mark – is a set of Byzantine bronze statues with four impressive horses in movement. The sculptures date back to the 2nd century AD, expressing perfection in motion and musculature. The figures have both a fantastic story and have had a long life. The statues originate from Byzantium, the city that later became Constantinople.

The four horses once decorated the entrance gate of the Hippodrome – the Roman arena for entertainment and horse racing. The horses were then brought to Venice as Constantinople fell in 1204 and placed at the entrance of St. Mark's Basilica, looking out over the city representing victory and triumph.

In 1797, Napoleon took The Triumphal Quadriga and moved it to Paris. He was manifesting his power and victory, showing Europe and the world that he was the new Emperor and successor.

After Napoleon's defeat, the horses were delivered back to Venice and St. Mark's Basilica. Until 1980, the original horses were placed outside the Basilica, but due to pollution, a replica was made, and the original statues are now to be found inside the Basilica. The Quadriga has experienced and seen a lot – what if they could tell us their story?

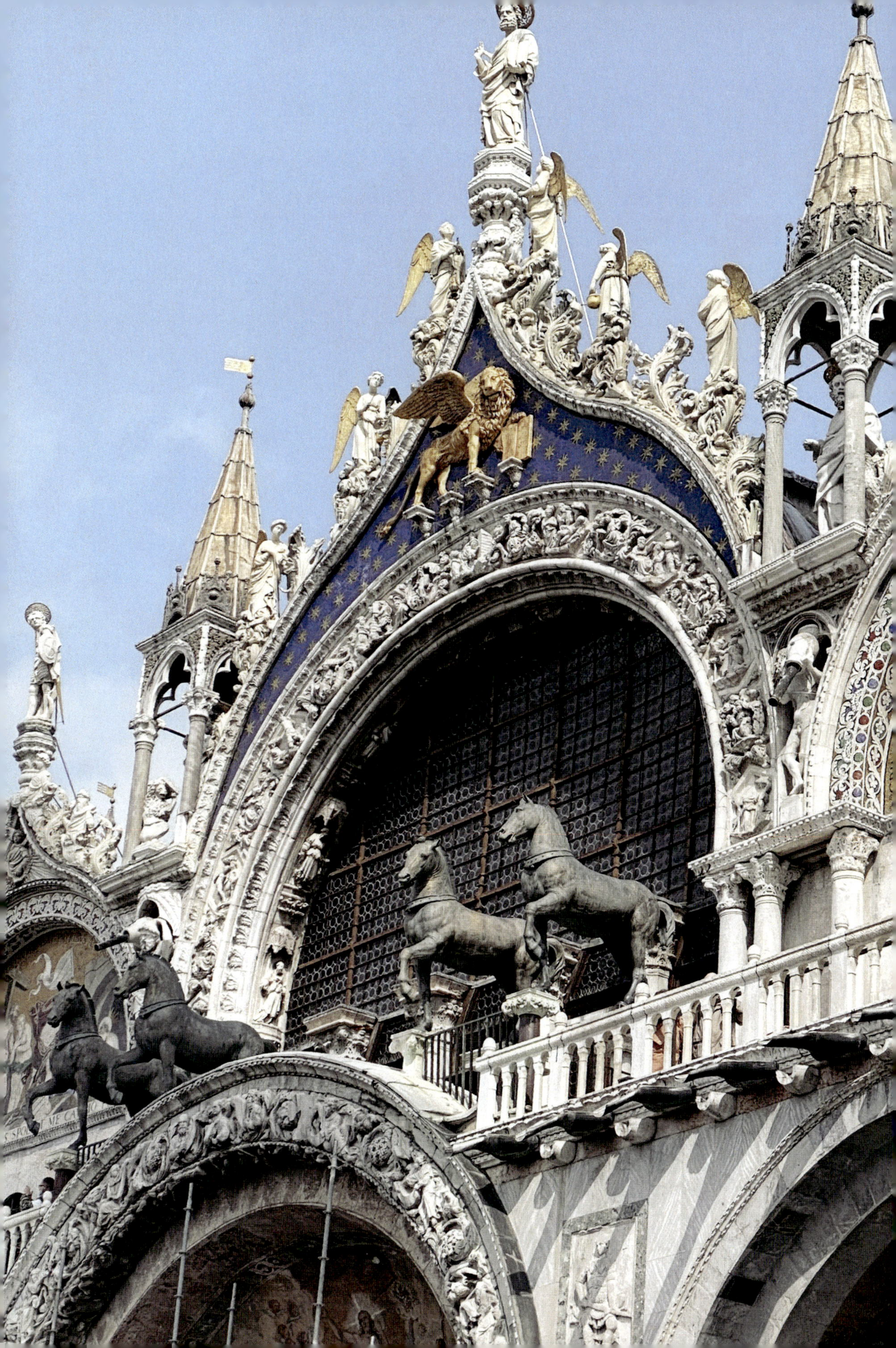

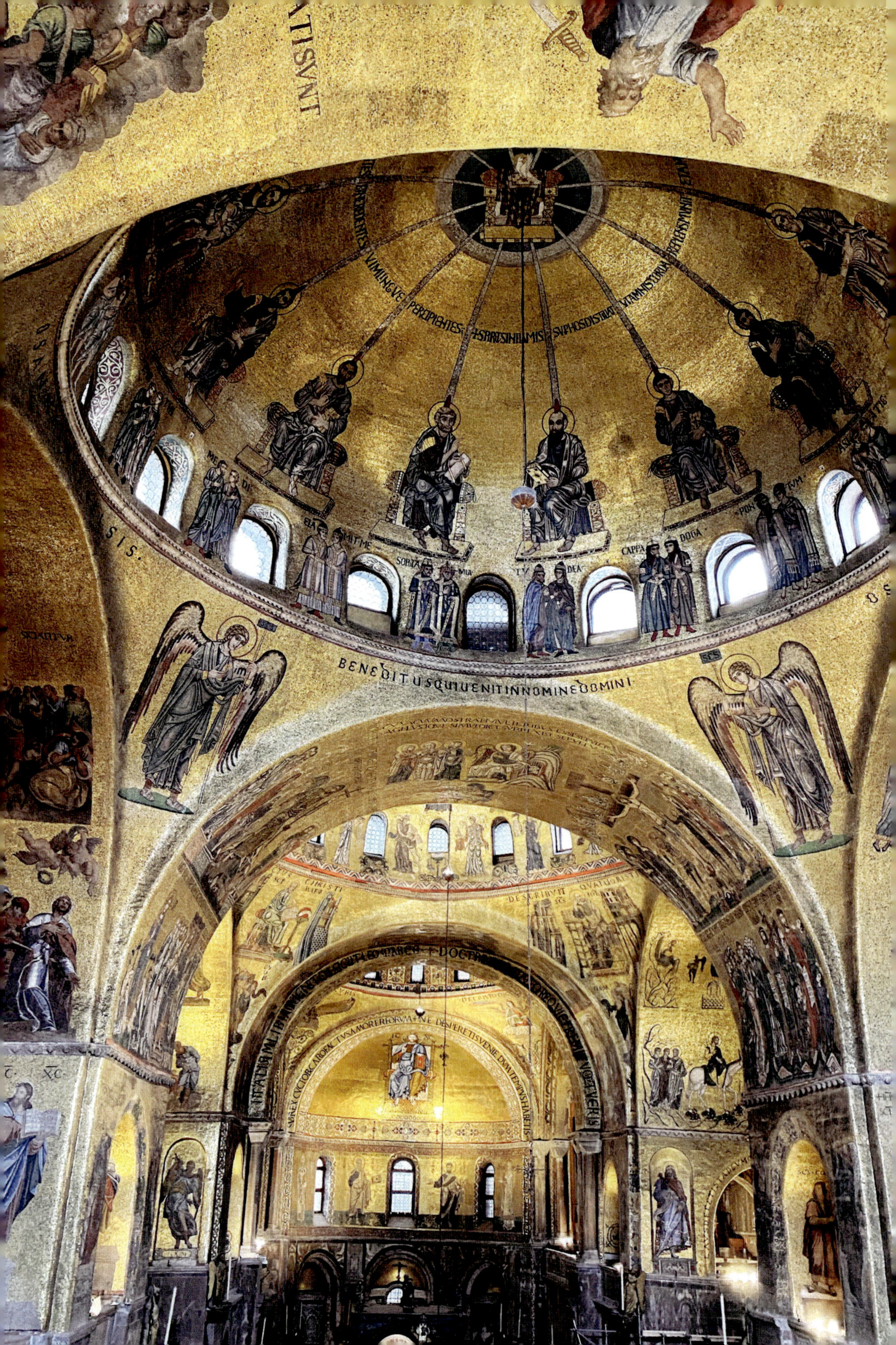
BENEDITUSQUIUENITINNOMINEDOMINI

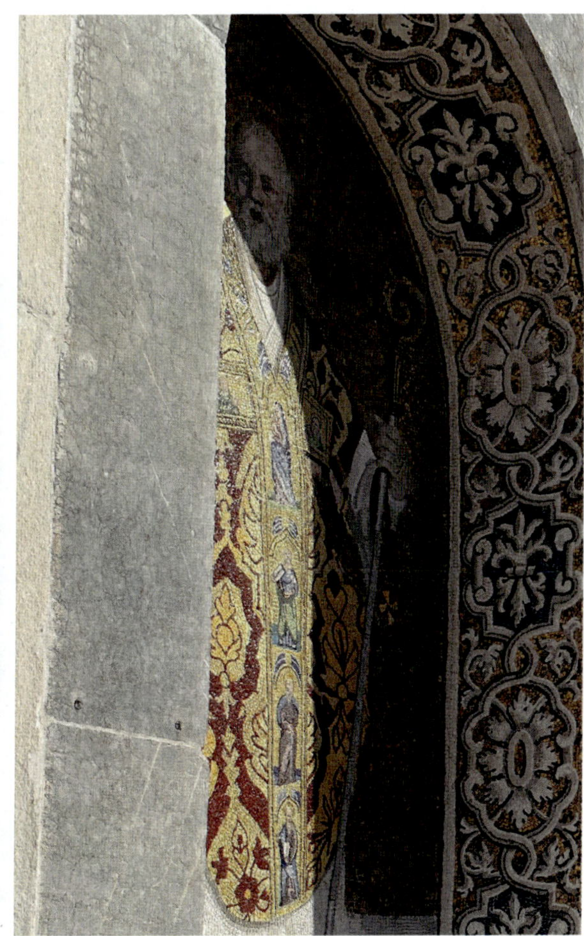

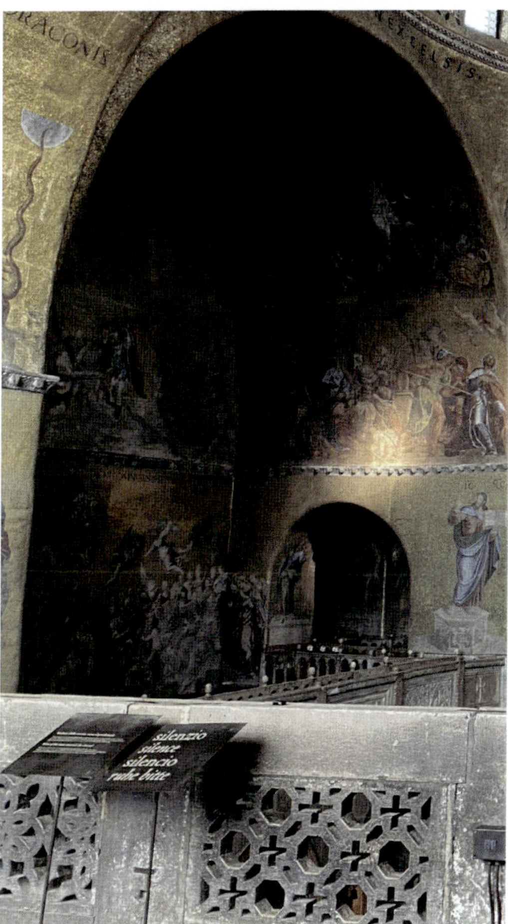

GOLDEN SHIMMER – STUNNING MOSAIC

Inside St. Mark's Basilica, the walls are covered with mosaics with golden backgrounds. It creates a golden shimmer over the entire indoor environment. The mosaics cover an area of more than 8,000 square metres. These mosaics were developed over eight centuries, so it has been an ongoing artistic work for centuries. The mosaics visualise a great selection of stories from the Bible and the lives of Christ, the Virgin Mary, and different Saints, with Saint Mark as the leading Saint and character. The ever-changing light during the day creates new visual effects depending on how the rays strike the golden mosaics.

WINDOWS WITH BEAUTIFUL PASTEL COLOURS

The colour of the glass plays with the colours of the marble in soft pastels of pink, green, brown, and purple. The windows are made of small pieces of circular glass and contrast with the clean and smooth surface of the marble. The coloured glass filters and softens the Venetian sunshine before entering the Basilica.

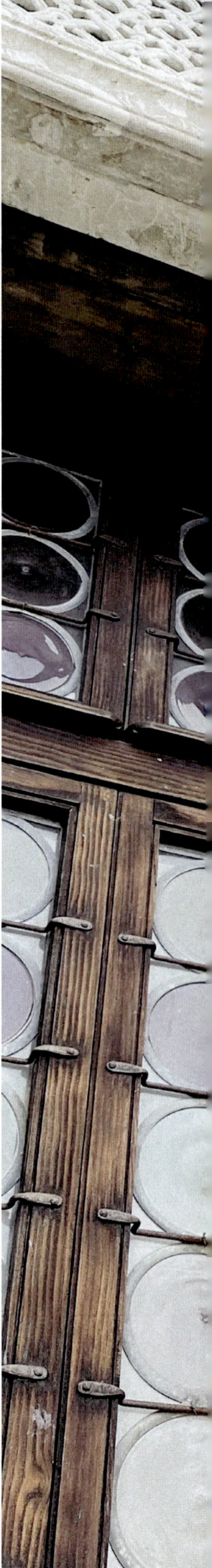

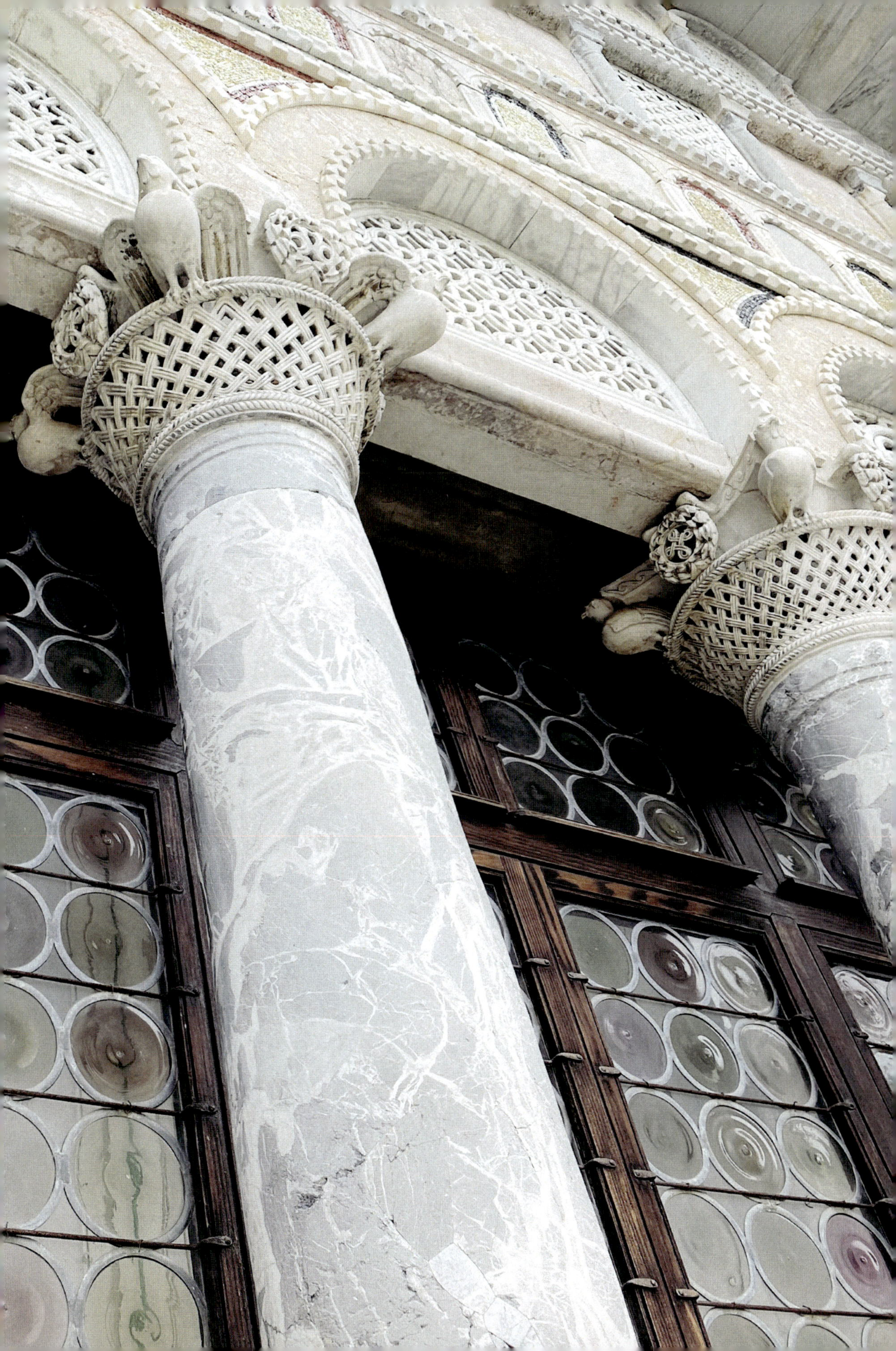

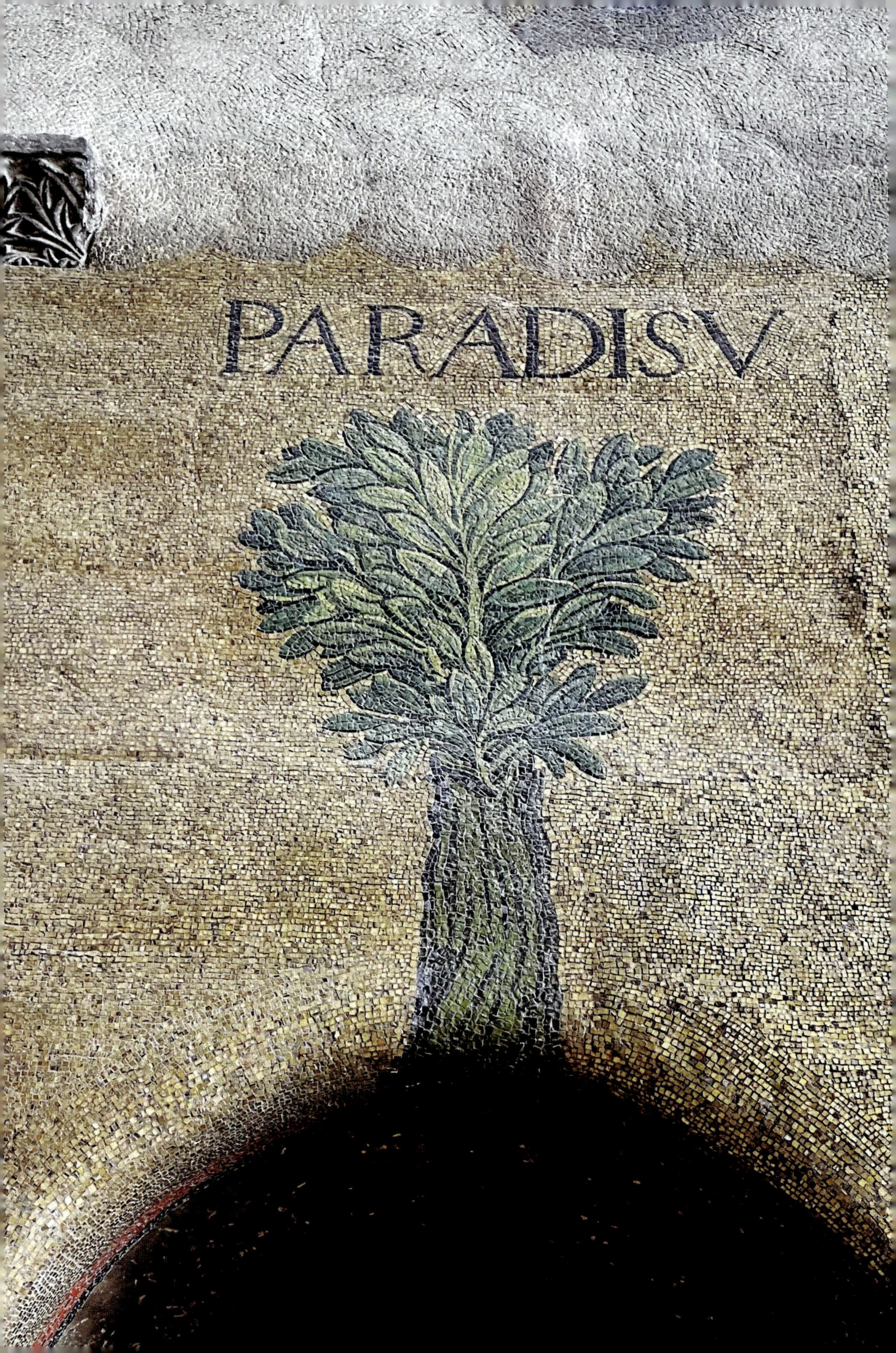
PARADISV

A PARADISE OF MOSAIC – THE GARDEN OF EDEN FOR ART

This beautiful mosaic tree from the Garden of Eden decorates one of the many vaults in the Basilica. The leaves are made using thousands of tiny pieces of tiles in different shades of green, giving the mosaic life, light, and motion. Even the inscriptions are written in mosaic, and the typography shows utmost perfection. The words are in Latin and give a deeper meaning to the mosaic. Each small part is a unique piece of art, telling its own story from the Bible.

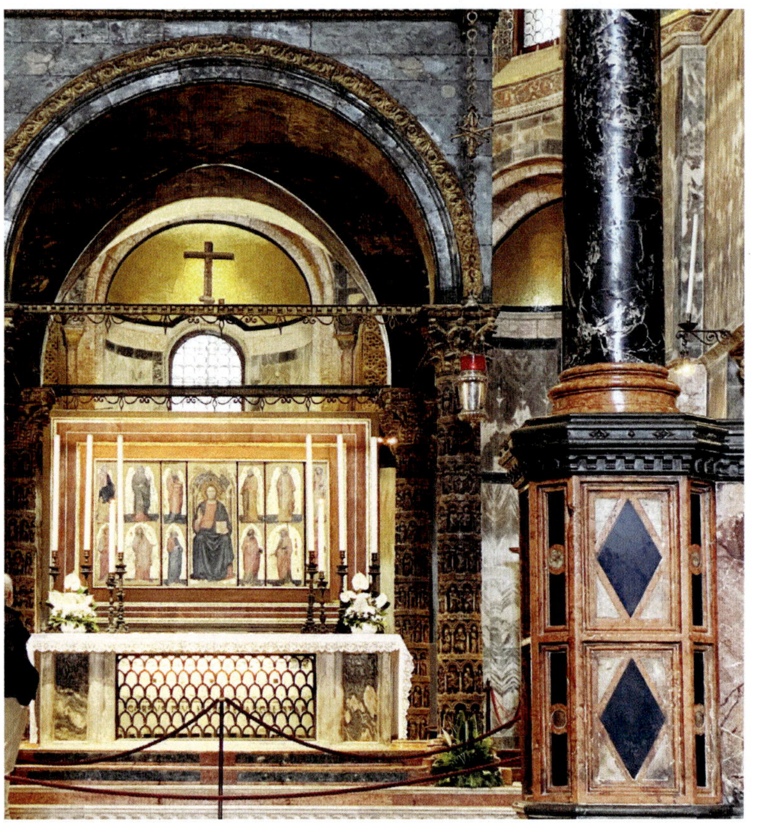

PALA D'ORO – THE HIGH ALTAR

Pala d'Oro is the incredibly precious altarpiece of St. Mark's Basilica. The Byzantine altar screen is gold and decorated with hundreds of gems – emeralds, sapphires, rubies, and amethysts – with over one thousand pearls. The precious stones embody the divine and light, and illustrate stories from the Bible – a masterpiece of unique craftwork. The high altar keeps the relics of Saint Mark. In the early 19th century, the Evangelist's relics were moved from the crypt and found a more central place in the heart of the Basilica.

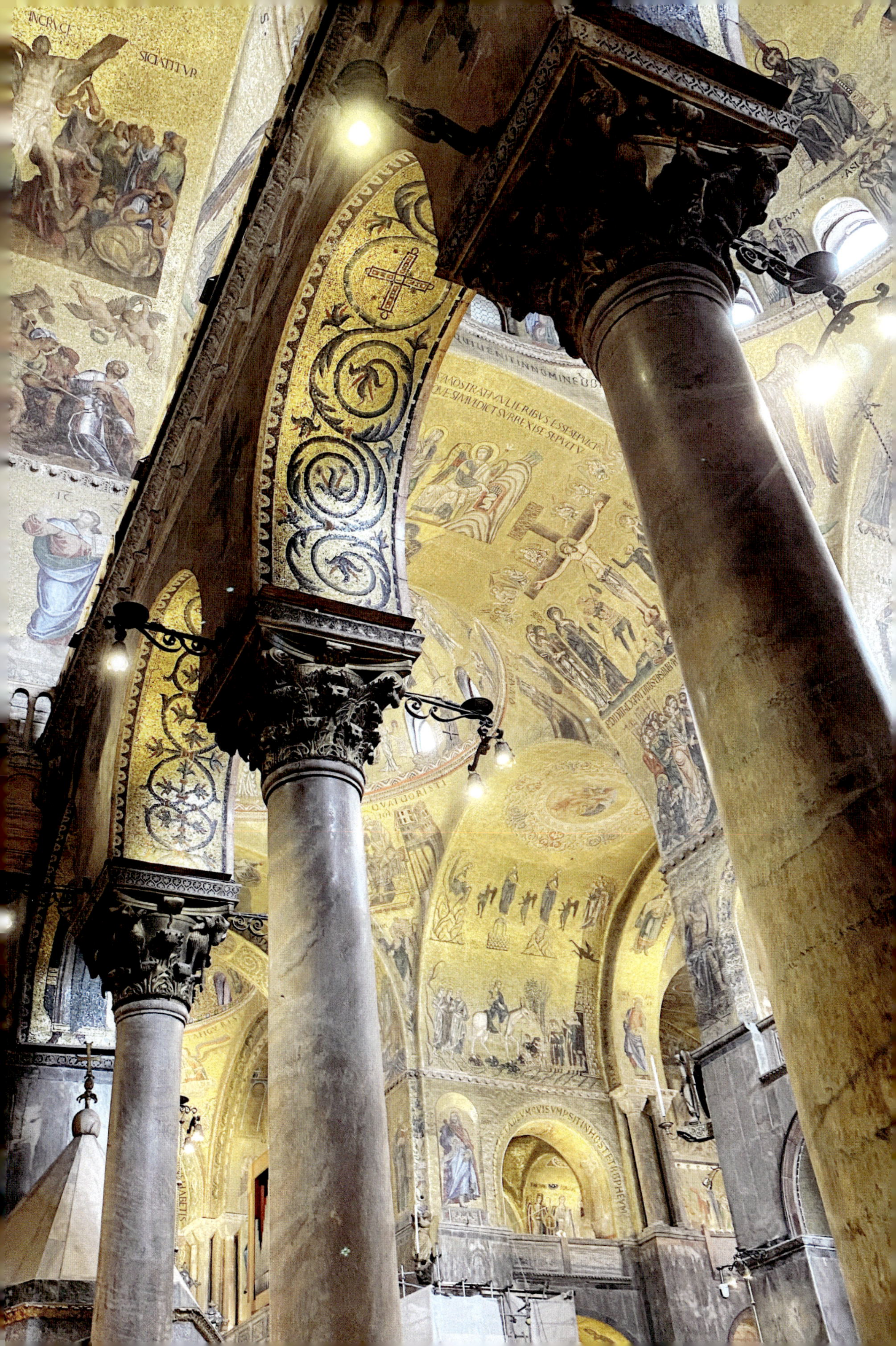

PIAZZA SAN MARCO – STYLISH PATTERNS, GREAT PERSPECTIVES

With its great perspectives, straight lines, perfect geometry, and architectural symmetry – the square and the grand buildings surrounding the square manifest the power of the Venetian Doges. St. Mark's Square (Piazza San Marco) is the true heart of Venice and has been for almost one thousand years.

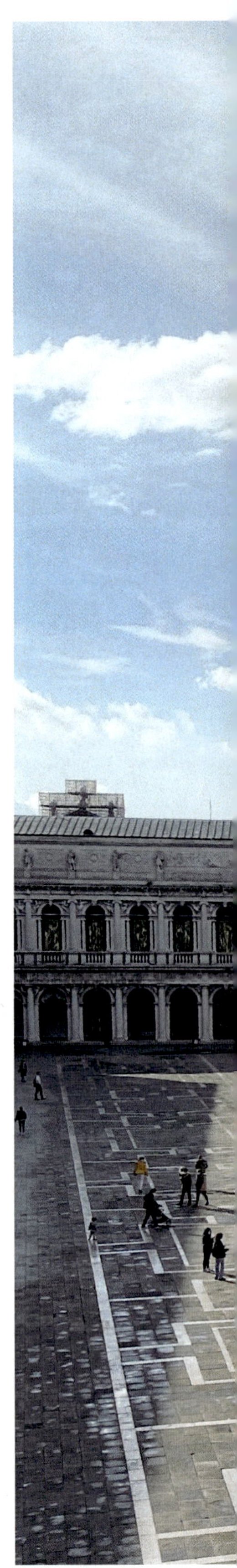

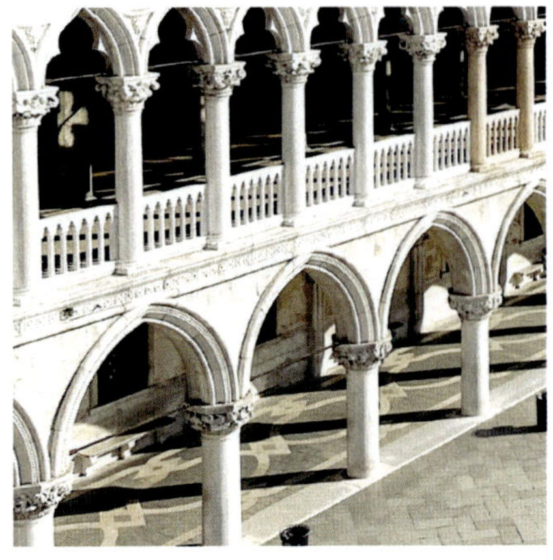

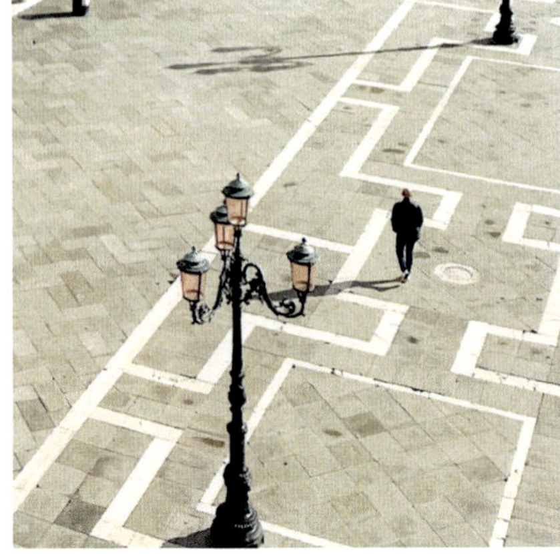

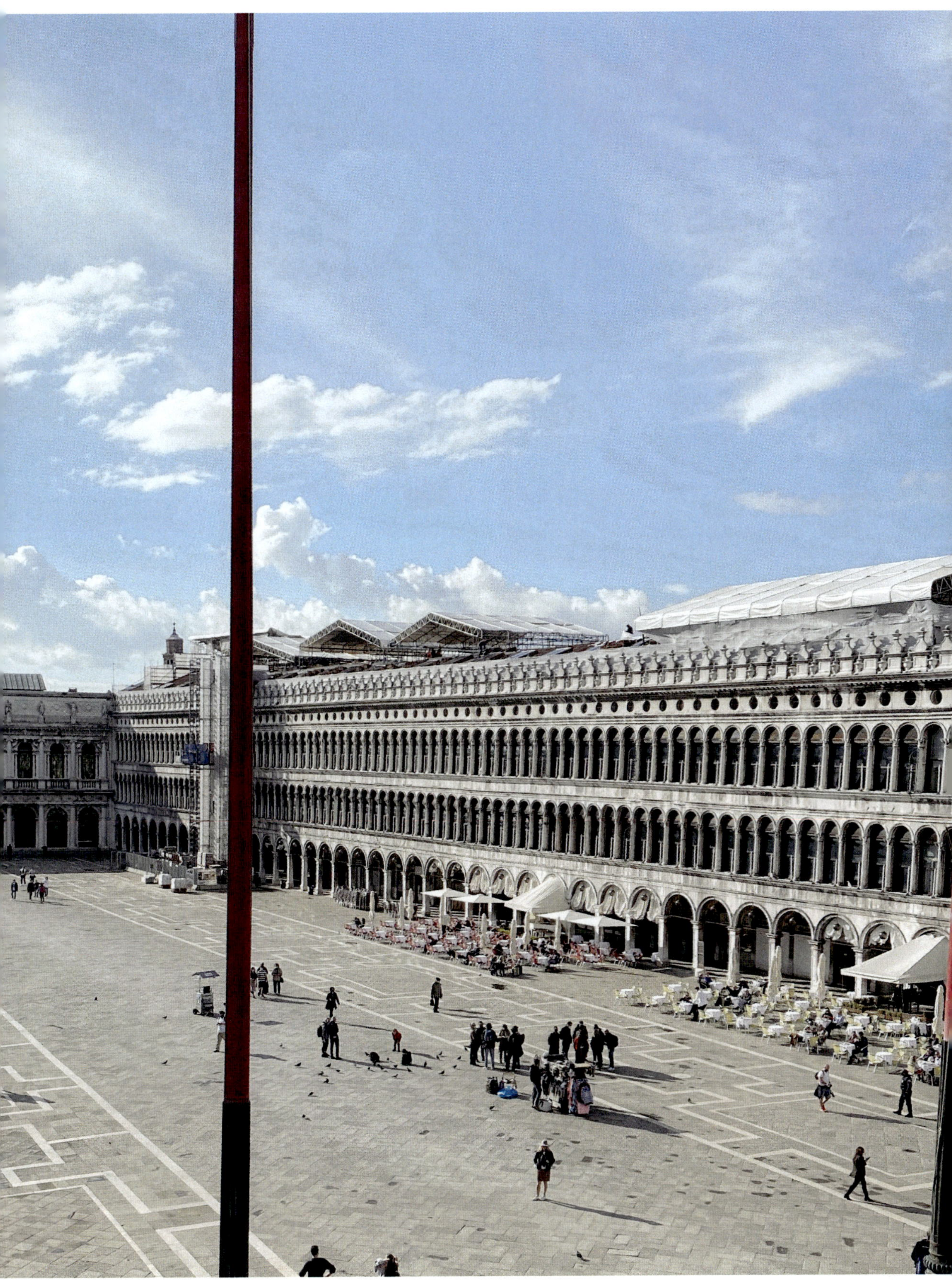

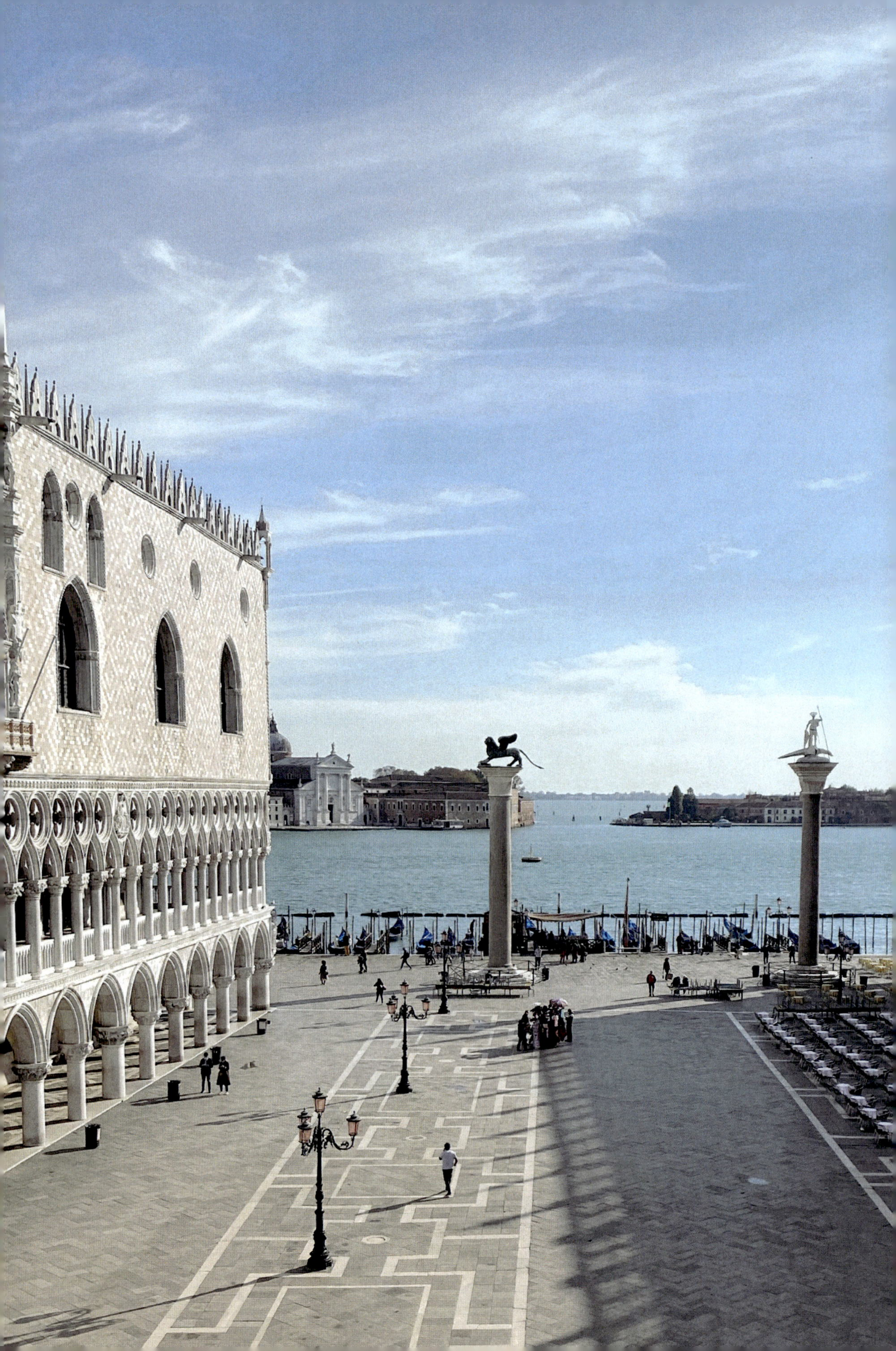

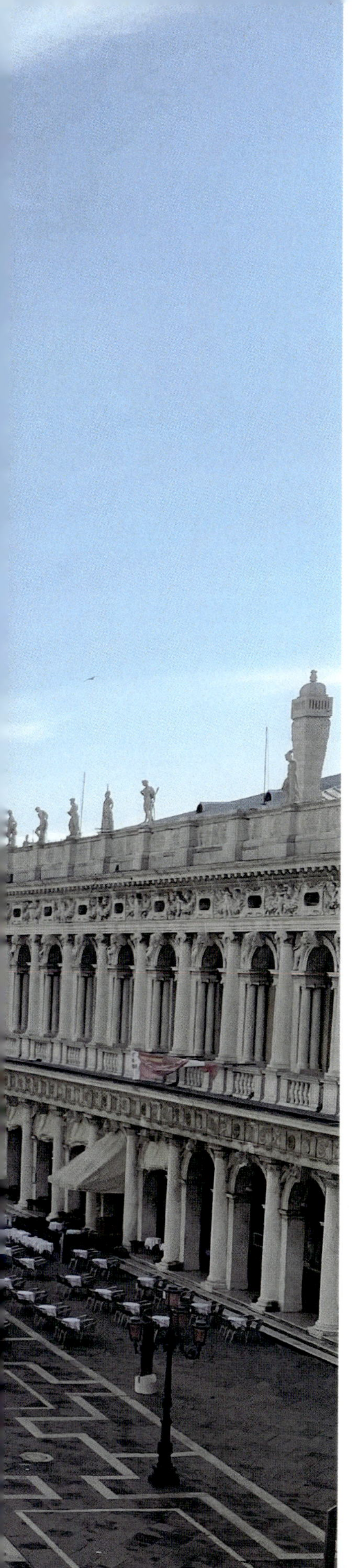

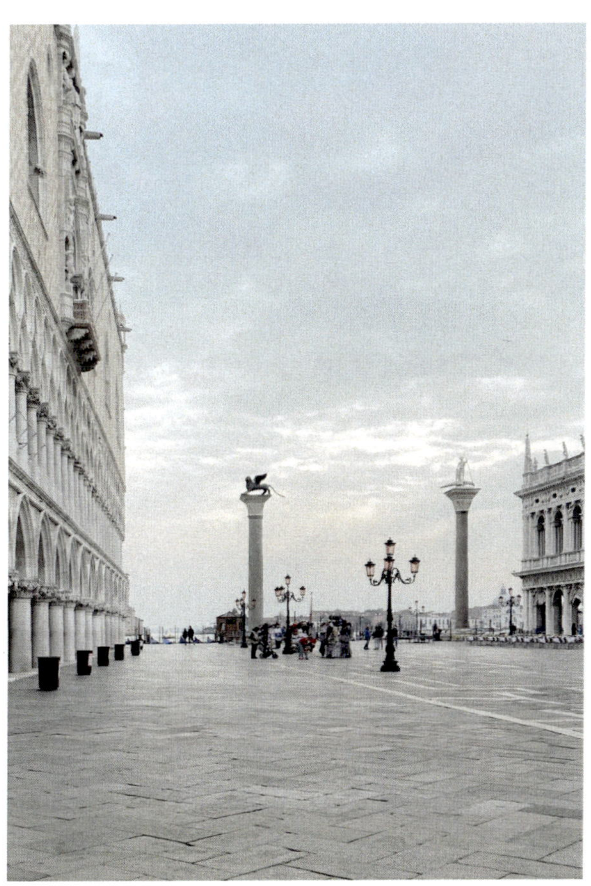

HERRINGBONE PATTERN

Once, the square was covered with grass before the stylish herringbone pattern was paved onto the court in 1264. The Piazza has also borrowed design influences from the Orient – with its large, oriental patterns and geometric design.

TORRE DELL'OROLOGIO – AN ASTRONOMICAL MASTERPIECE

The beautiful Venice astronomical clock was completed in 1499. St. Mark's Clock (Torre dell'Orologio) displays time, the moon's phase, and the Zodiac's dominant sign.

The clock tower originally housed a clock keeper who lived there with his family. The job of the clock keeper was to take care of the clock, have complete control over its complicated engineering, and ensure that every part of the astronomical clock worked adequately.

Five hundred years later, St. Mark's Clock powers on in Venice!

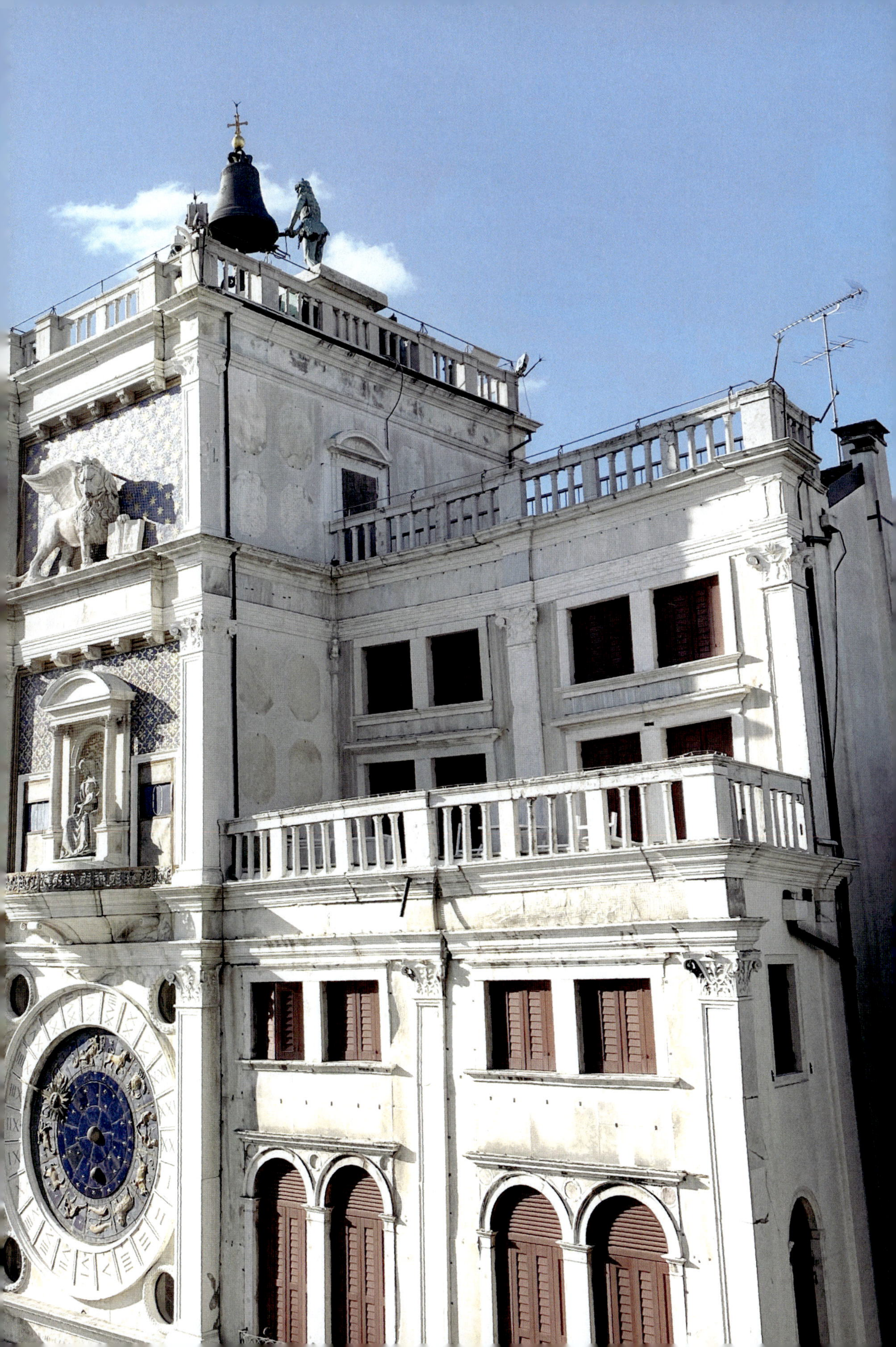

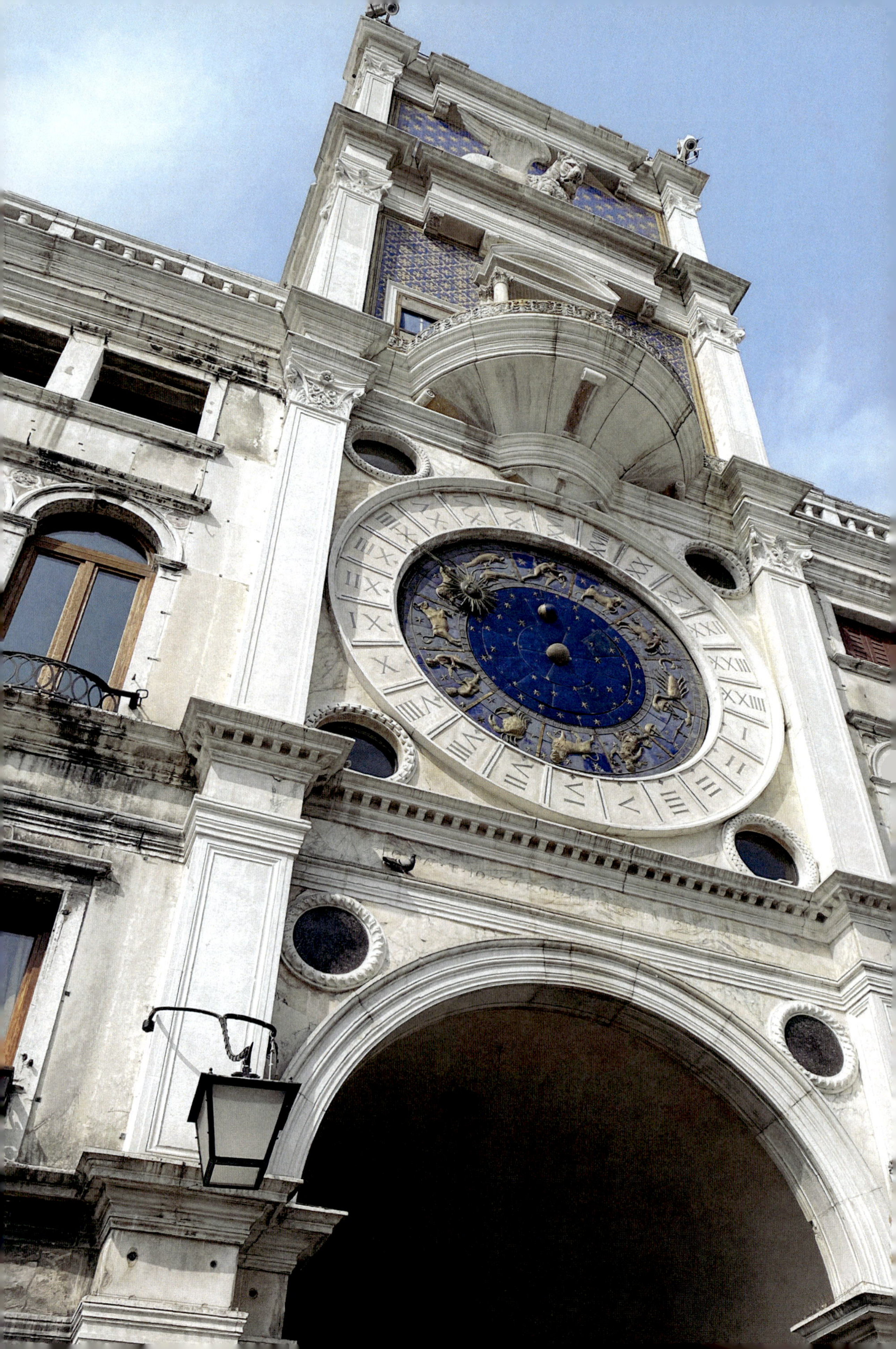

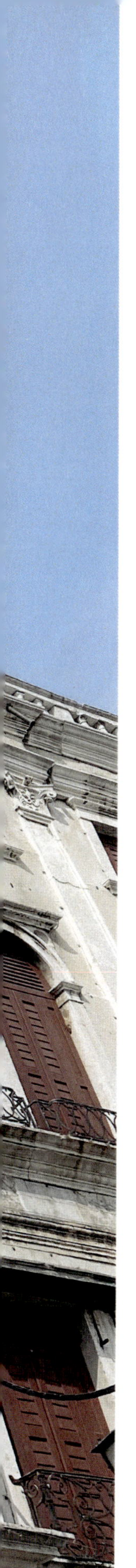

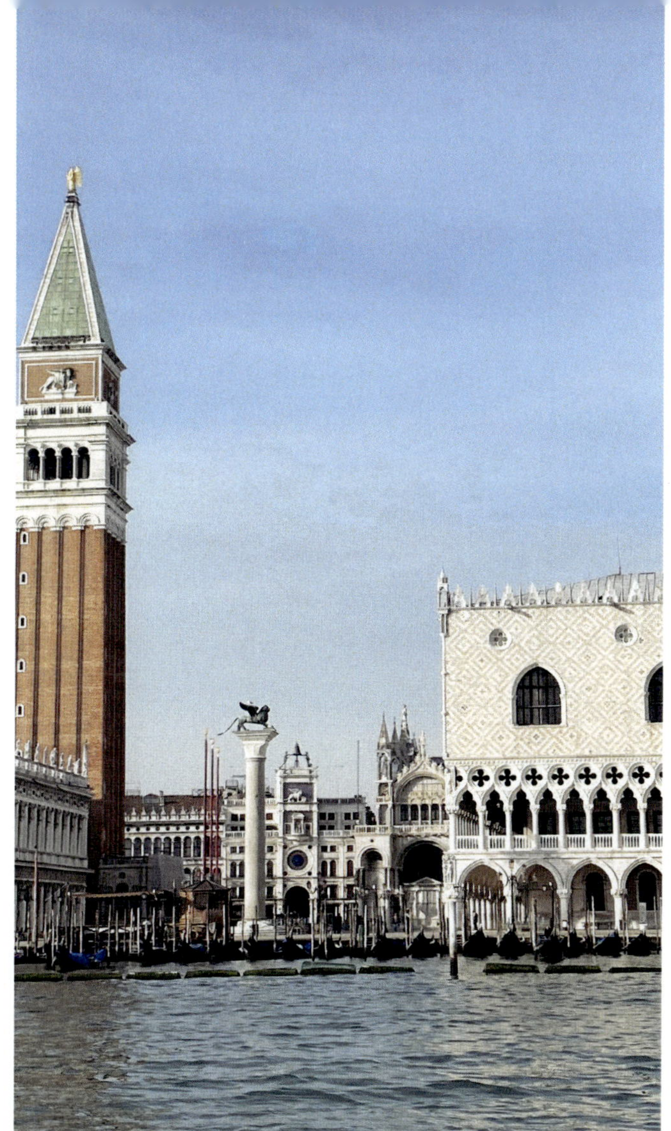

FACING THE LAGOON – THE ENTRANCE TO MERCERIE

The St. Mark's Clock (Torre dell'Orologio) stands proudly on the north side of St. Mark's Square, and the beautiful Renaissance building faces the lagoon. The clock tower is also the entrance to the Mercerie area leading up to Rialto.

THE CAFÉS OF SAN MARCO – EUROPE'S FIRST COFFEE HOUSES

St. Mark's Square is surrounded by cafés, all with a great heritage and past. Napoleon described St. Mark's Square as the Salon and Drawing Room of Europe. It is undoubtedly a fashionable meeting point for Venice visitors. It is a suitable place to take a break and enjoy the beauty of the fantastic buildings and the waterfront of the lagoon.

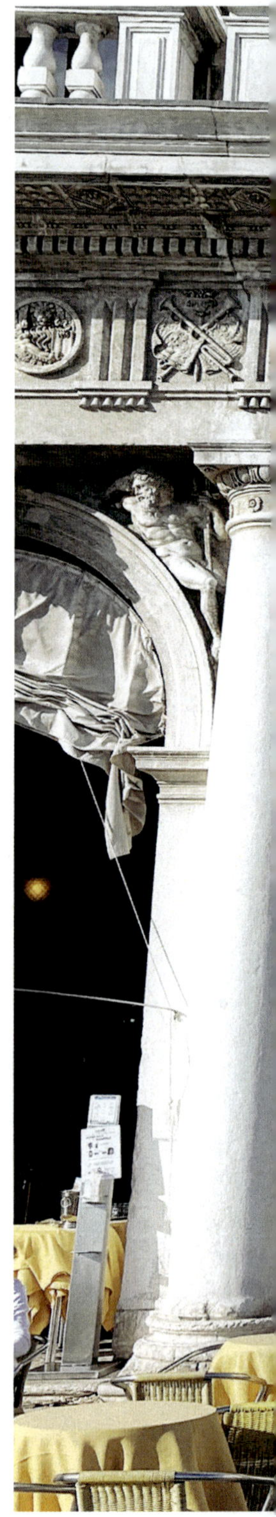

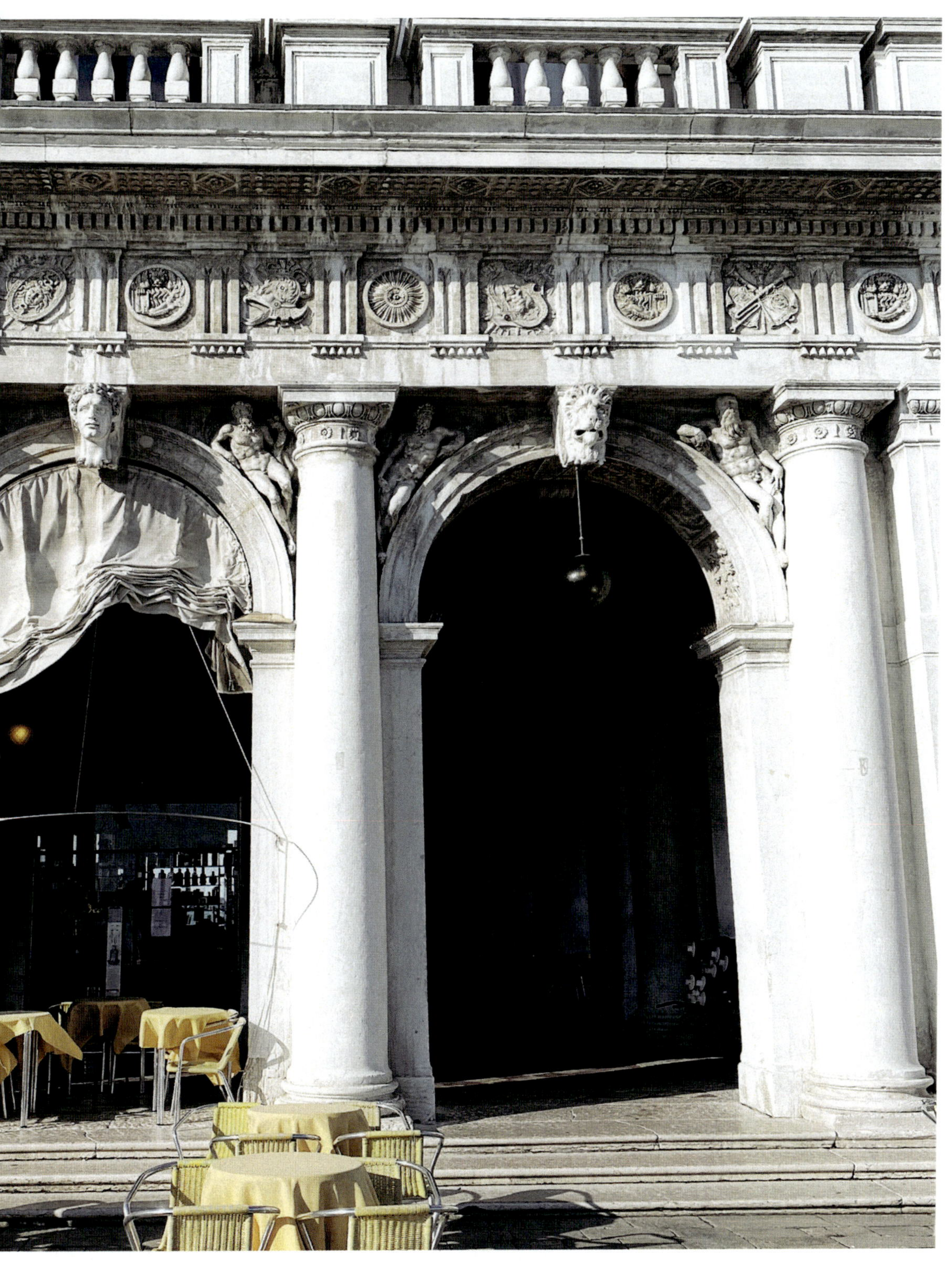

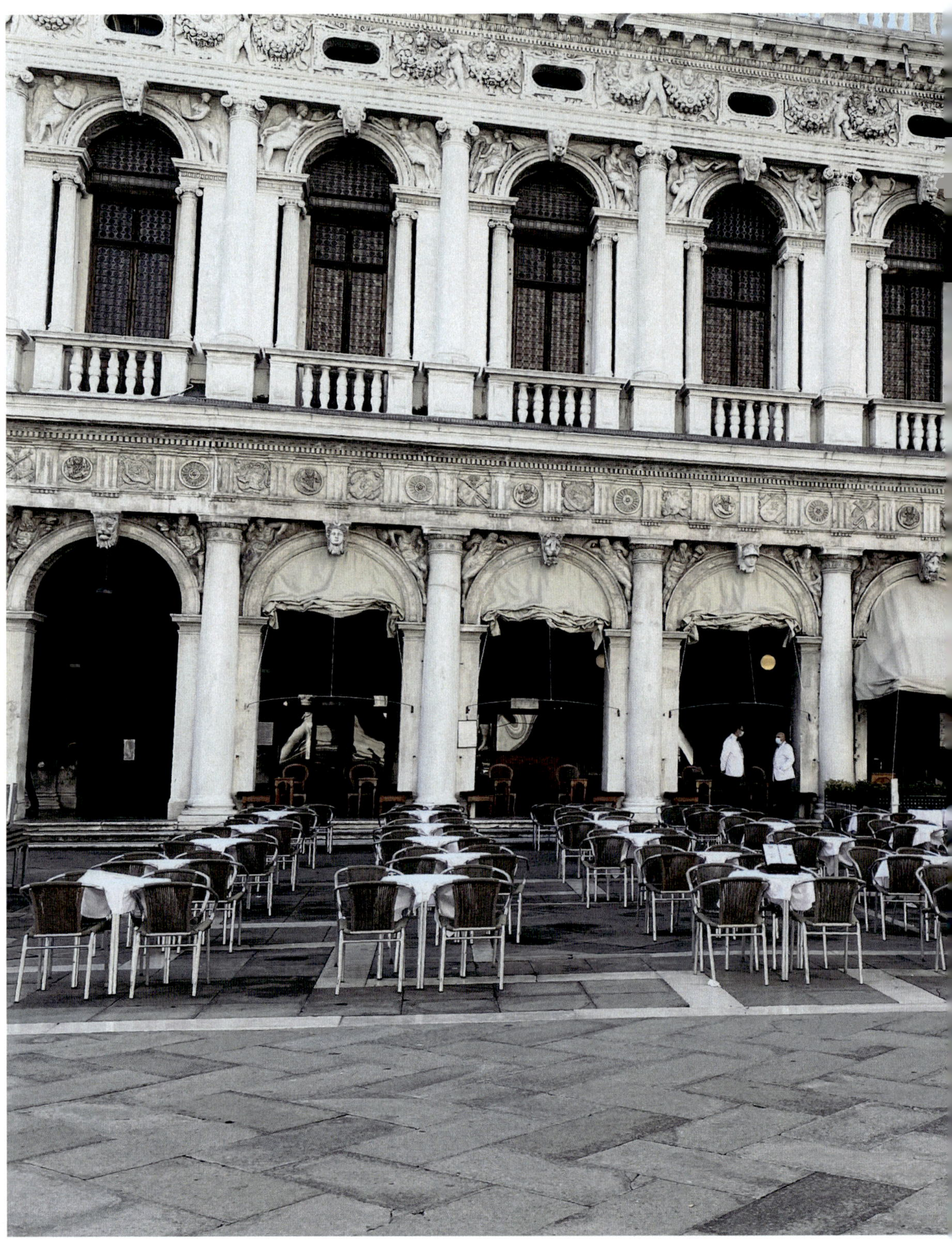

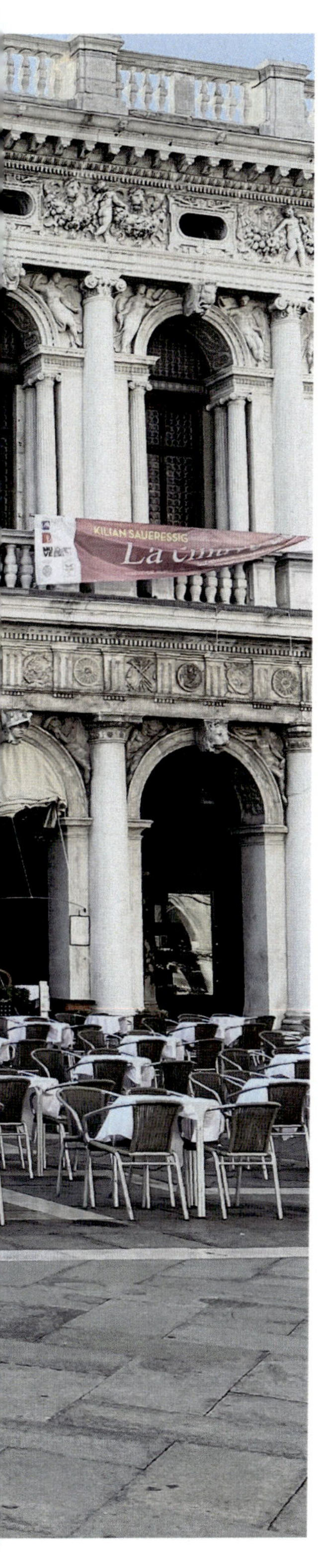

ALPINI – THE FATHER OF ITALIAN COFFEE

The Italian coffee culture came to light in Venice. The Italian botanist, Prospero Alpini, who had lived for a long time in Egypt, introduced coffee to the Venetians at the end of the 16th century.

Alpini laid the foundation for the great Italian coffee culture that was then developed. A hundred years later, coffee drinking was a part of the social culture, and the first coffee houses were established around St. Mark's Square.

One of the most famous coffee houses on St. Mark's Square is Caffè Florian. The coffee house opened in 1720 and is one of Europe's oldest cafés. Here, Goethe and many other famous European writers, poets, and politicians enjoyed a precious coffee moment.

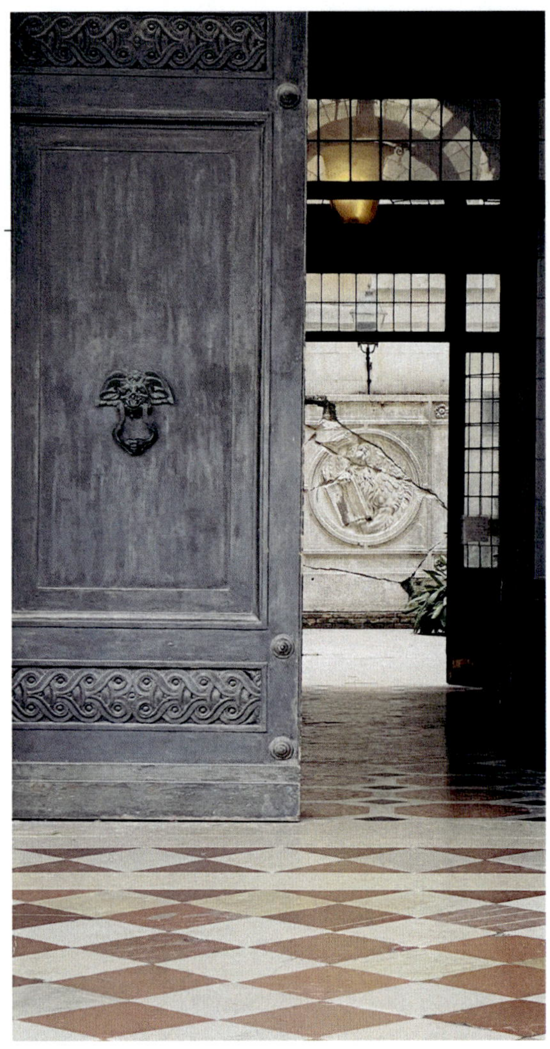

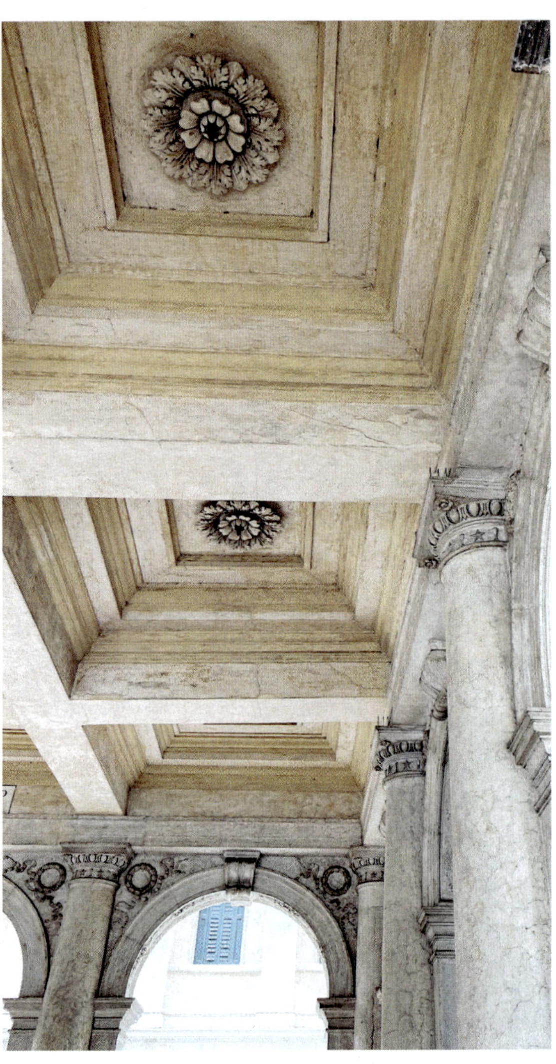

THE AMBIANCE OF PIAZZA SAN MARCO

From glory days to darker times, the square has conquered time with its beauty. Since the medieval ages, a bustling square has been in the centre of Venice. It is one of the most beautiful piazzas in the world. The Basilica di San Marco, the Palazzo Ducale, impressive government buildings, and cafés – frame the square.

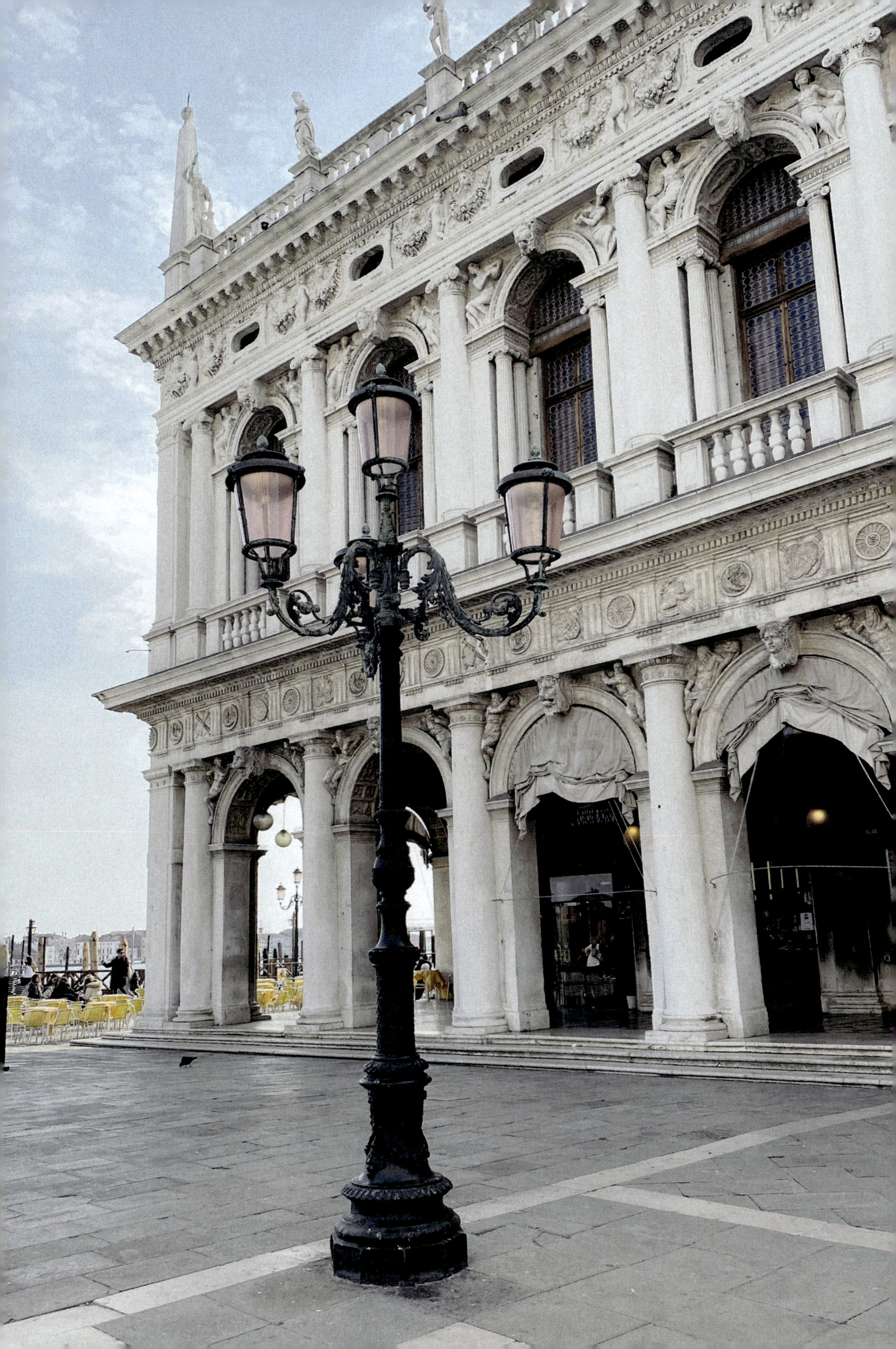

IV

PONTE DI RIALTO

THE RENAISSANCE BRIDGE WITH VAULT DESIGN

The beautiful vault architecture, light limestone surfaces, and the stairs' design make the bridge a beloved Venice masterpiece. The Rialto Bridge (Ponte di Rialto) is the natural connection between San Polo and San Marco, as it is the narrowest point of the Canal Grande. The bridge is an example of brilliant and purposeful Renaissance design and architecture since it enables both pedestrians and boats to pass and has small shops for commerce. In addition, its beauty and sustainable building materials have made it a true icon for Venice. The Istrian stone (Pietra d'Istria) of the Rialto Bridge has mastered time with grace.

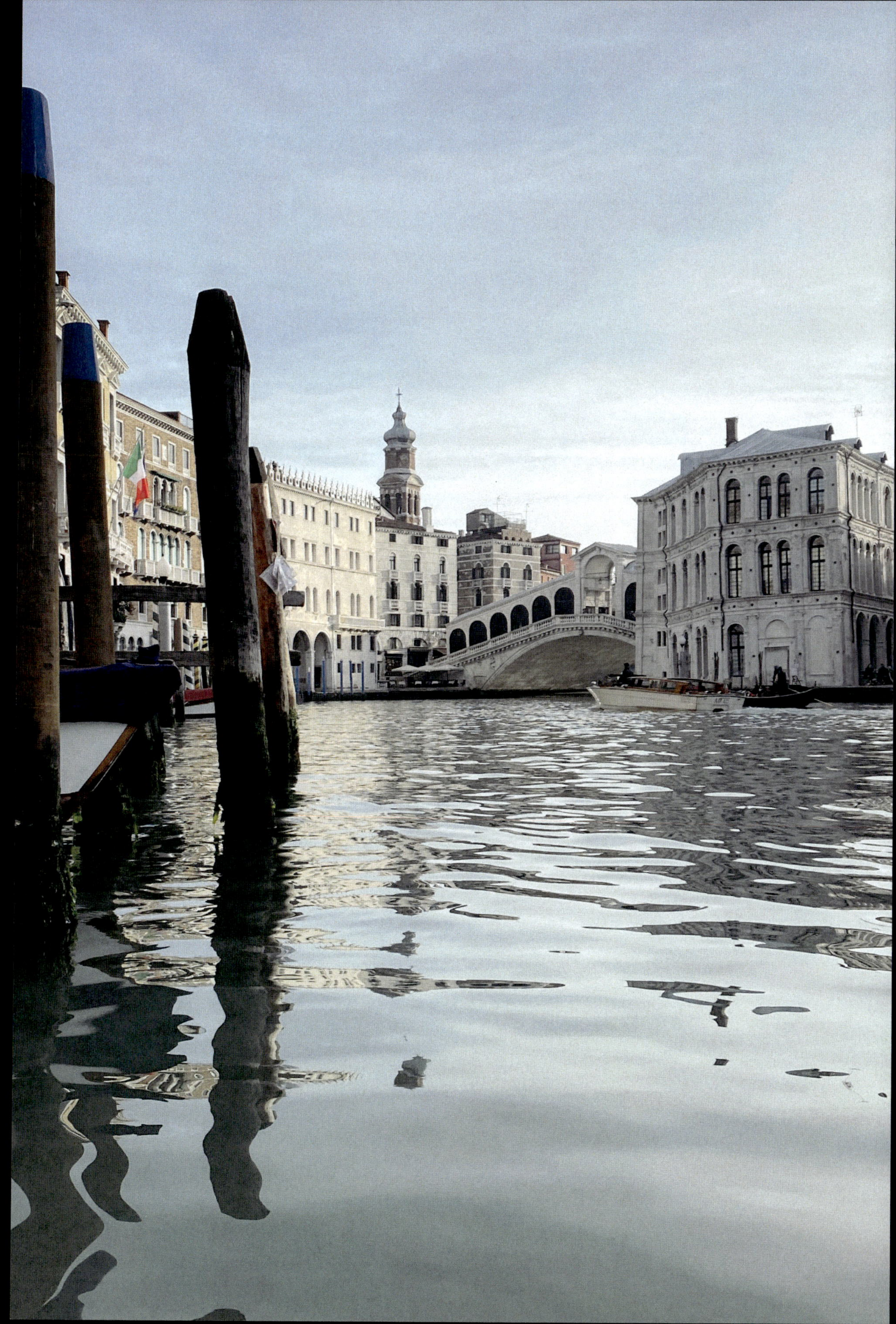

PONTE DI RIALTO

The Rialto Bridge (Ponte di Rialto) in Venice attracts the eye in many ways. The beautiful vault architecture with its light stone surfaces, the design of the stairs leading up to and down from the bridge, and the exciting idea of integrating small shops into the bridge. After competing with many bridge proposals, the architect and engineer Antonio da Ponte got the assignment to build the bridge. The bridge was finished at the end of the 16th century and has been a beloved spot for visitors to Venice ever since. The Rialto Bridge is an example of good, purposeful design. It combines easy and smooth pedestrian movement over the bridge, boats and gondolas underneath, as well as beauty, into one engineering and architectural solution.

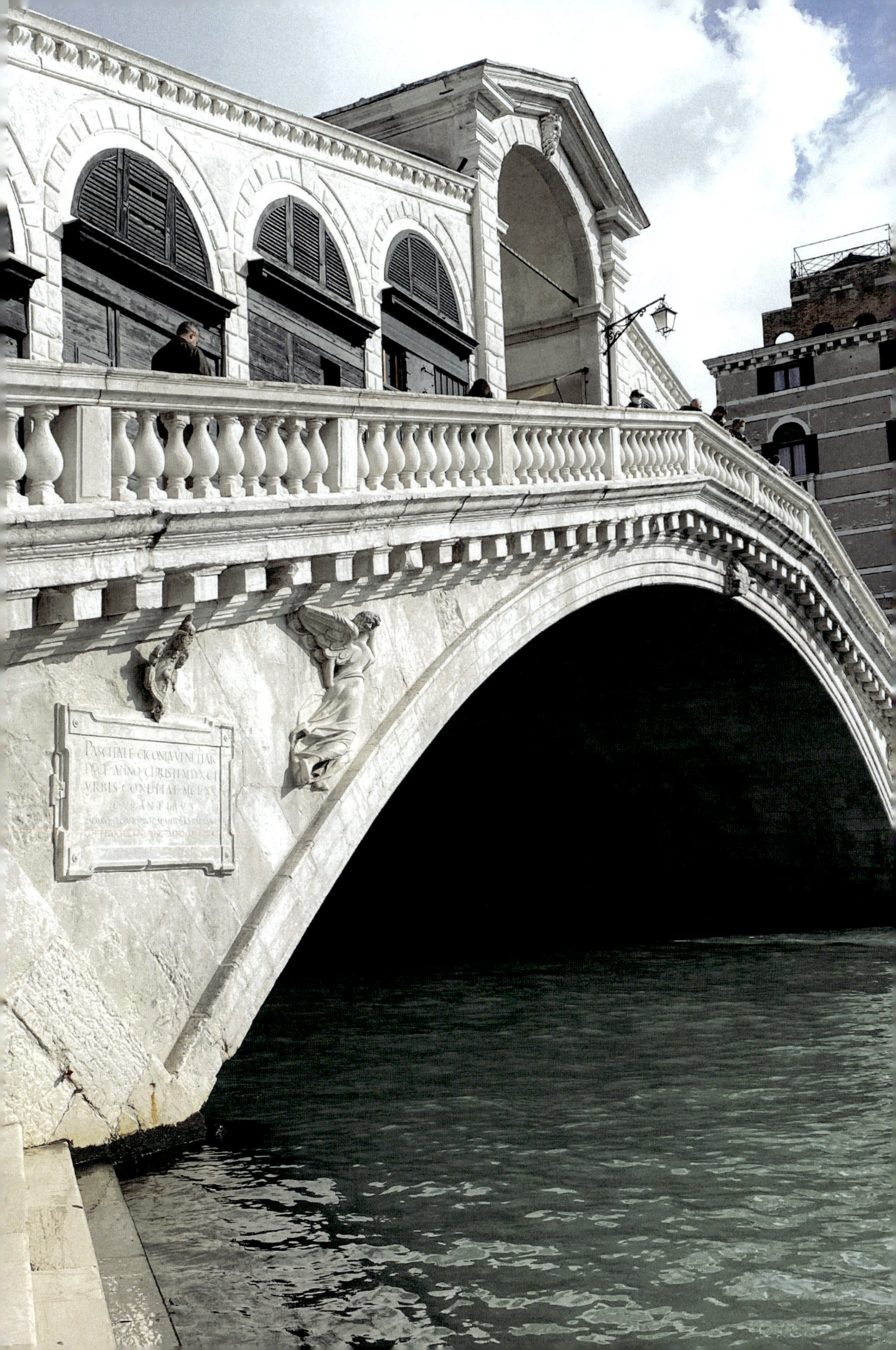
PASCHALE CICONIA VENETIAR

RIALTO BRIDGE SHOPS

The Rialto Bridge has two rows of small shops, covered with blue wooden shutters when closed. The Renaissance architect Antonio da Ponte was forward-thinking when integrating small shops into the Rialto Bridge construction. He created a Renaissance shopping experience for the pedestrians passing over the bridge. Over 400 years later, these well-designed small shops are still trading at the Rialto Bridge. After closing, the shop is sealed with the wooden shutter to cover the windows.

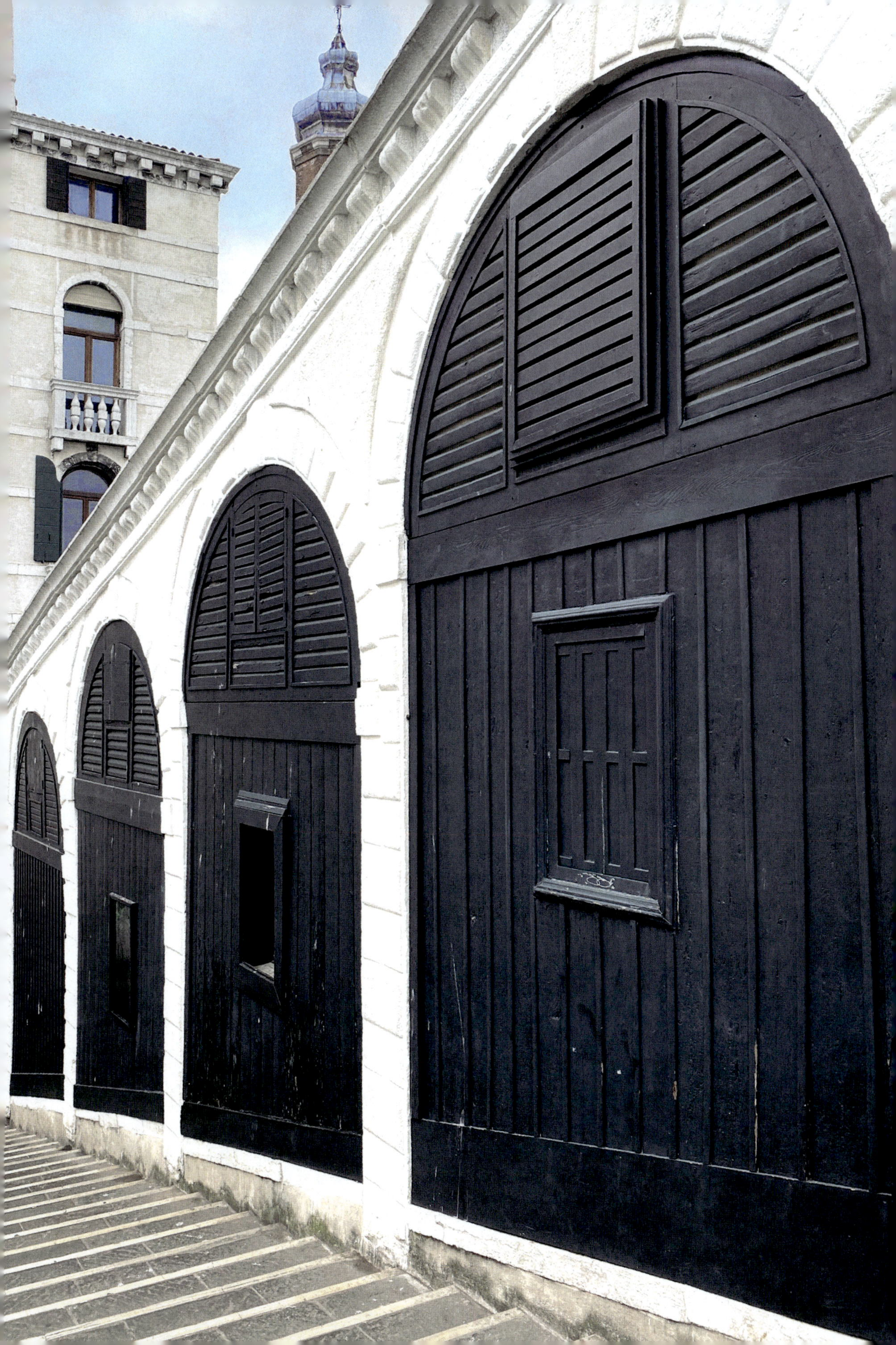

RIALTO FOOD MARKET – 1,000 YEARS OF DAILY COMMERCE

The Rialto district developed into the heart of trade and a central point for social life in Venice, with restaurants and small shops, where the Rialto food market has played an essential role in supplying food to the city. It is fascinating that fish, vegetables, and fruit have been traded for over 1,000 years in the same marketplace. The Venetians have done their daily food shopping here and found everything necessary for the typical Venetian cuisine and continue to do so today.

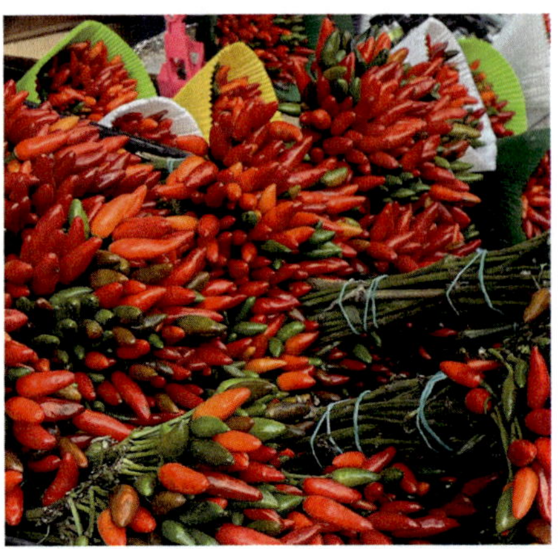

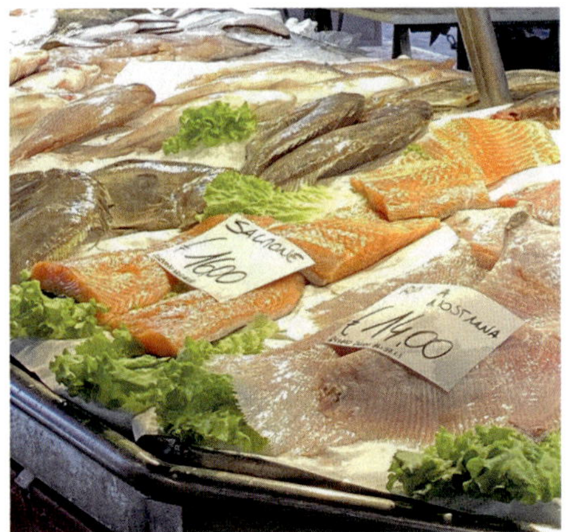

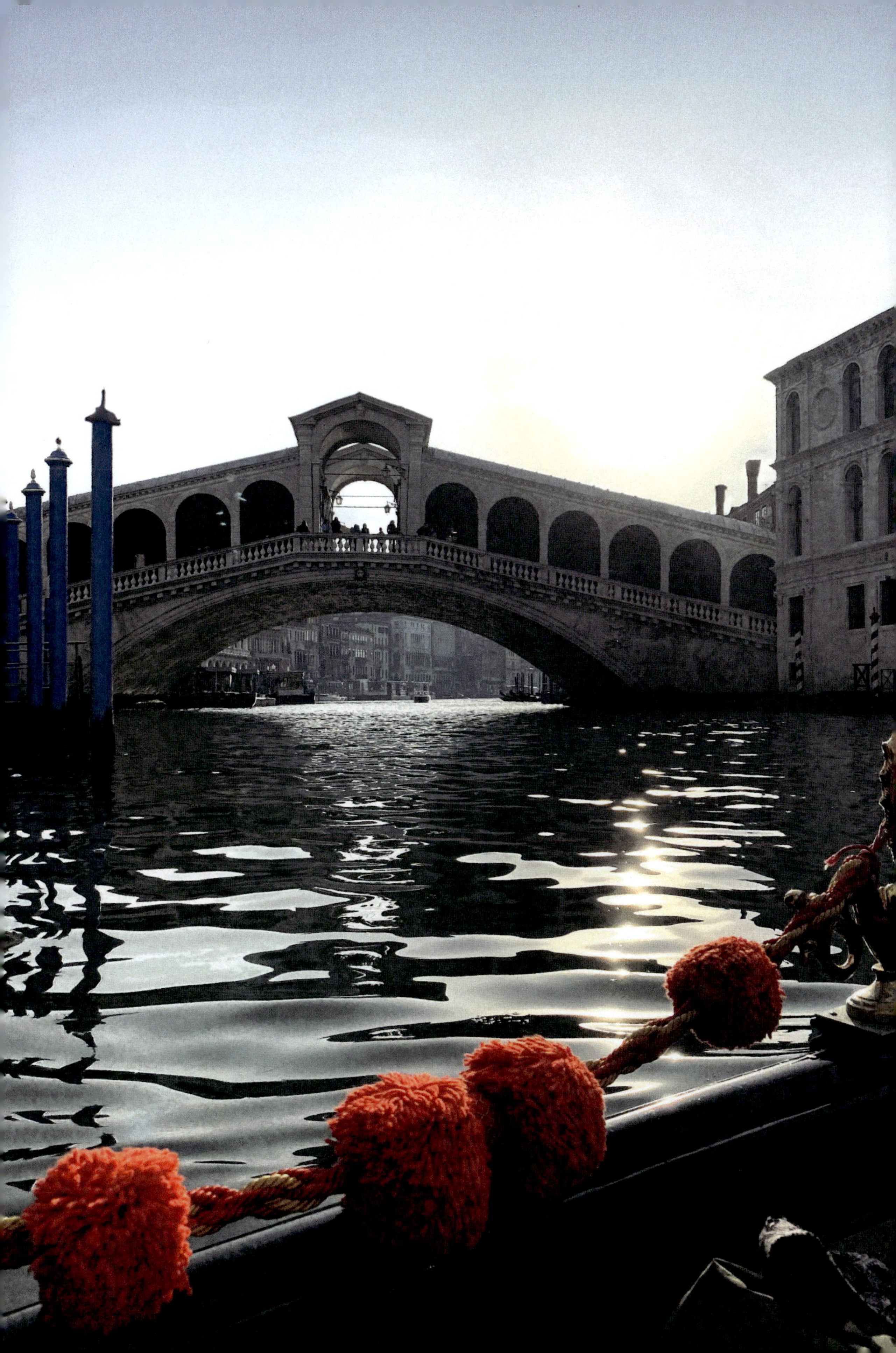

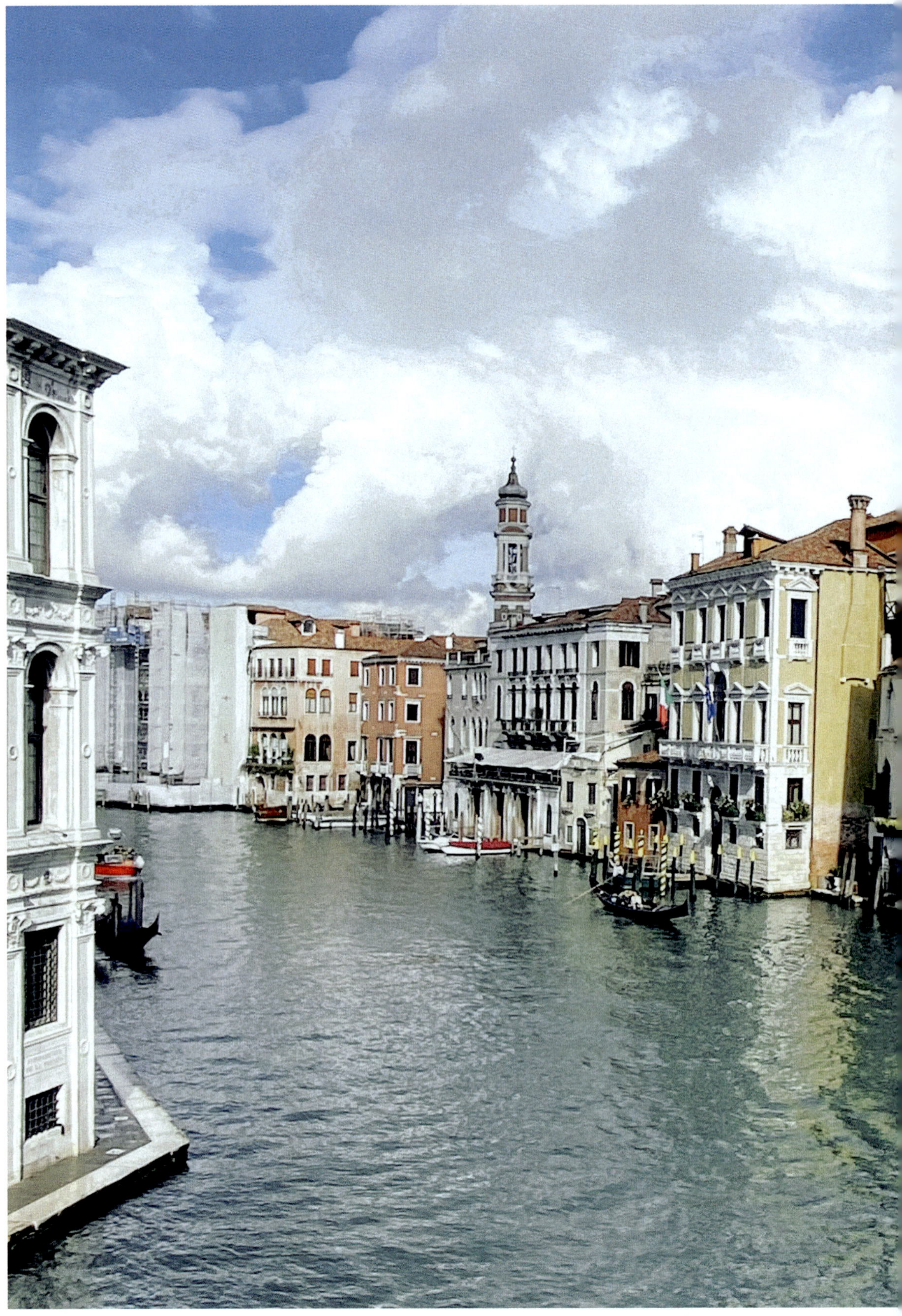

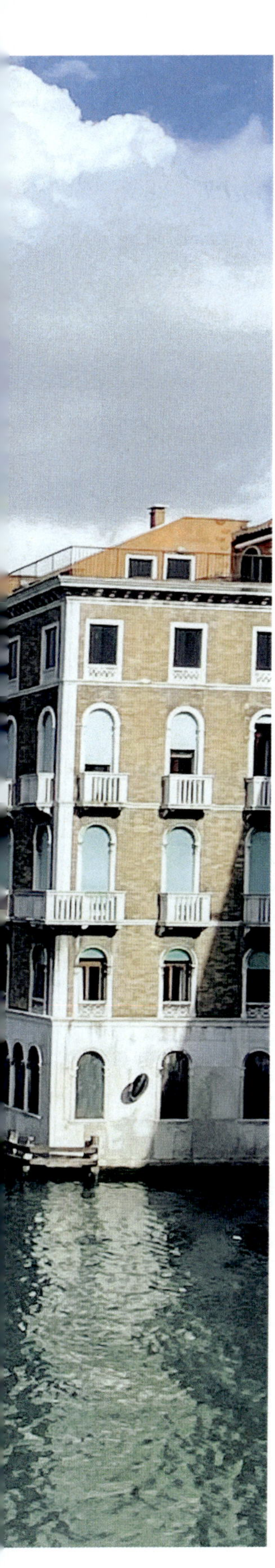

CANAL GRANDE – GREAT VIEWS FROM EVERY ANGLE

From the Rialto Bridge, you have great views of the Grand Canal and the stunning collection of small Palaces facing the canal. It is just as enchanting to view the bridge from the water level in, for example, a gondola. A great thing about Venice is that you are left breathless by its beauty, no matter the viewing perspective.

V

PALAZZO DUCALE

NEPTUNE BY SANSOVINO – STANDS FIRM WITH A CONFIDENT POSTURE

This magnificent marble statue of Neptune stands at the top of the Giant's Staircase (Scala dei Giganti) that leads up to the Palace from the courtyard. On the opposite side stands the statue of Mars. The great postures of these giants express self-confidence and strength and frame the impressive marble staircase. The marble statues of Neptune and Mars were created by the sculptor Jacopo Sansovino – an influential Italian sculptor and architect during the Venice Renaissance. The Giant's Staircase leads into the heart of the Doge's Palace (Palazzo Ducale).

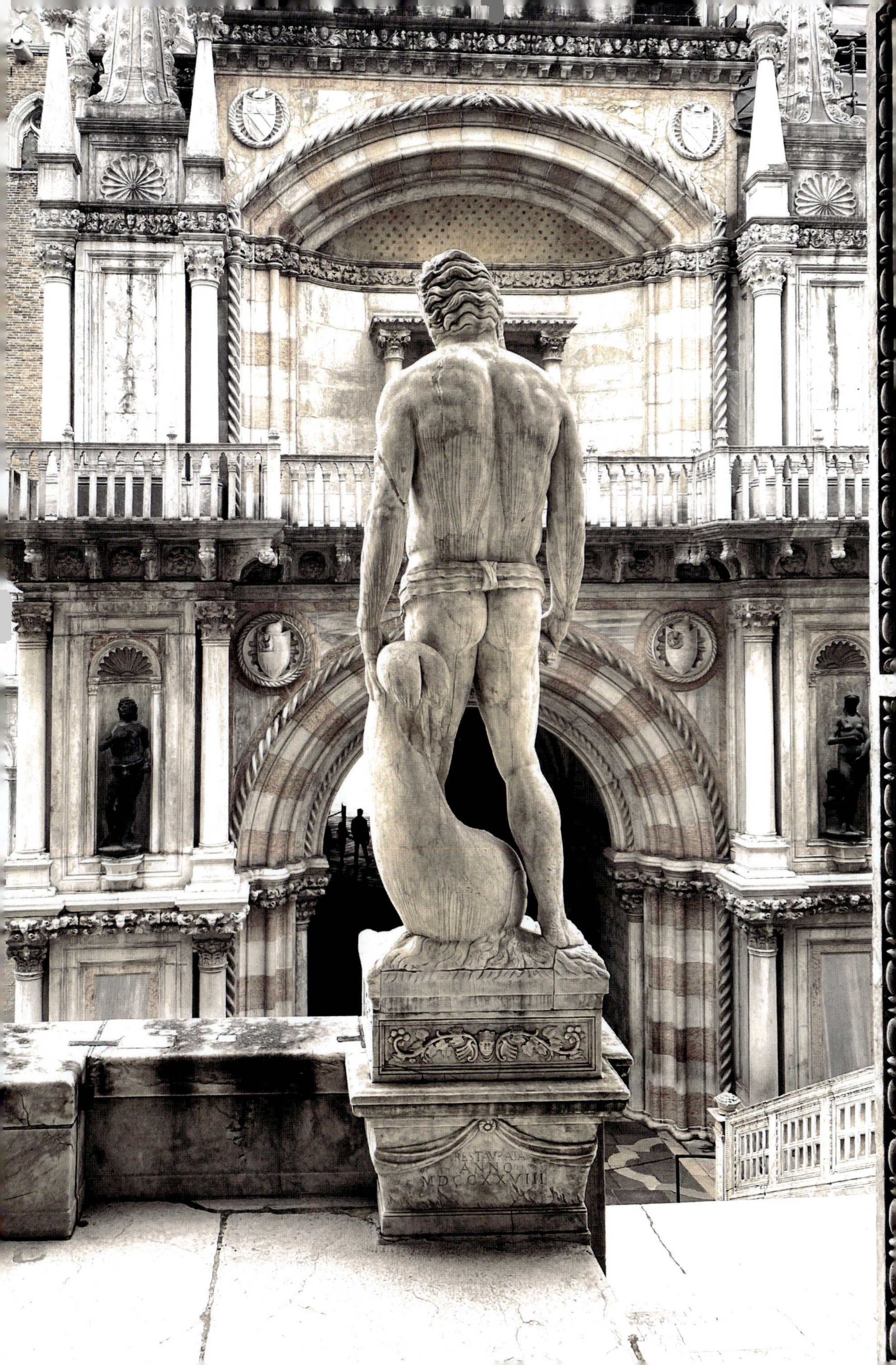
RESTAVRATA
ANNO
MDCCXXVIII

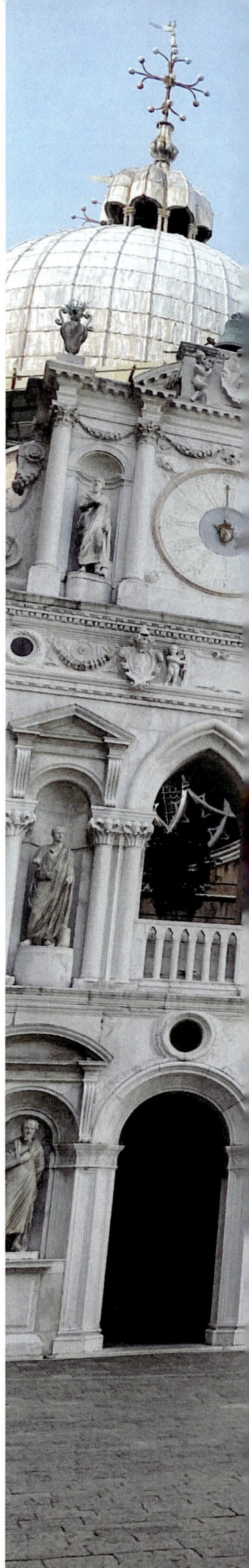

THE COURTYARD – CEREMONIES, CORONATIONS AND TOURNAMENTS

The Palace's beautiful courtyard has experienced fancy coronations, thrilling tournaments, and festive ceremonial events. The main entrance connects elegantly to St. Mark's Square and St. Mark's Basilica. The Doge and his court could attend the events taking place around the Palace with great convenience, only a couple of steps away.

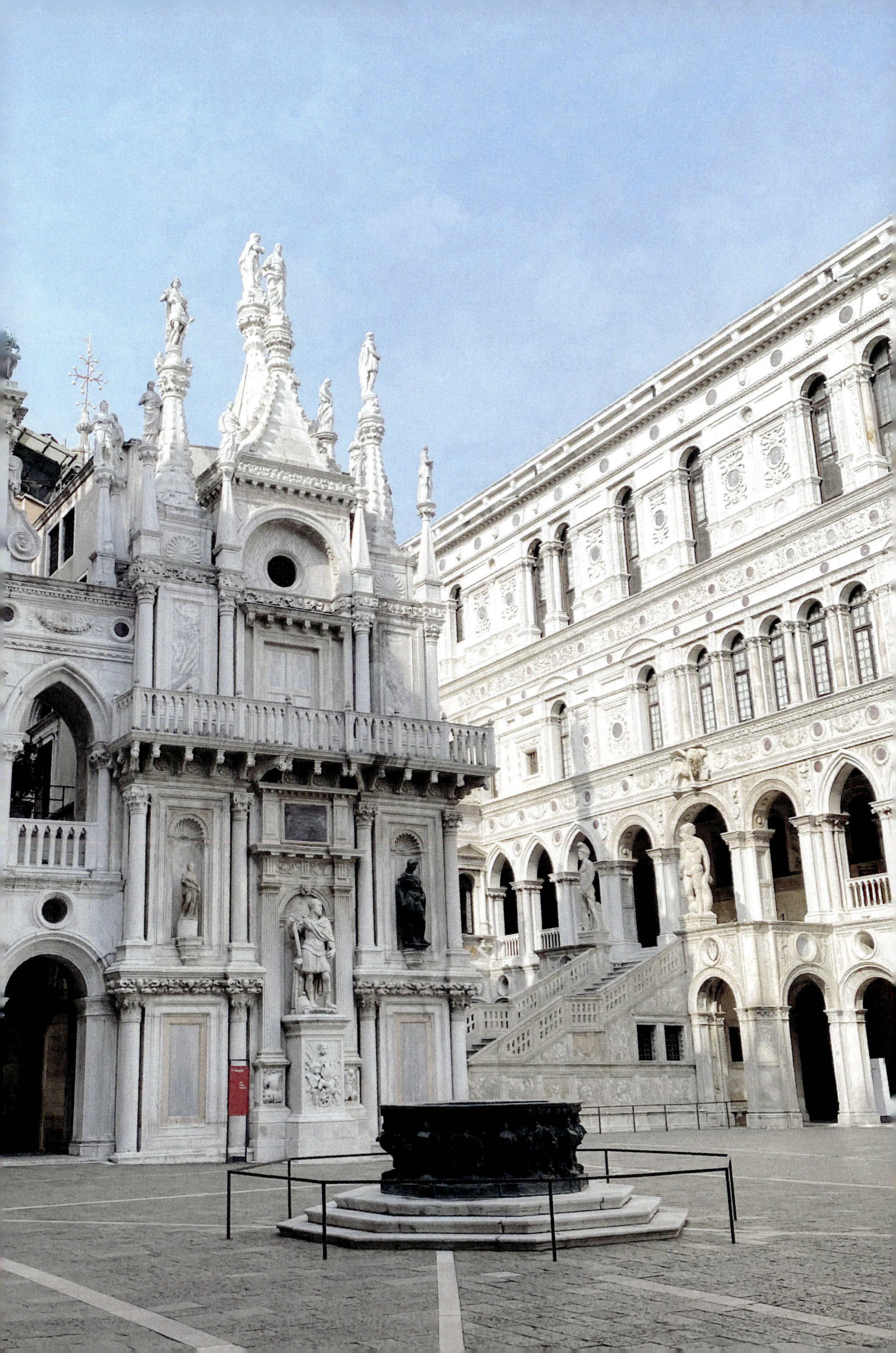

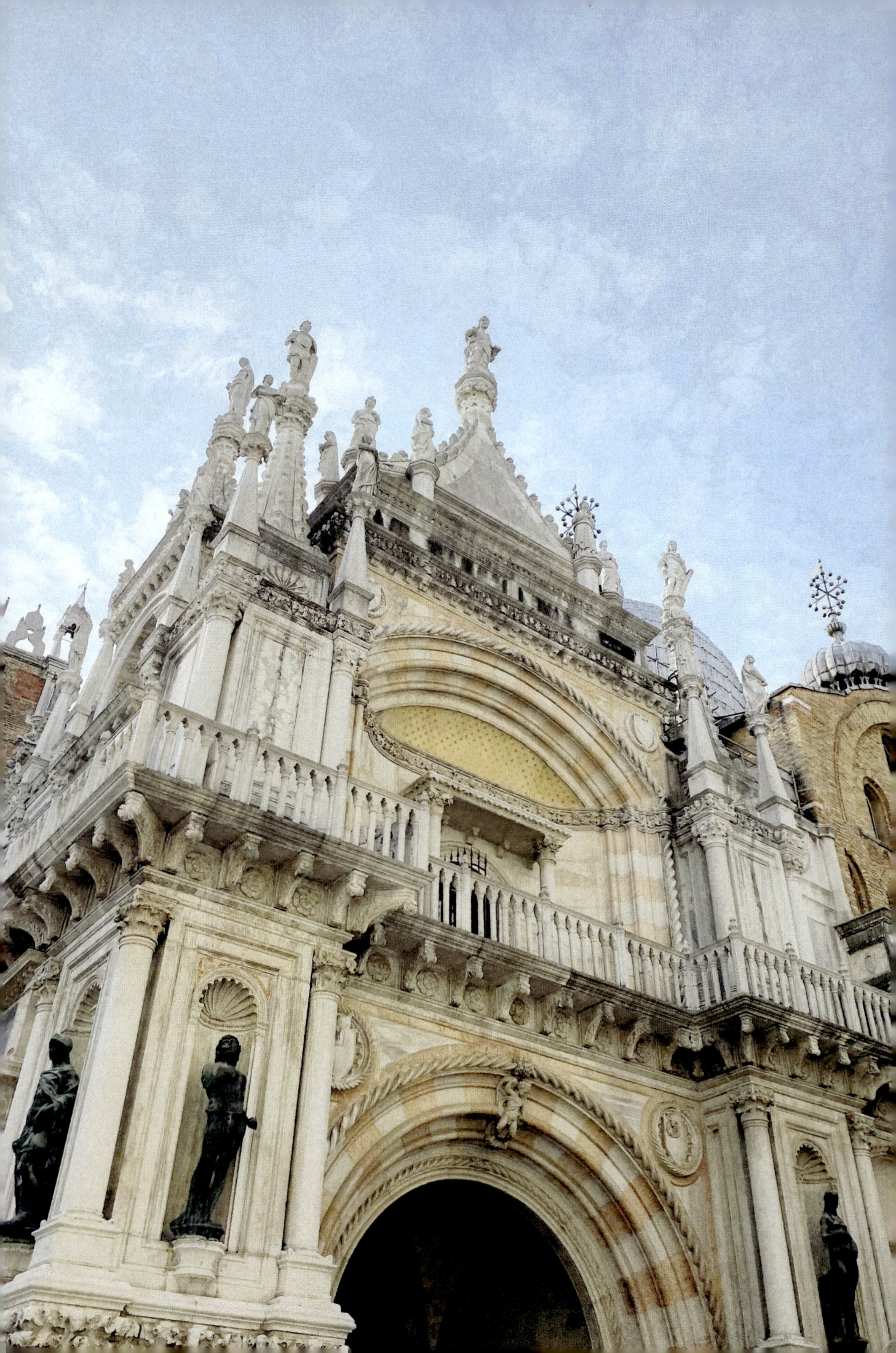

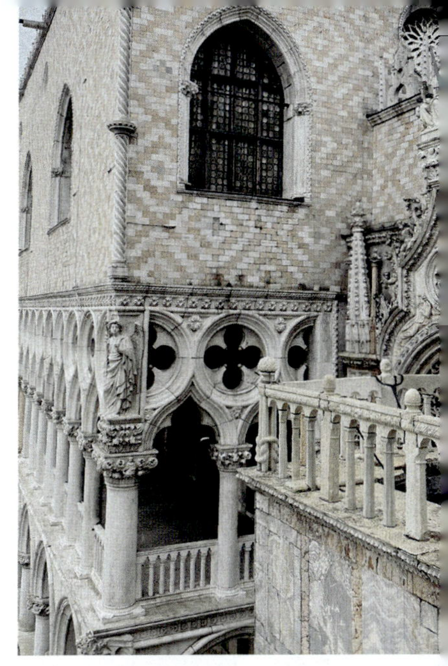

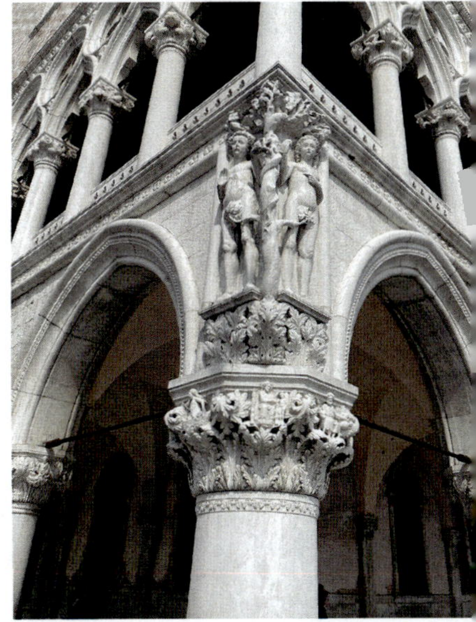

ARCO FOSCARI – GOTHIC TOWERS AND ORNAMENTS

A beautiful section of the courtyard is the Foscari Arch (Arco Foscari), a true masterpiece with its gothic towers and beautiful ornaments in marble and stone. The architect and sculptors Bartolomeo Bon, Antonio Bregno, and Antonio Rizzo collaborated on creating the magnificent arch.

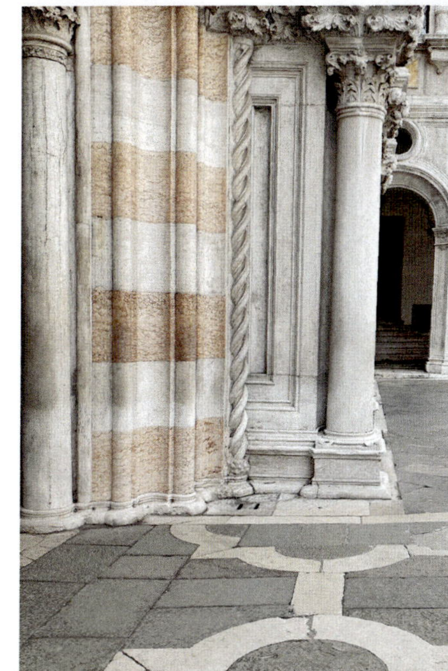

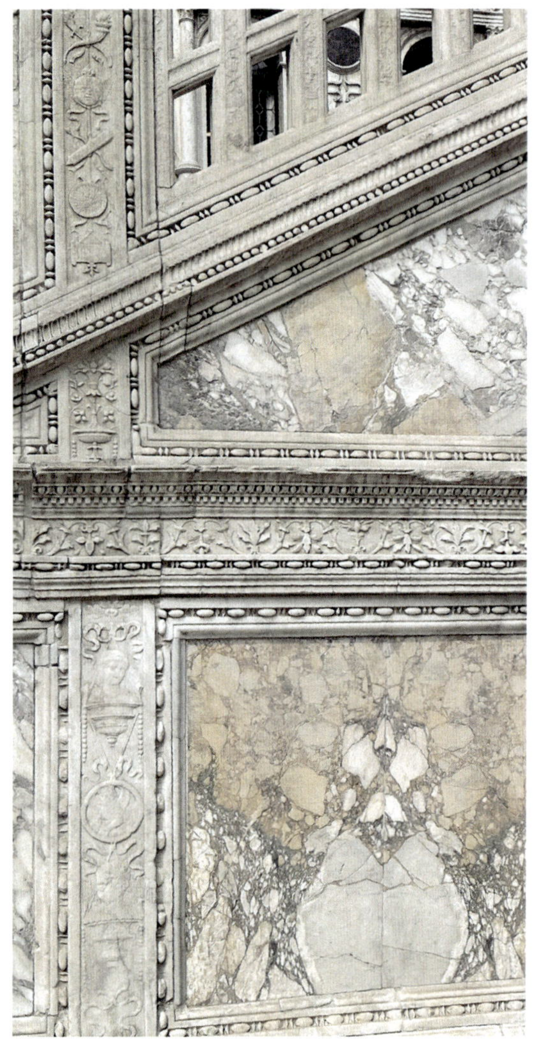

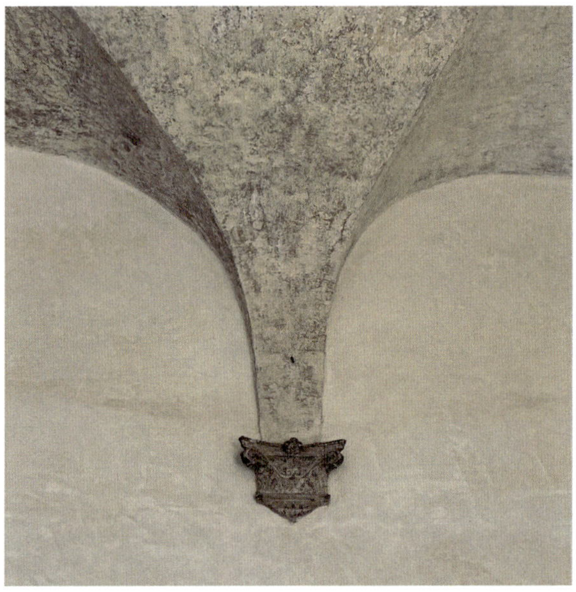

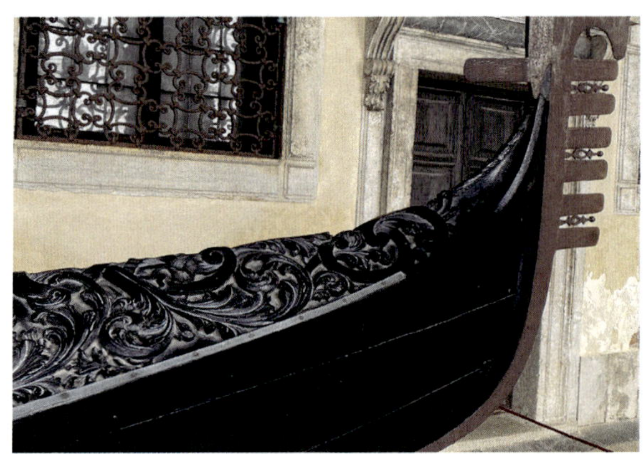

SCALA DEI GIGANTI – A MARBLE DREAM

This magnificent marble statue of Neptune stands at the top of the Giant's Staircase (Scala dei Giganti) that leads up to the Palace from the courtyard. On the opposite side stands the statue of Mars. The great postures of these giants express self-confidence and strength and frame the impressive marble staircase. The marble statues of Neptune and Mars were created by the sculptor Jacopo Sansovino – an influential Italian sculptor and architect during the Venice Renaissance.

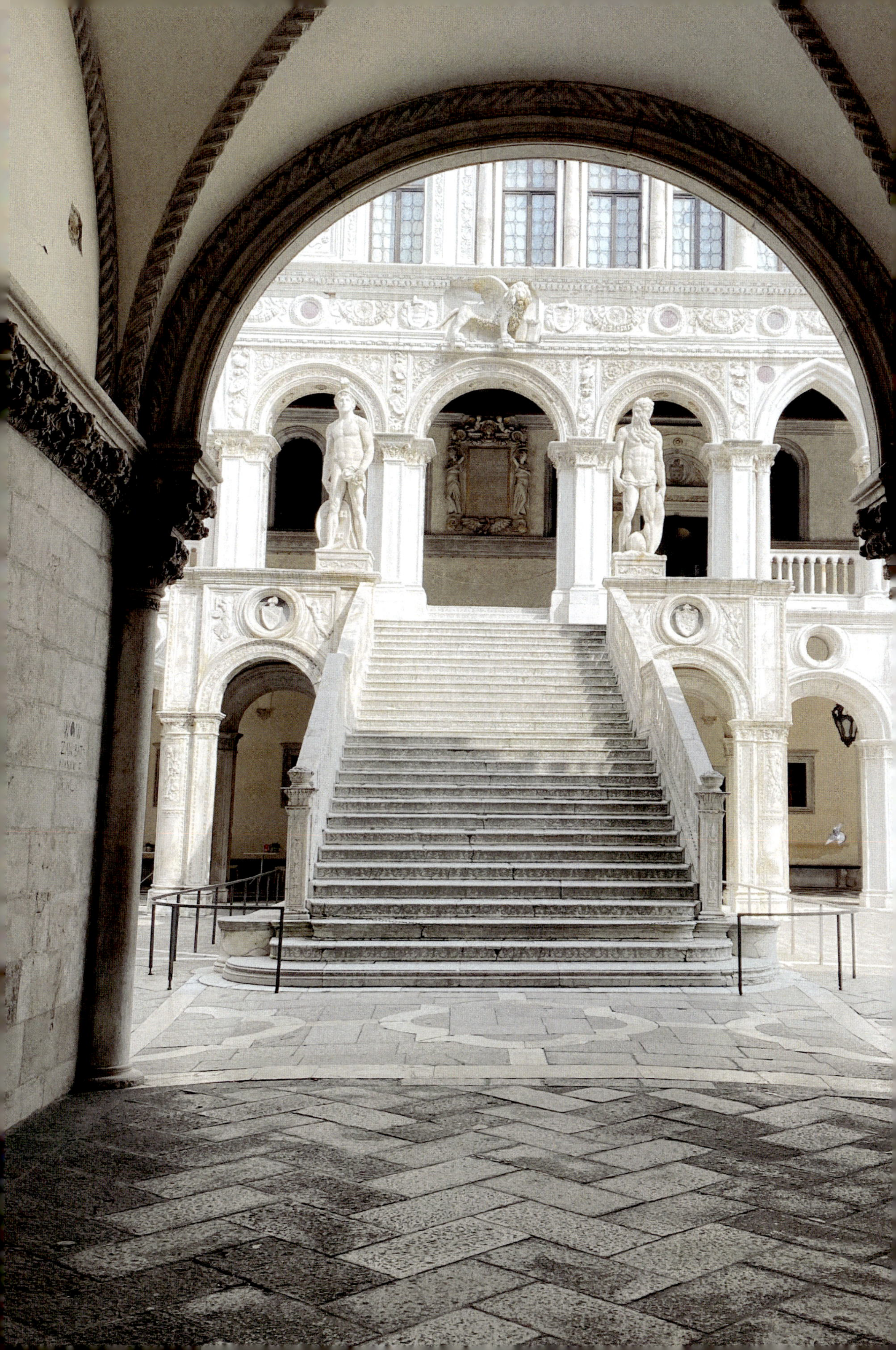

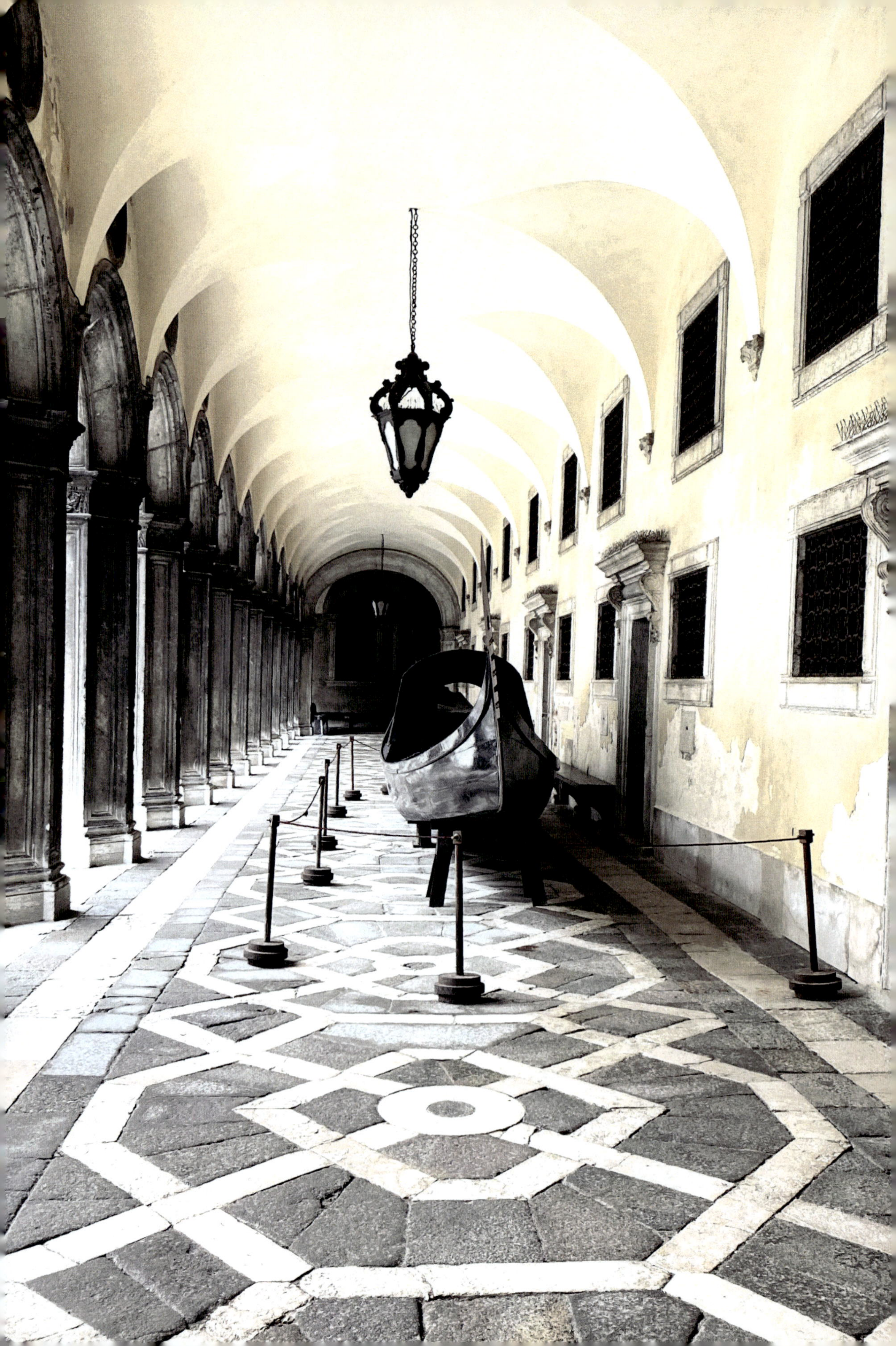

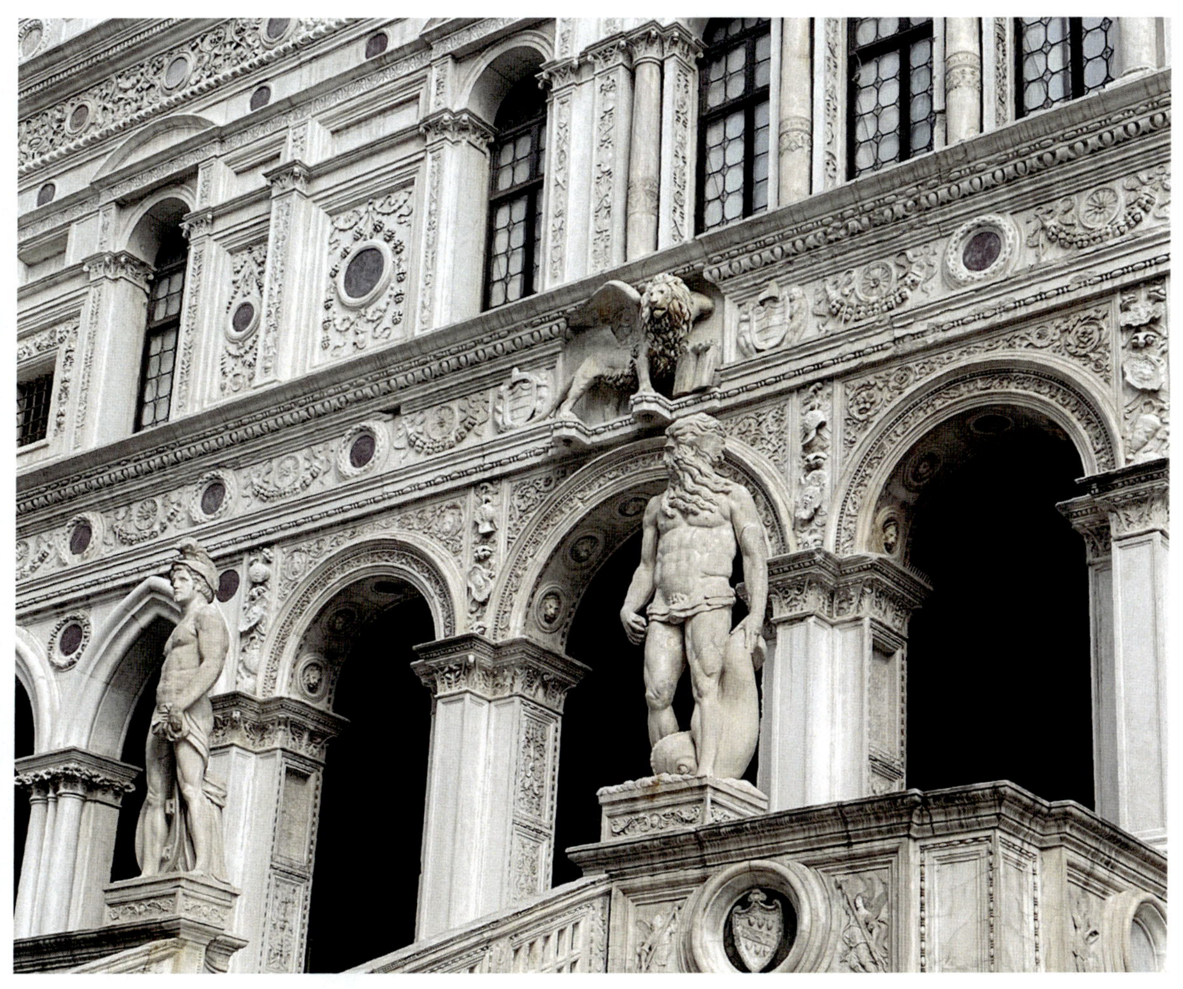

THE ANTIQUE GONDOLA – A BLACK BEAUTY

A vintage gondola from the 18th century stands in the Palace courtyard. Once, it carried prominent members from the Palace on their excursions through the city canals of Venice. Now, the gondola has found rest in the shadow, under the vaults, keeping its secrets and stories to itself.

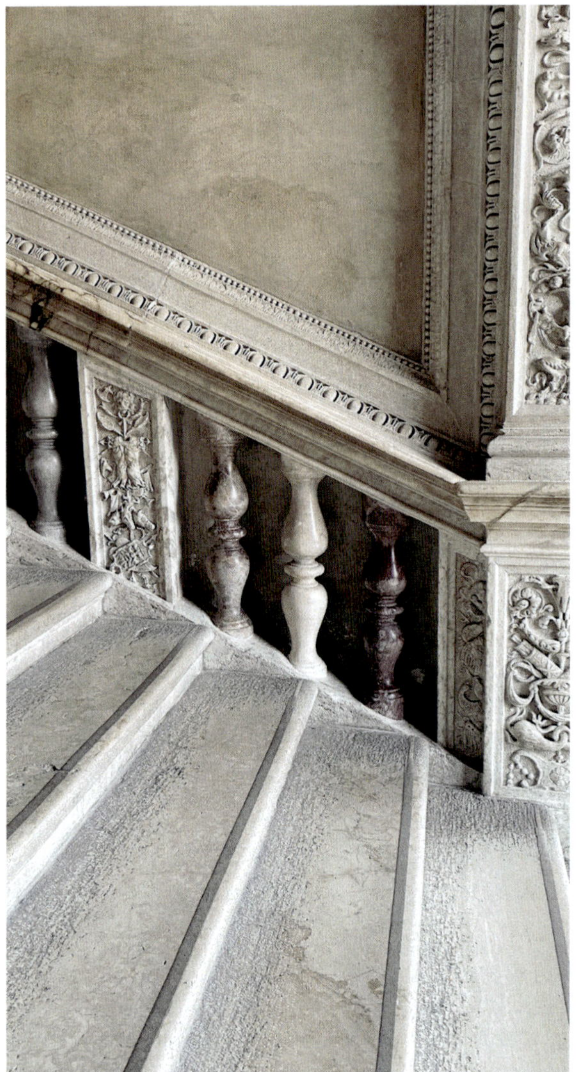

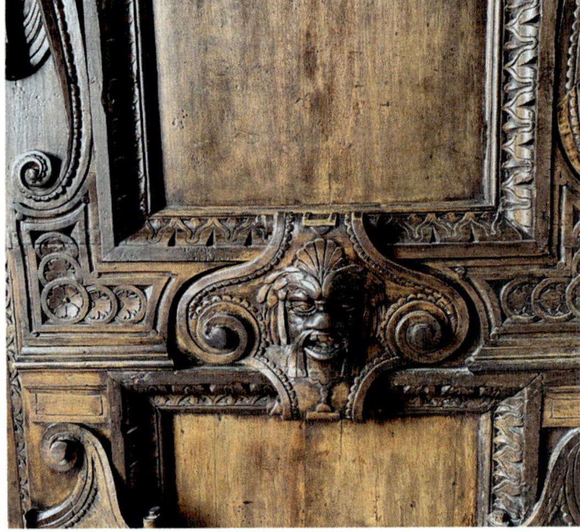

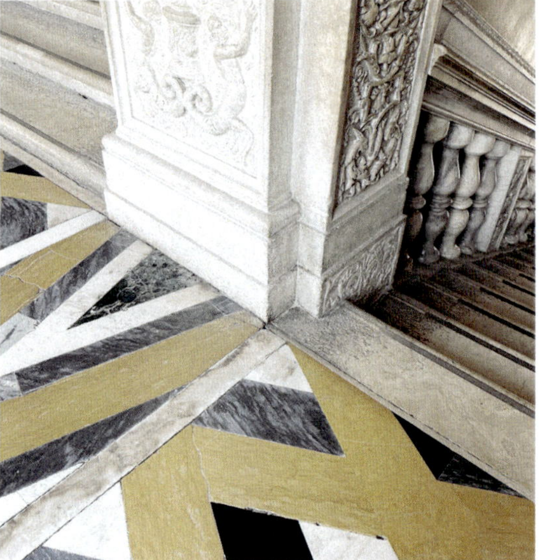

LA SCALA D'ORO

The Golden Staircase (La Scala d'Oro) leads from the Giant's Staircase into the Palace and is a splendid walk. The first part of the stairs leads to the Doge's apartment of honour and then further right to the heart of the Palace. The sculptor Alessandro Vittorio created the decoration of the white stucco and gold covering of the ceiling, and the painter Giambattista Franco oversaw the frescoes of the staircase.

The sidewalls of the staircase are without any decoration. The grey creates a subtle transition between the marble and the ornate ceiling. The marble floor has a square, symmetric pattern, creating optical illusions when viewed from a distance. It is composed of yellow, black, grey, and white marble. The Golden Staircase is a true gem of beauty.

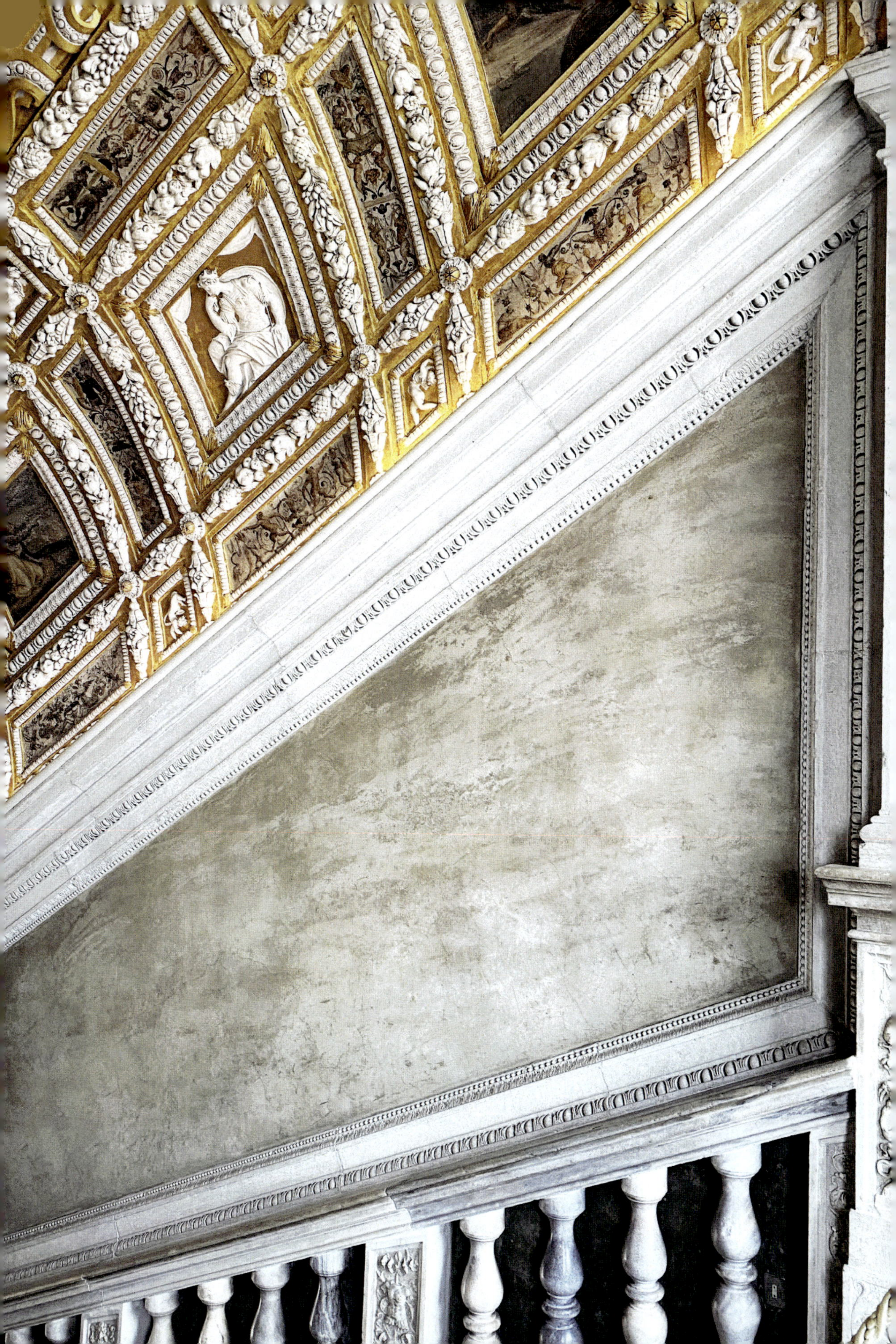

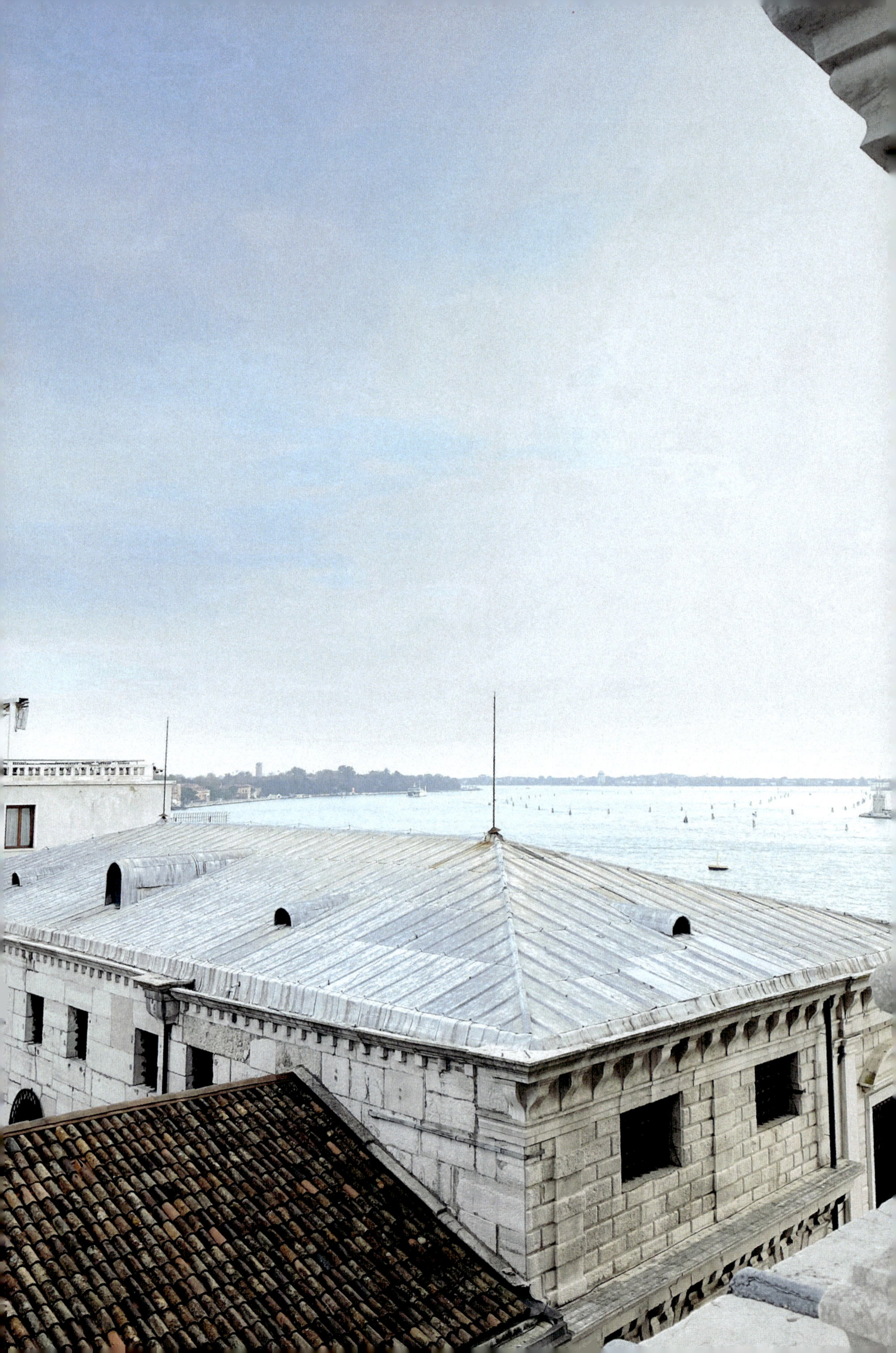

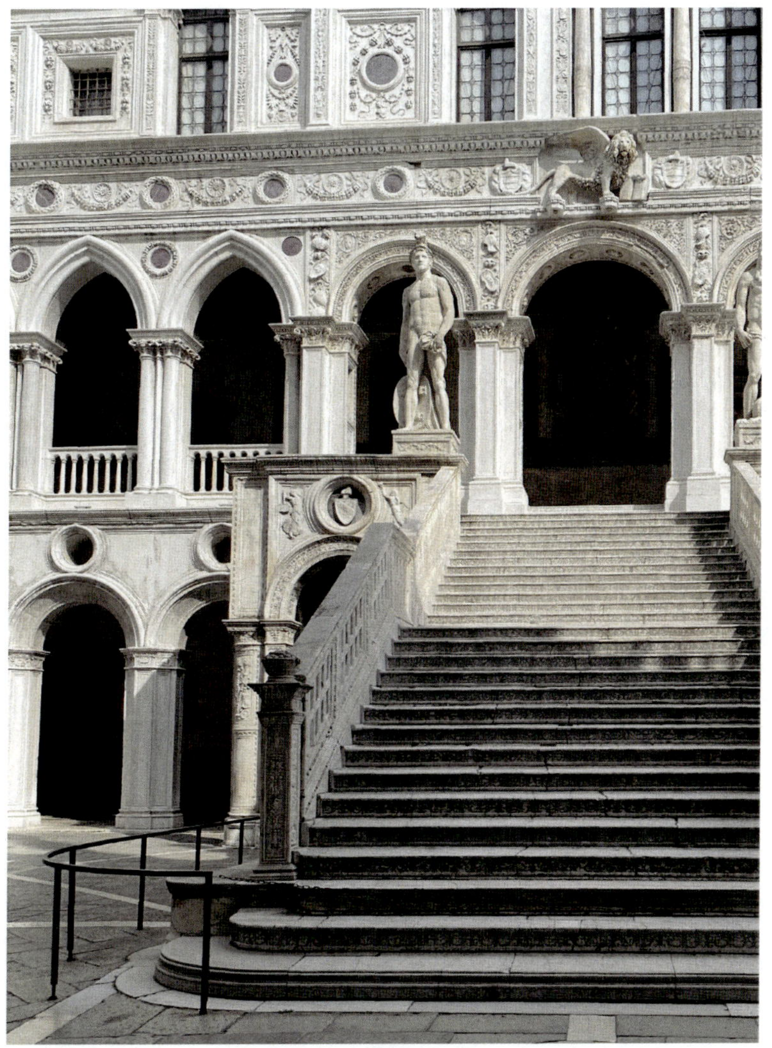

A ROOM WITH A VIEW OF THE ADRIATIC SEA

The views from the Doge's Palace towards the Adriatic Sea are relaxing. The Rulers of Venice could sit and watch the ships and vessels passing by on the horizon at sea. The soft light reflects the sea with a blueish shimmer.

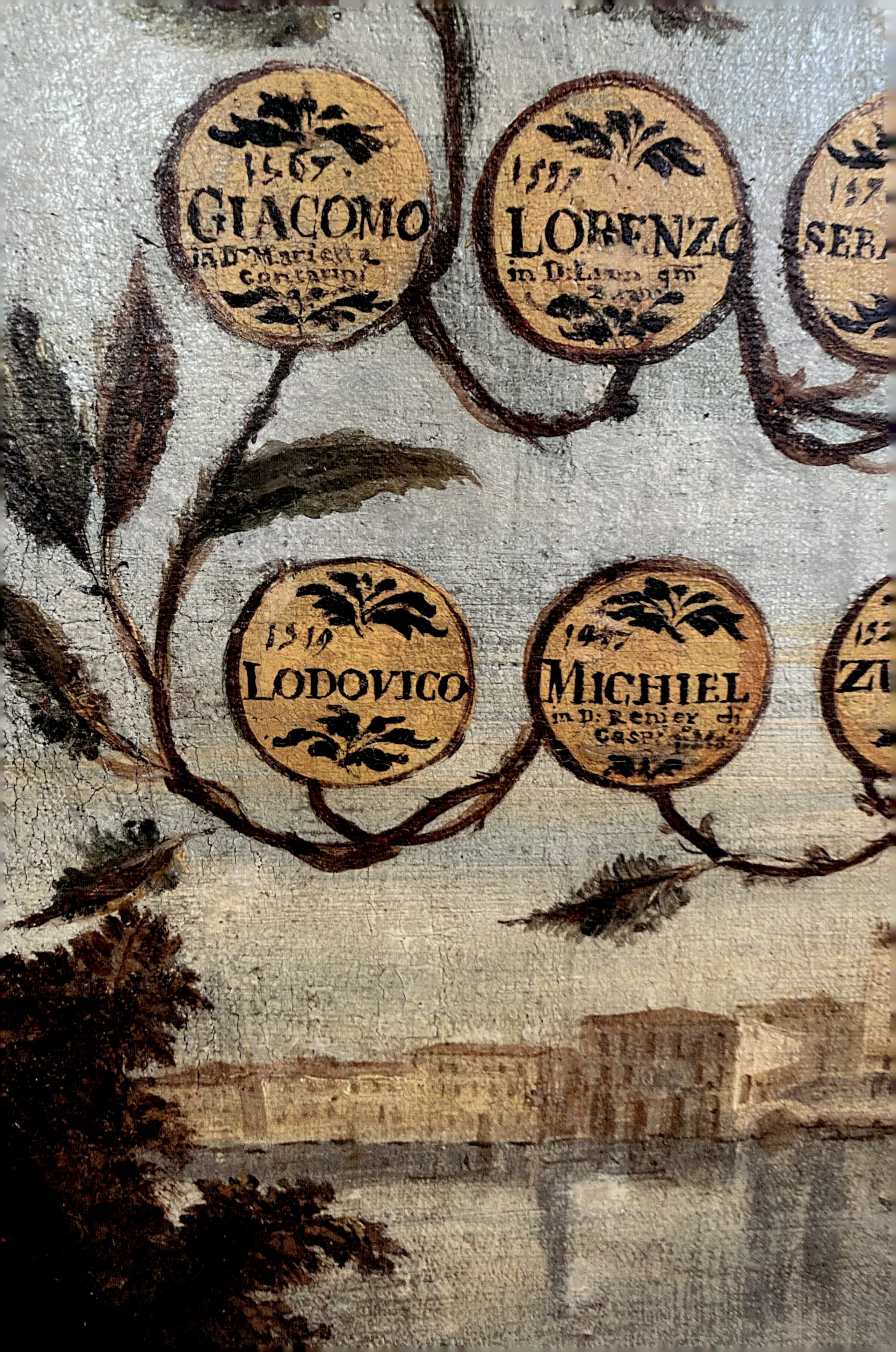
1567.
GIACOMO
in D. Marietta
Contarini
1557
LORENZO
in D. Lucr.
LODOVICO
MICHIEL
in D. Renier di

THE FAMILY TREE OF DOGE FOSCARI

The painting of the family tree of the Doge Foscari hangs in the Doge's Palace (Palazzo Ducale). The House of Foscari was one of Venice's noble families.

Venice had 120 Doges before the Venetian Republic ended after having existed for a thousand years. In the year 810, the Doge Agnello Participazio moved from the area of Rivoalto and decided to build the first version of the Palazzo Ducale. By this time, Venice was an outpost in the Byzantine Empire. Over the years, Venice became more powerful and gained independence from Byzantium. The Doges were selected for life and could rule for a lifetime. They came from noble Venetian families, and the election was complex. The very last Doge abdicated in 1797 as Napoleon captured Venice.

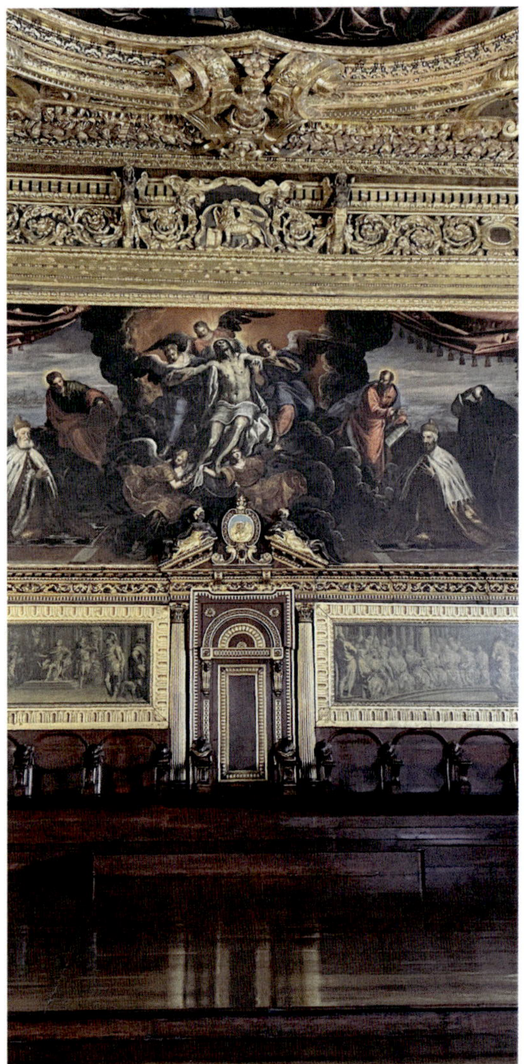

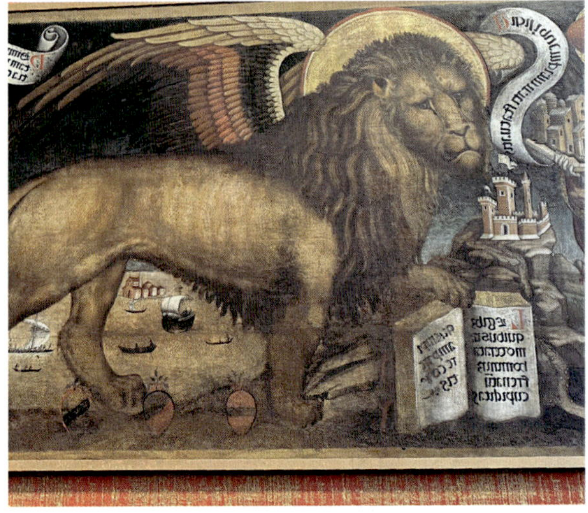

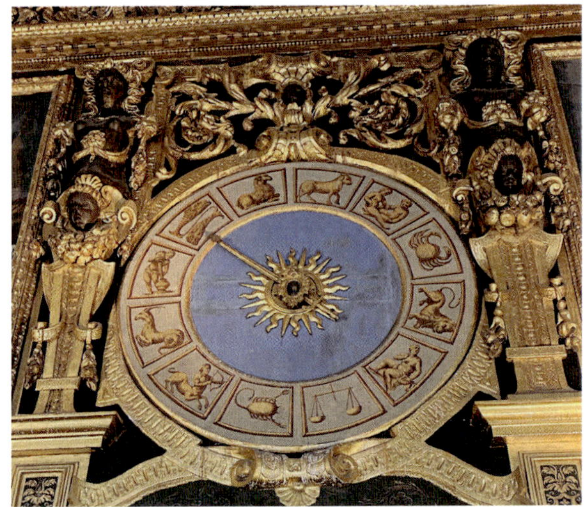

THE GREAT COUNCIL – POWER AND GLORY

The Doge had his throne in the impressive and opulent Chamber of the Great Council (Maggior Consiglio). Here, the Great Council handled all political and administrative matters in the Republic of Venice. The painting "Il Paradiso" by the Italian Renaissance artist Tintoretto decorates the entire wall behind the throne. A striking astrological clock with zodiac symbols shines in gold and blue. Another iconic Palace painting is Vittore Carpaccio's "Winged Lion of Saint Mark".

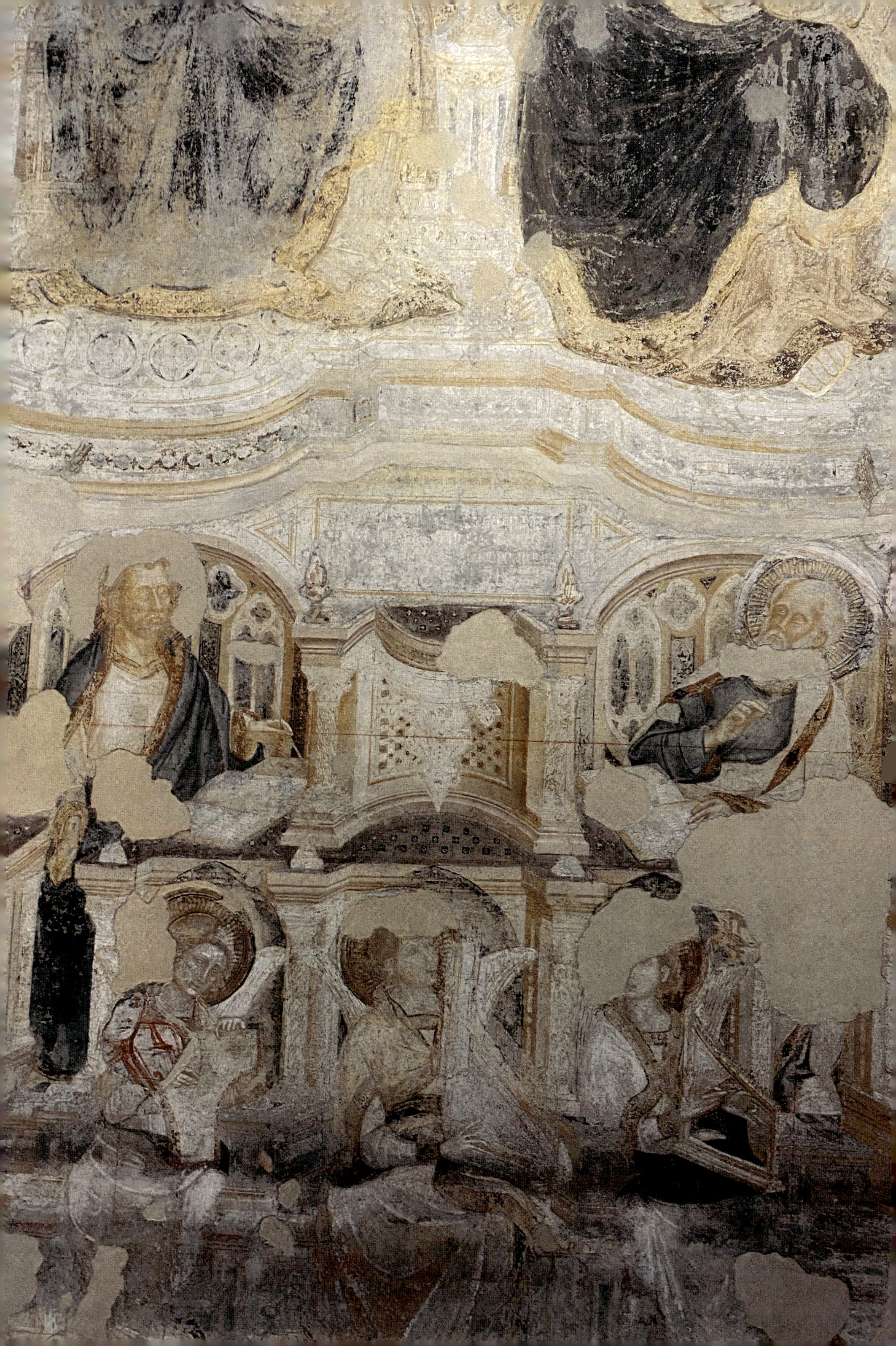

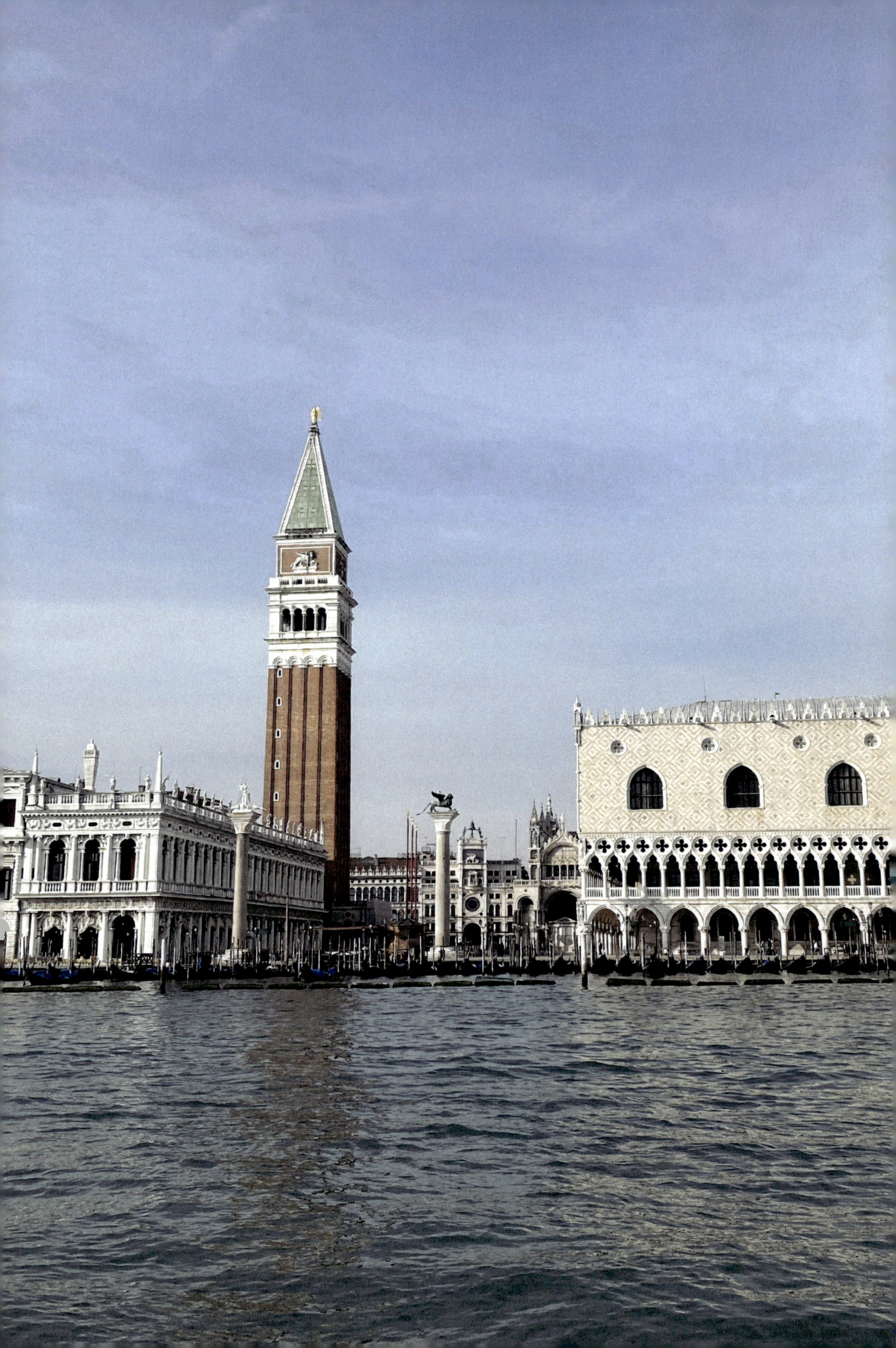

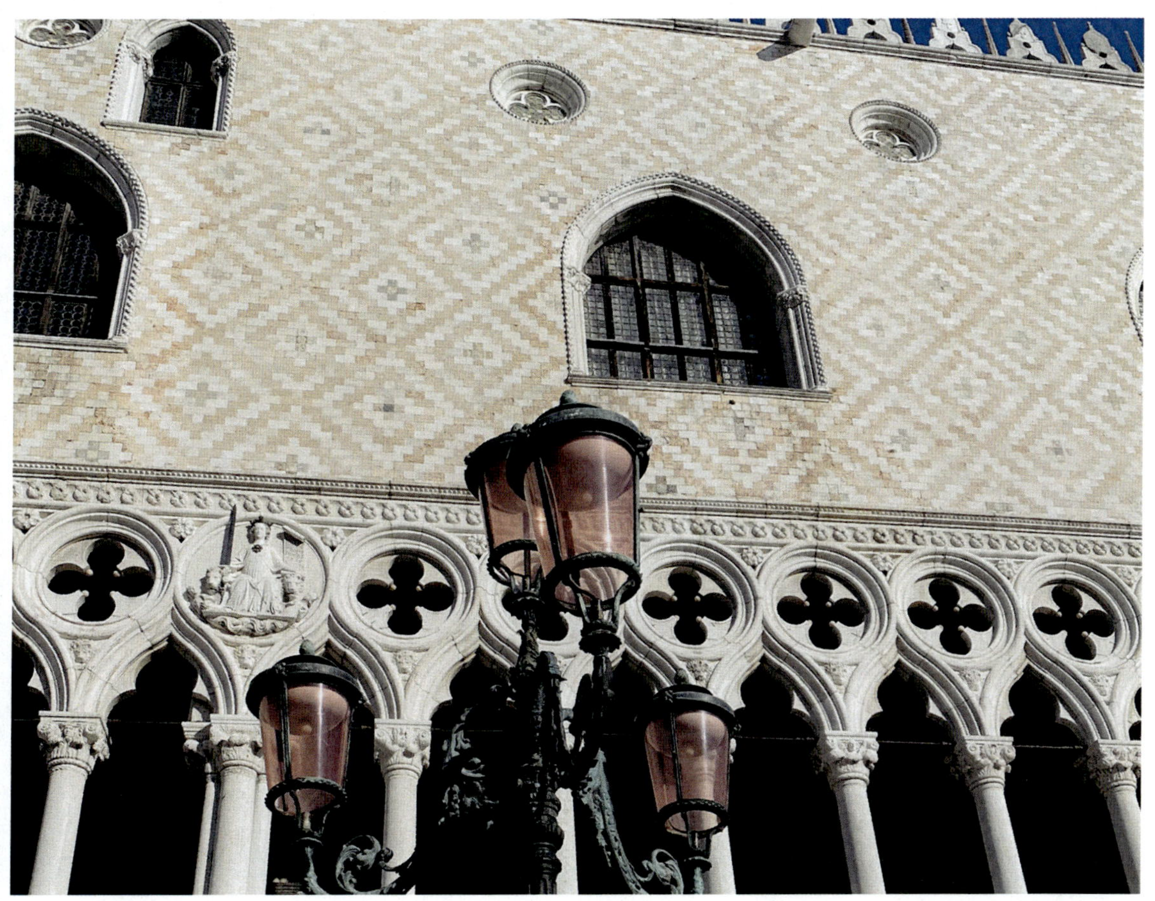

VENICE – THE QUEEN OF SEAS

With a view over the Adriatic Sea, the different Doges ruled from the magnificent Doge's Palace (Palazzo Ducale) for over a thousand years. The Doge's Palace was built and decorated over a long period of time and is a true masterpiece of Gothic and Renaissance architecture. The Venetian Republic grew strong, a maritime superpower and main port towards the Orient. The fortunes of Venice and its success in so many different areas – from political stability, navy skills, military strength, and economic growth to artistic and cultural expressions – made Venice unique and the absolute Queen of the Adriatic Sea.

VI

PONTE DEI SOSPIRI

A LAST SIGH, A LAST VIEW OF FREEDOM

The Bridge of Sighs (Ponte dei Sospiri) by the architect Antonio Contino is one of the most famous bridges in the world. Built of white limestone over the narrow canal Rio del Palazzo, it connects the Doge's Palace with the Doge's Prison. Imagine the last view of the blue Venetian Lagoon, the final breath of clean air, and the last sigh before entering the dark Prison. The famous Venetian and romantic adventurer Giacomo Casanova is one of the few who escaped the Doge's Prison. In 1755, he walked over the Bridge of Sighs into the Doge's Prison. The bridge also has a romantic and iconic air – a kiss in a gondola under the Bridge of Sighs, and you will find eternal love. Contino's masterpiece has left an impression on the world.

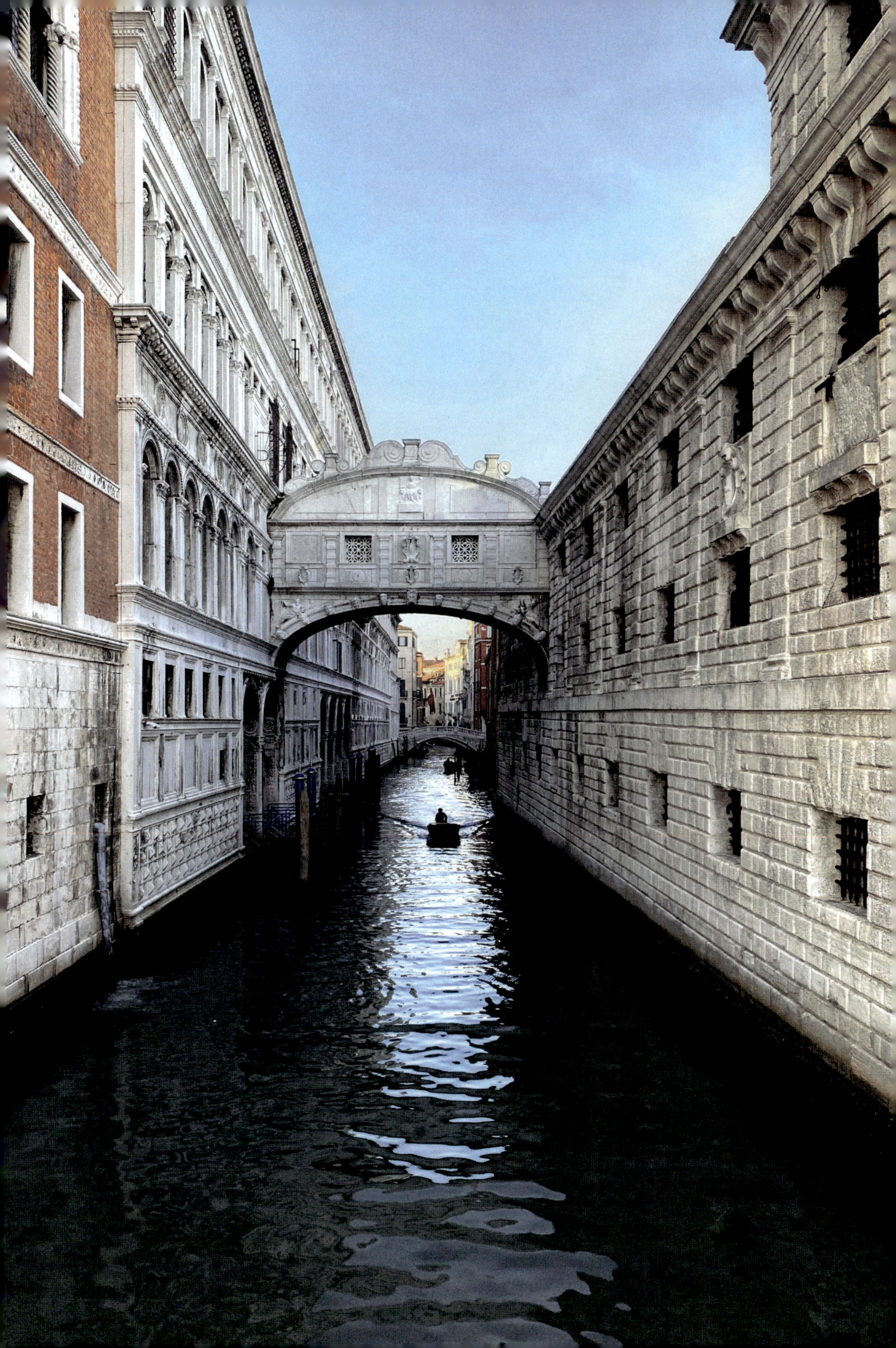

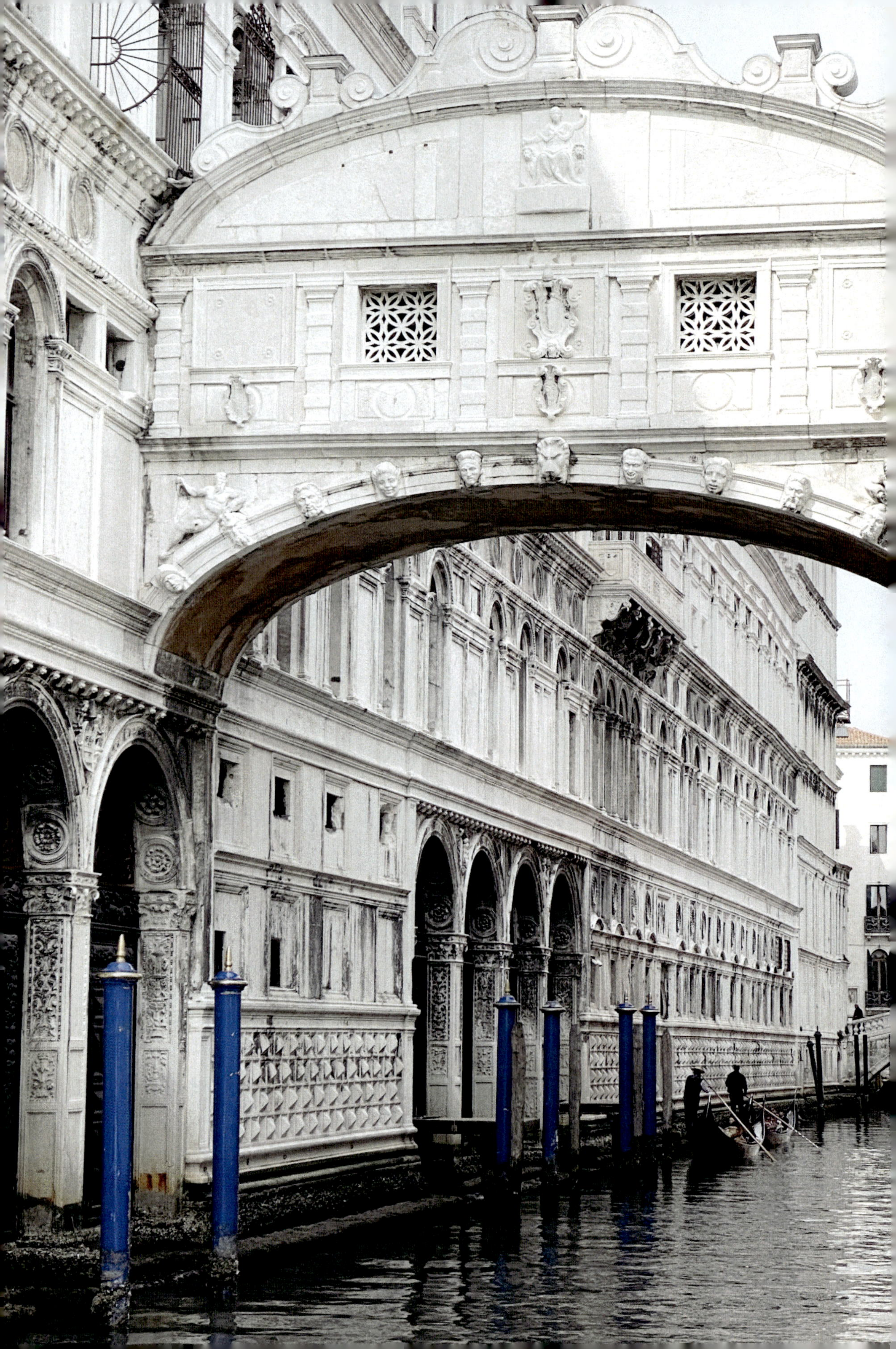

WHITE LIMESTONES OVER RIO DEL PALAZZO

The Bridge of Sighs (Ponte dei Sospiri) connects the Doge's Palace with the Prison. It was the architect, Antonio Contino, who created the impressive design.

The bridge is made of white limestone over the narrow canal Rio del Palazzo. The limestone is Istrian stone, iconic for Venetian architecture. The Bridge of Sighs was completed in 1614 and has since become one of the world's most famous bridges. The saying goes, if you kiss under the Bridge of Sighs in a gondola, you will enjoy eternal love! It is a bridge connected to strong emotions, from love to despair.

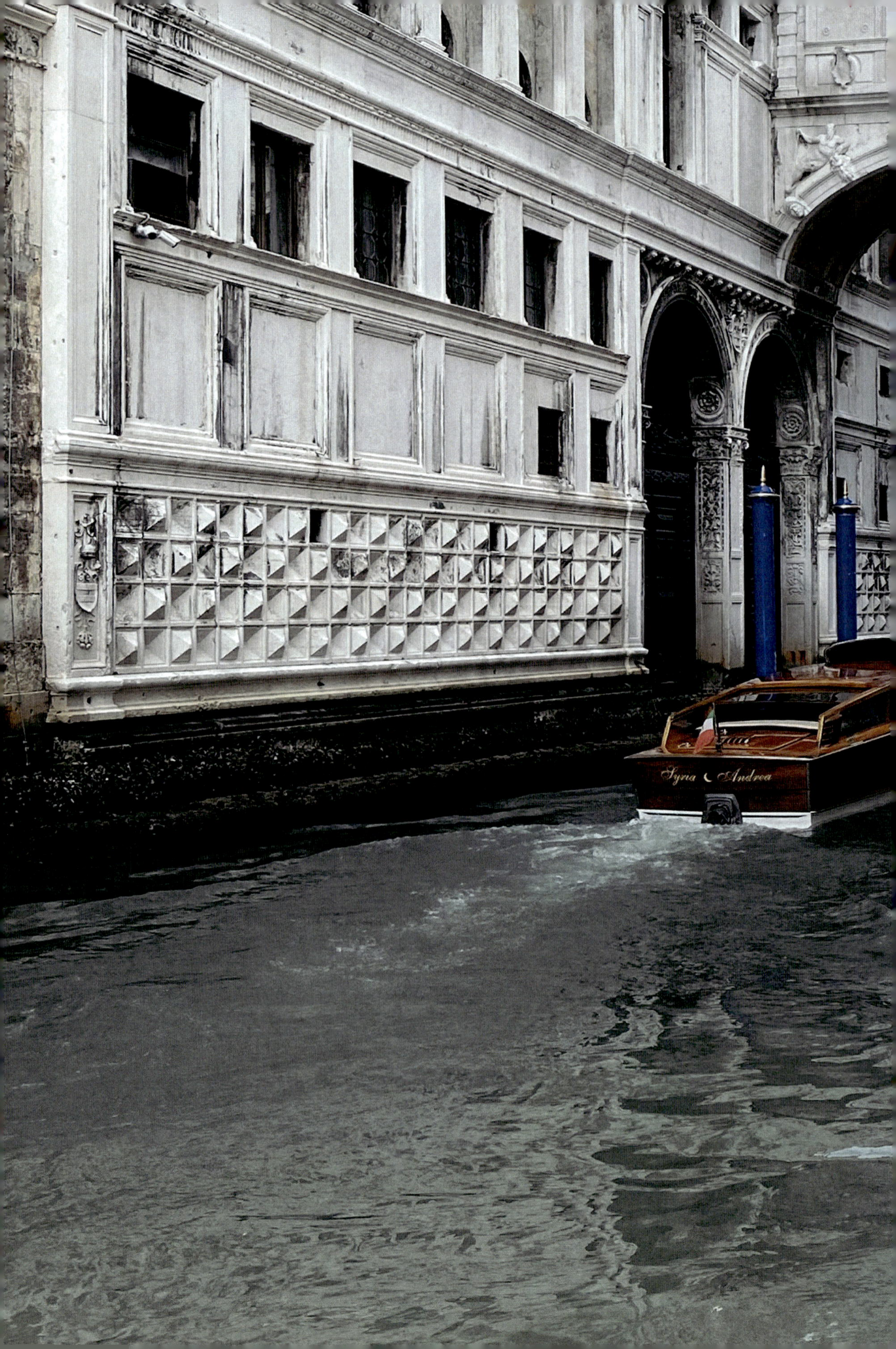
Syria Andrea

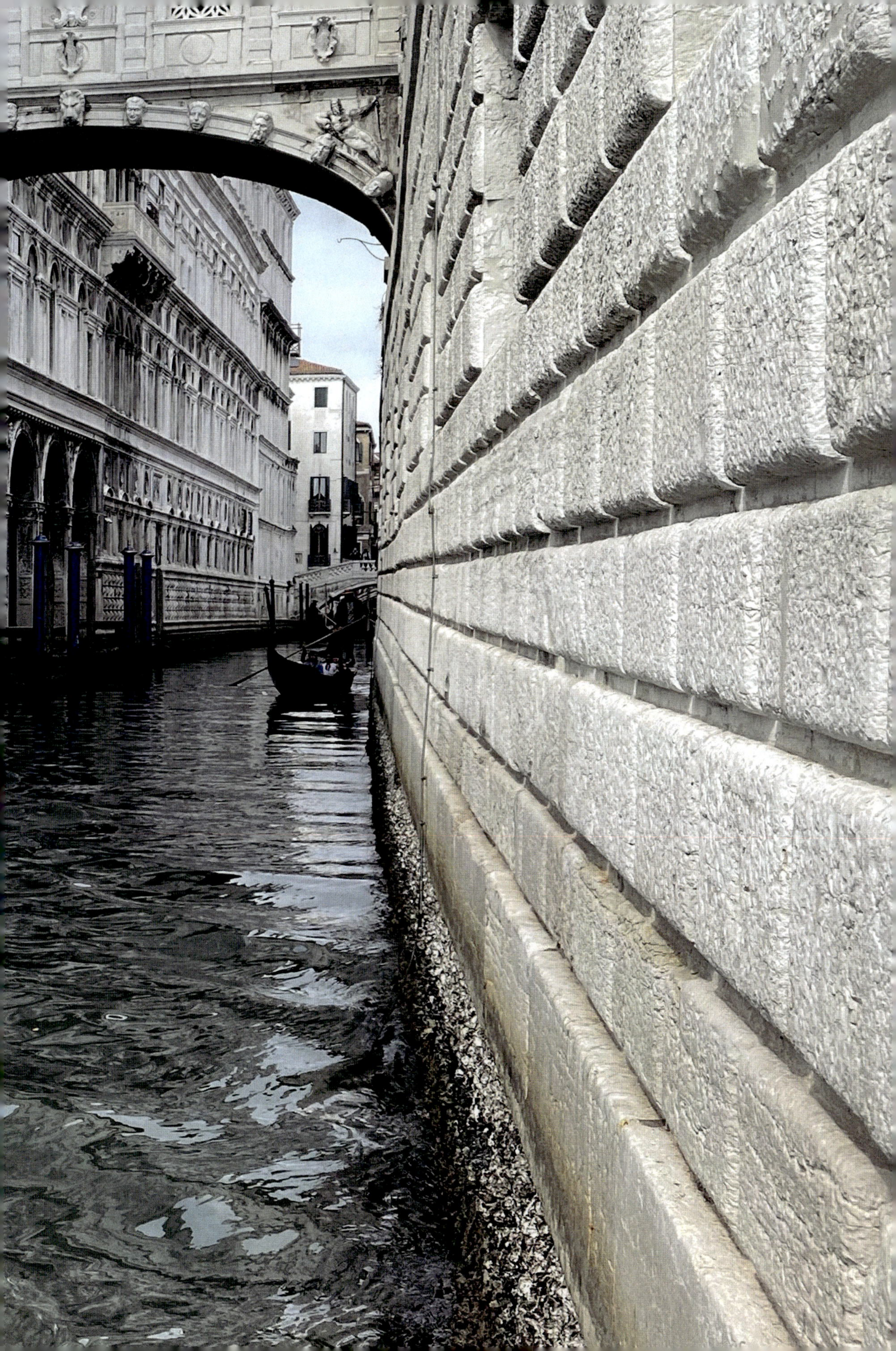

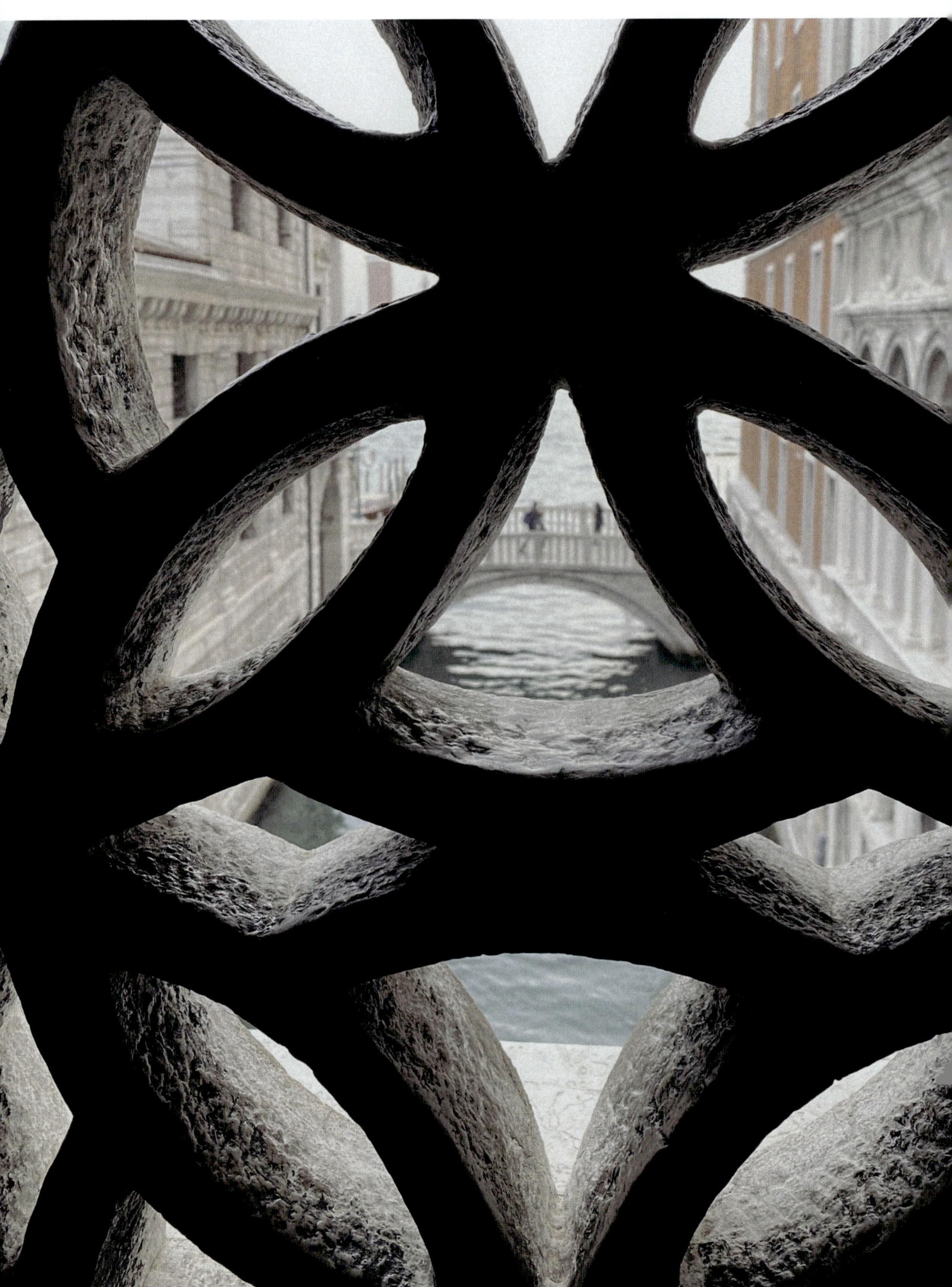

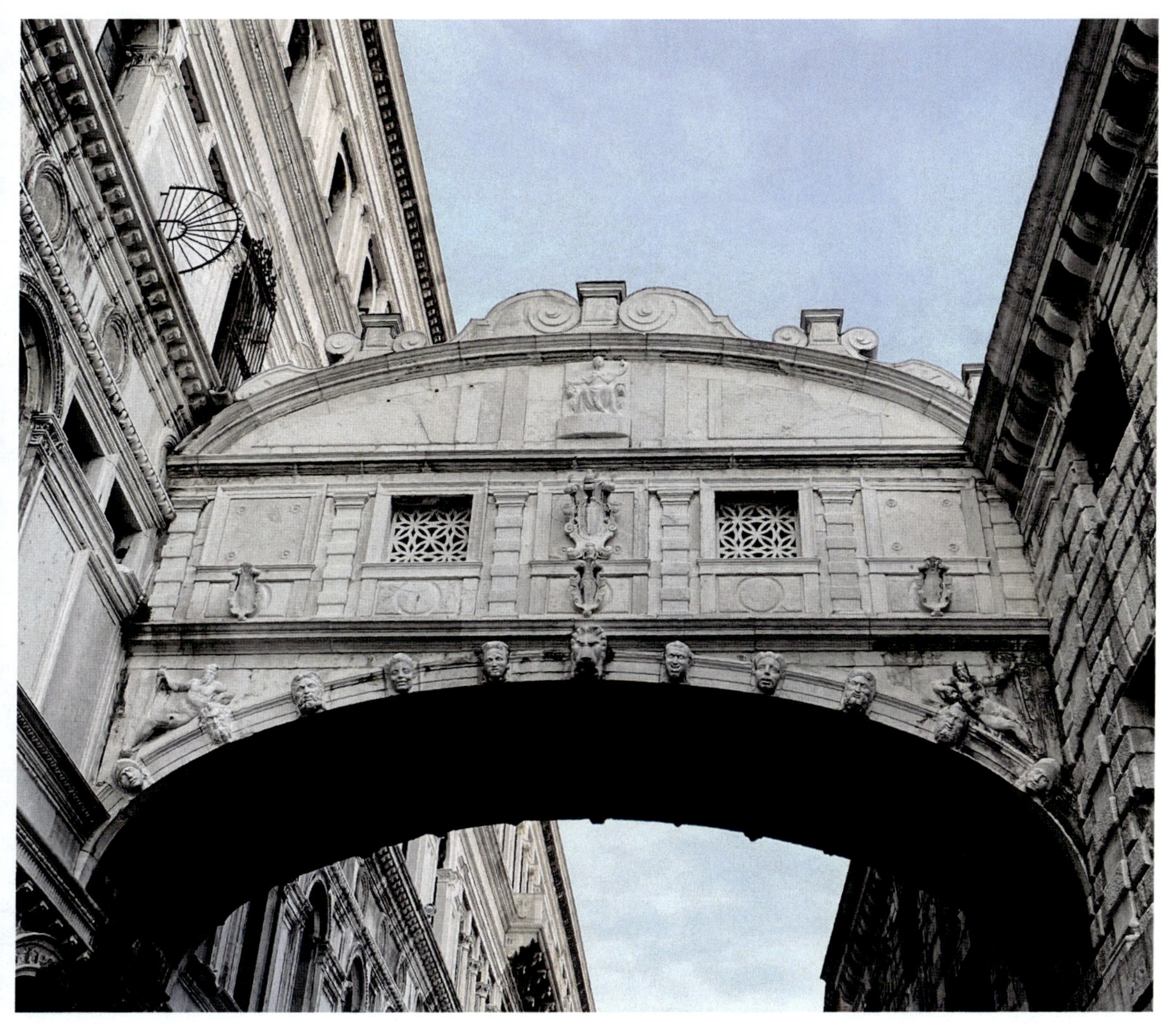

A LAST DEEP SIGH – A LAST BREATH OF FRESH AIR

The emotional bridge name refers to the sighs the condemned prisoners uttered when making their last walk from the courtroom in the Doge's Palace to Prison. The final view of the turquoise Adriatic Sea, the fresh sea breeze, and the last breath of clean air. Goodbye to freedom – in many cases, forever. Prison life was not so likely to survive.

THE ESCAPE OF CASANOVA

In July 1755, one of the most famous Venetians, Giacomo Casanova, walked over the Bridge of Sighs on his way to the Prison. Thirty years old and condemned for five years by the Council of Ten.

Casanova's cell was in the Leads (Piombi) just under the Prison roof. The name refers to the slabs of lead used for the roof. Only one year later, Casanova and another fellow prisoner, Father Marino Balbi, escaped together through the roof. It was their second attempt, and this time, they succeeded. Casanova is not only famous for his romantic adventures around Europe. He is also one of the few to escape from the Doge's Prison.

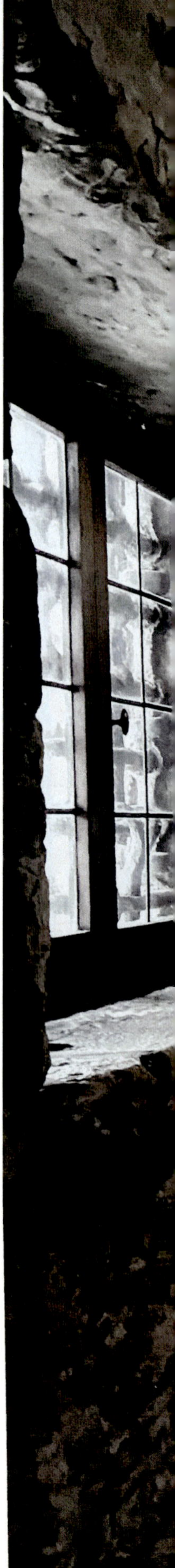

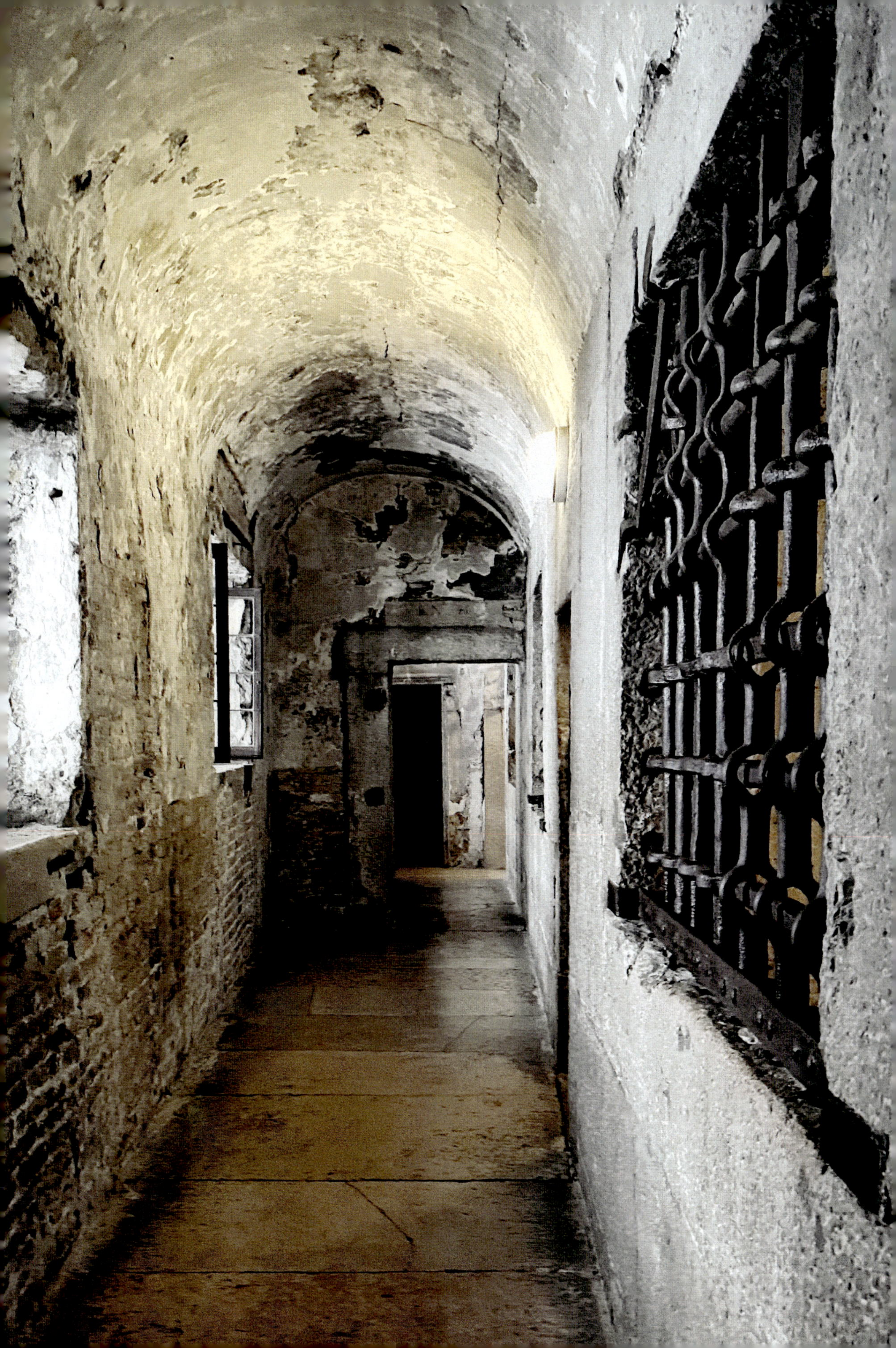

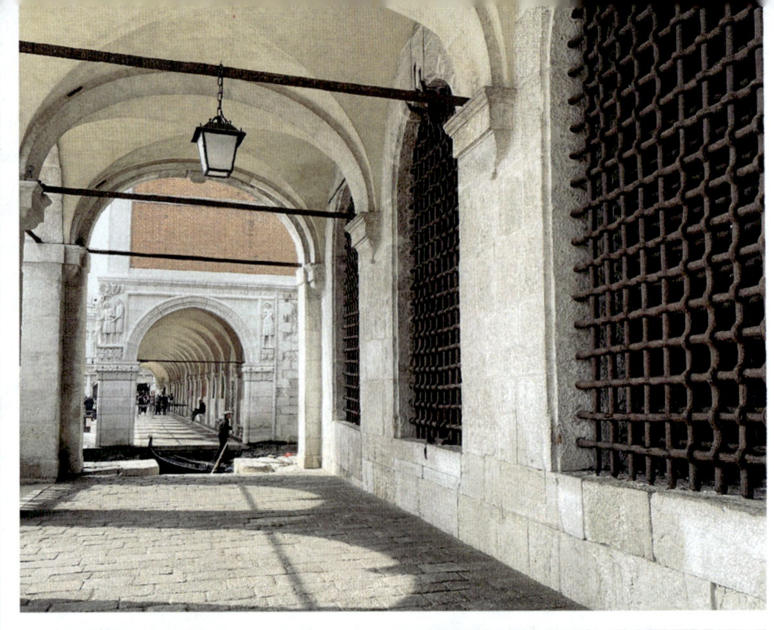

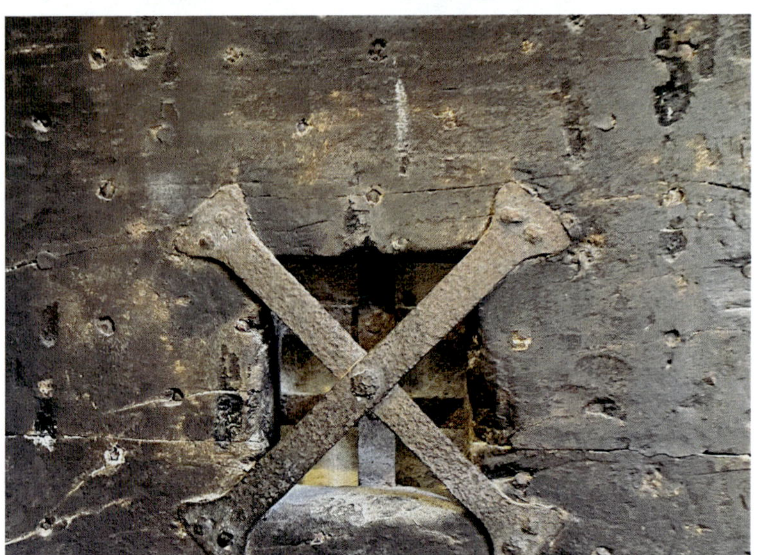

IRON, STONE, AND WOOD – STRONG CRAFTSMANSHIP

Just as magnificent as the Bridge of Sighs and the Doge's Palace look from the outside, just as robust and raw is the prison inside. The Prison walls are thick and massive, the wood bold, and the iron locks and hinges unbreakable. It is impressive craftsmanship in every detail with persistent and sustainable materials that have stood the test of time.

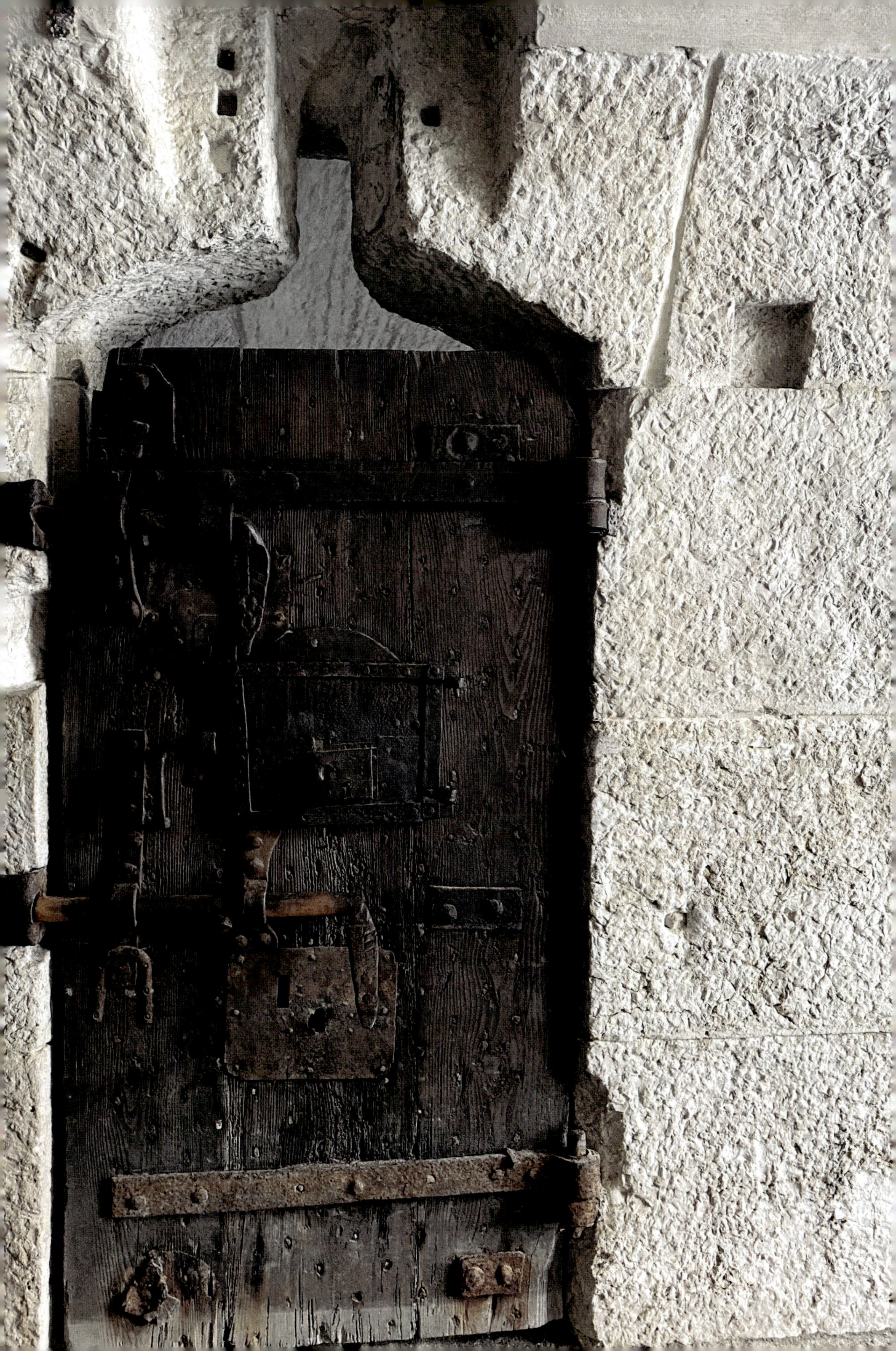

THE LAST VIEW OF FREEDOM

Imagine a last glimpse of the blue sea with the church of San Giorgio Maggiore on the opposite side of the lagoon. It is time to enter the dark prison cell, where the rays of light from the sun seldom reach. This last view of the Venetian Lagoon is beautifully framed by the massive rose windows made of thick stone. It is practically impossible to escape.

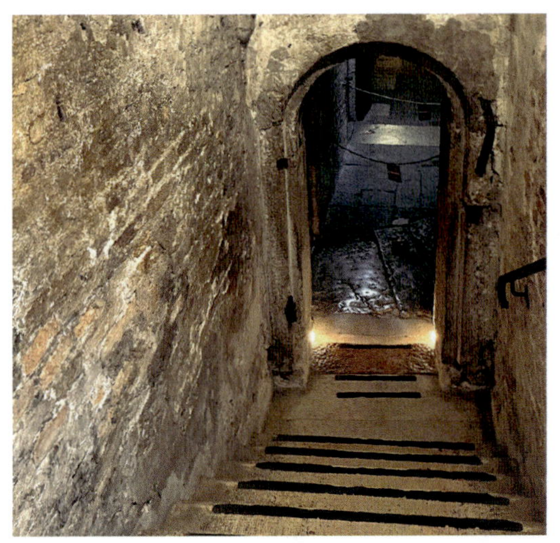

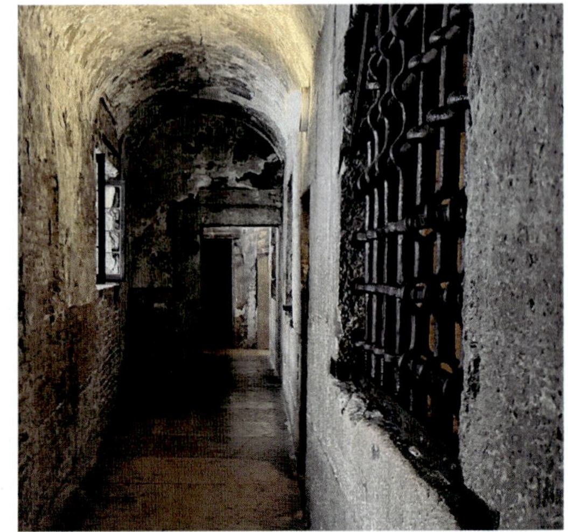

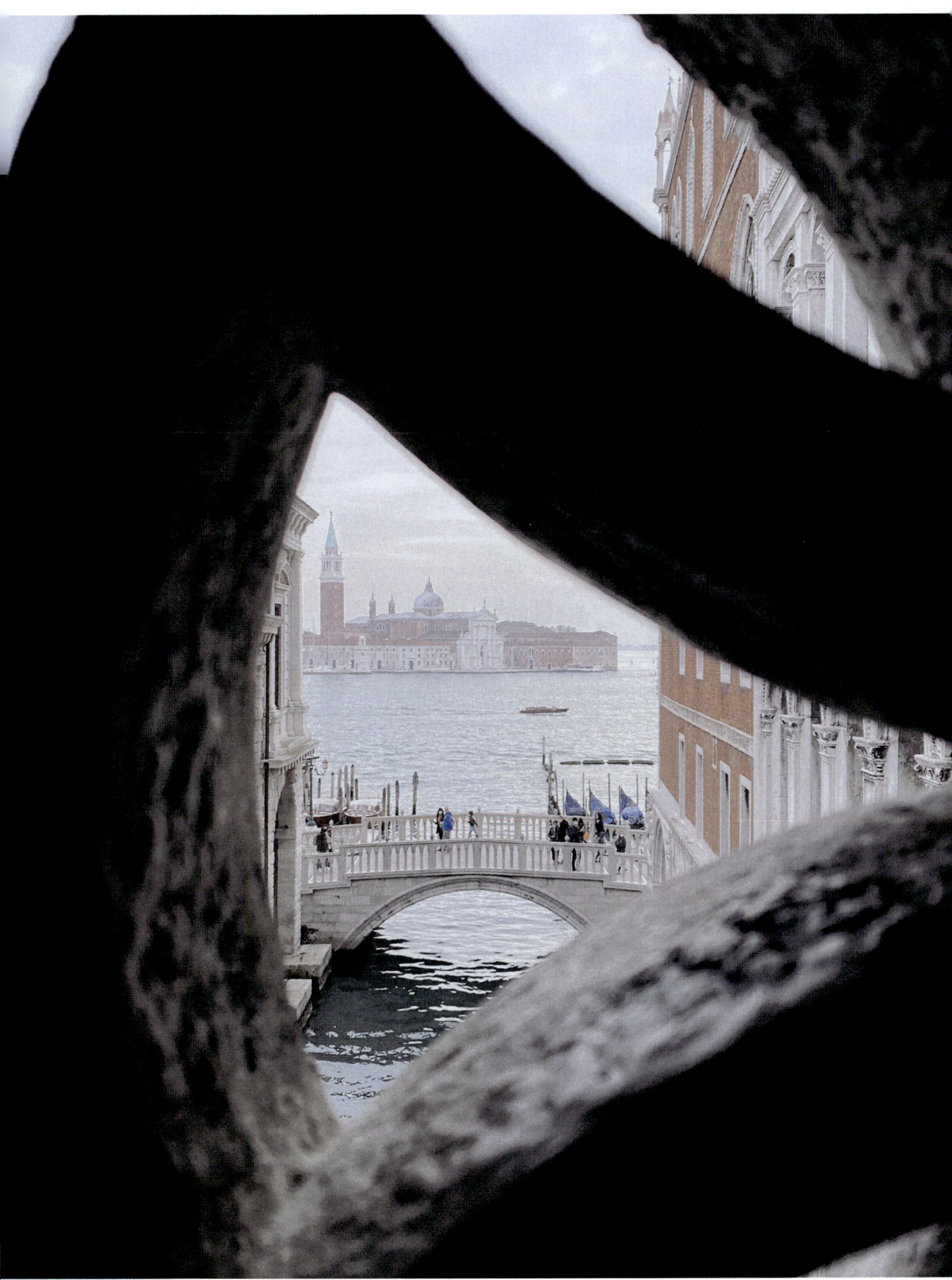

VII

CANAL GRANDE

THE TURQUOISE HIGH STREET

The Canal Grande is the most important of the canals in Venice. The colour of the water varies beautifully with the sky, often with a bright turquoise-green colour. The canal is the Venice high street dividing the city into two. Across the channel, four bridges connect the different districts. The most famous of the Canal Grande bridges is the iconic Rialto Bridge. The Canal Grande curls through Venice and makes two great curves, forming an inverted S-shape. Along the almost four-kilometre-long canal are around 180 impressive Palaces, each with its own signature and story.

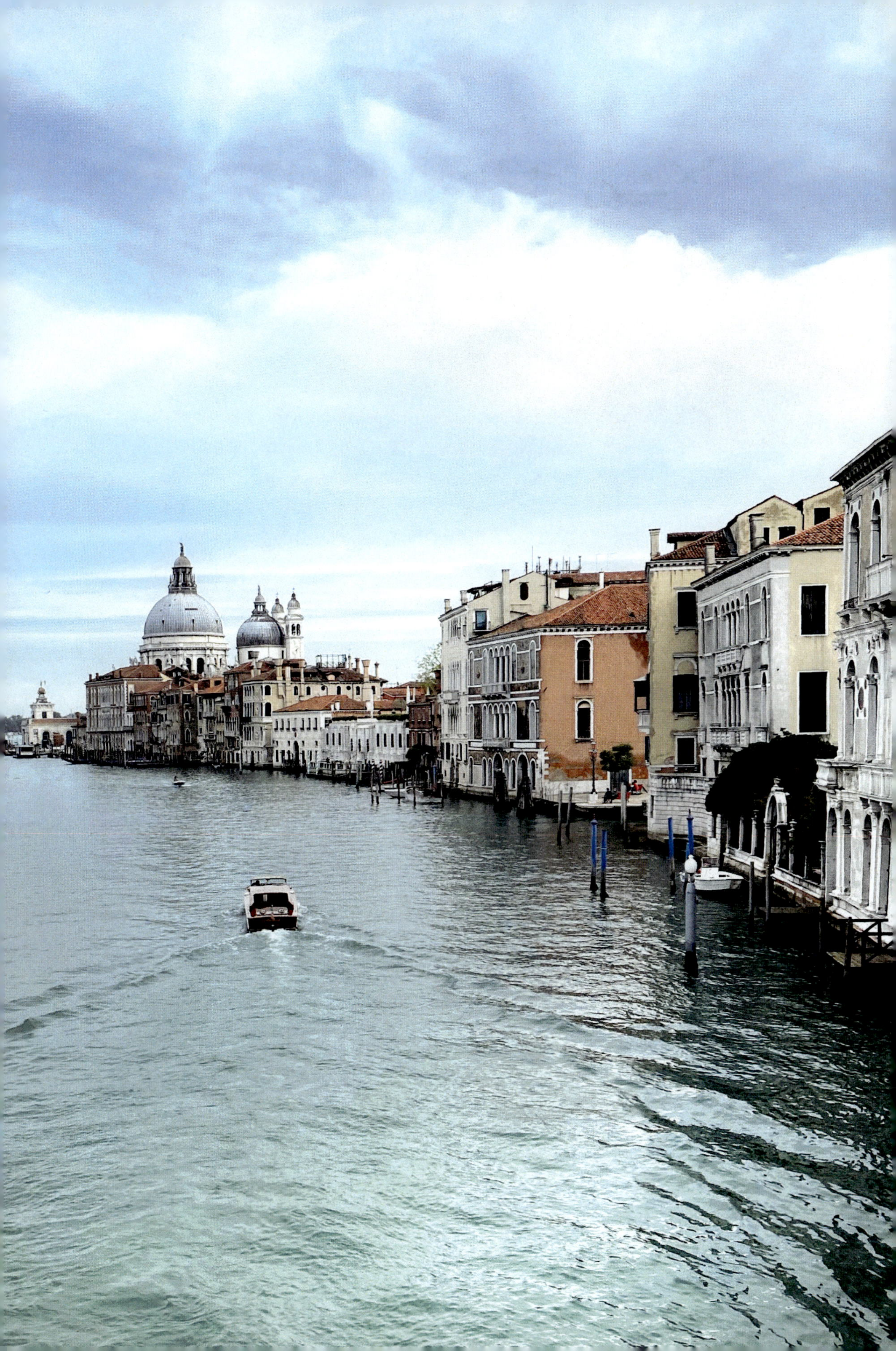

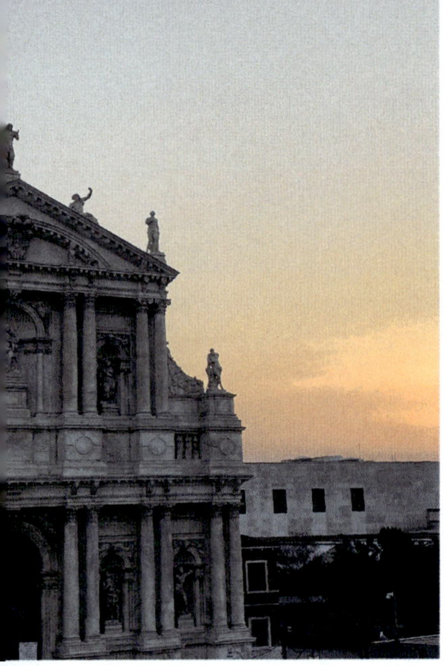

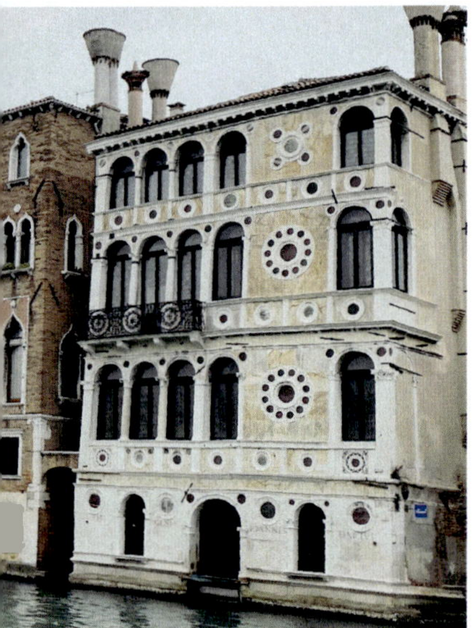

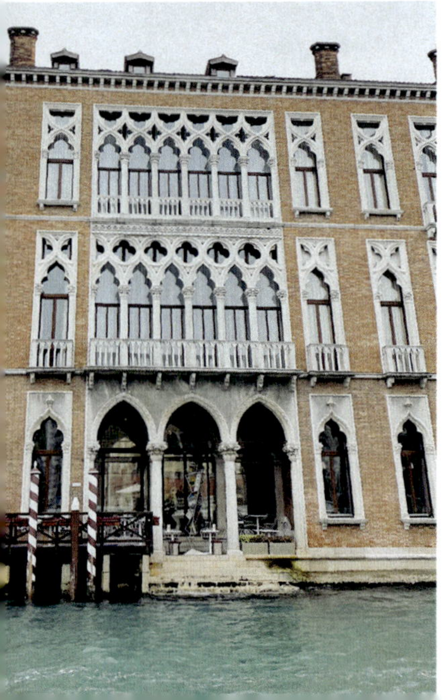

MAGNIFICENT PALACES OF CANAL GRANDE

Over the centuries, the Canal Grande has been important for commerce, and the Palaces could be built from the wealth generated from intensive trade and commercial activities. Venice dominated trade on the Mediterranean Sea and connected Europe with North Africa and Asia. The Canal Grande is like an exclusive City Boulevard with fantastic Gothic architecture constructed with the finest marble and stone. Some Palaces catch the eye more than others. Palazzo Dario, with a colourful, playful marble façade; Palazzo Giustinian, with its late Venetian gothic architecture; or Ca d'Oro, one of the most beautiful Palaces along the canal.

UNIQUE IMPRESSIONS OF THE VENETIAN ARISTOCRACY

The Venetian aristocracy did their very best to impress their peers, and the palace façades played a significant role in contributing to its imposing grandeur and uniqueness. It was part of the noble family brand. The palaces had a relatively limited space on the ground floor. Therefore, having a garden is not typical in Venice; the water and light connection is more important. The Palaces line up after one another, closely connected to the waterfront. It is undoubtedly a gallery of architecture from the 12th century to the 18th century – from Byzantine, Gothic, and Renaissance to Baroque. Many noble families had one or several family members elected to be Doge and rule over the Venetian Republic.

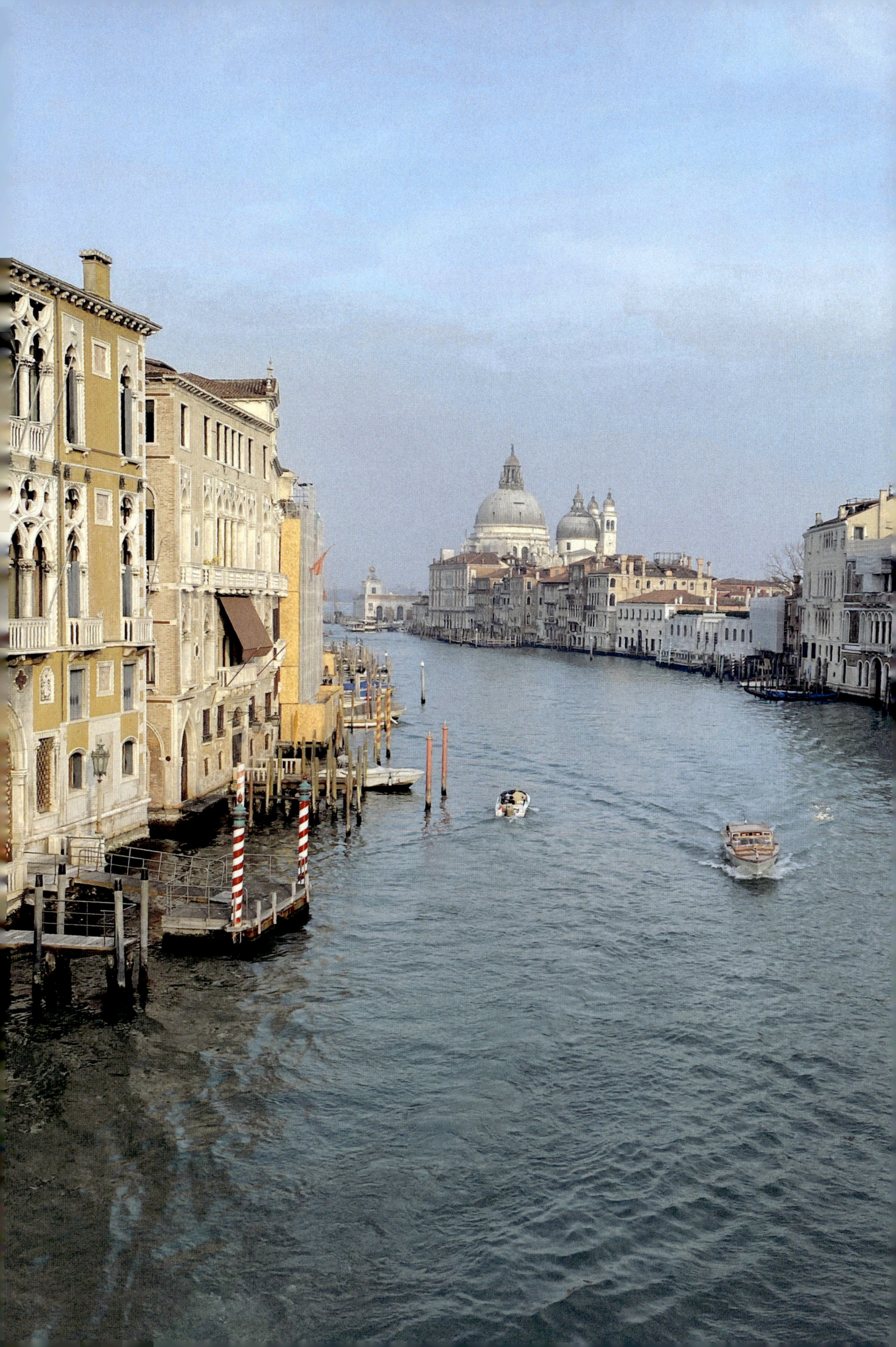

CA' D'ORO – A GOTHIC DREAM

It is one of the finest examples of Venetian architecture. A beautiful Renaissance Palace with Byzantine and Gothic elements. It was built in the early 15th century for residential purposes for the noble Contarini family. The marble tracery was formerly covered in gold leaf; therefore, the name – the House of Gold – Ca' d'Oro. Imagine the glory when the Palace was fully built and the materials were new and shiny.

The Palace attracts the eye, something extraordinary and almost divine in its aesthetic. It is true craftsmanship in every detail and one of Venice's gems.

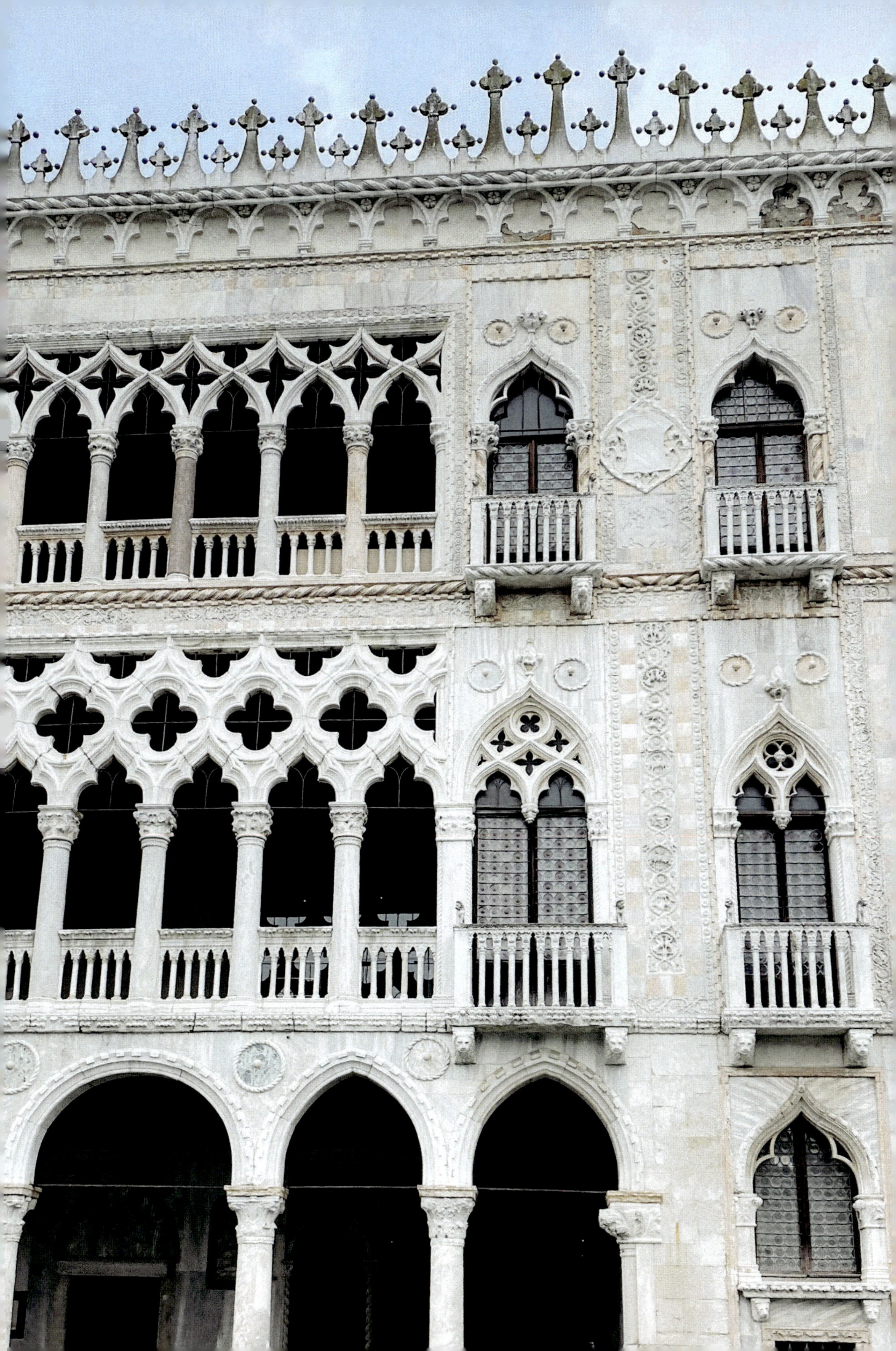

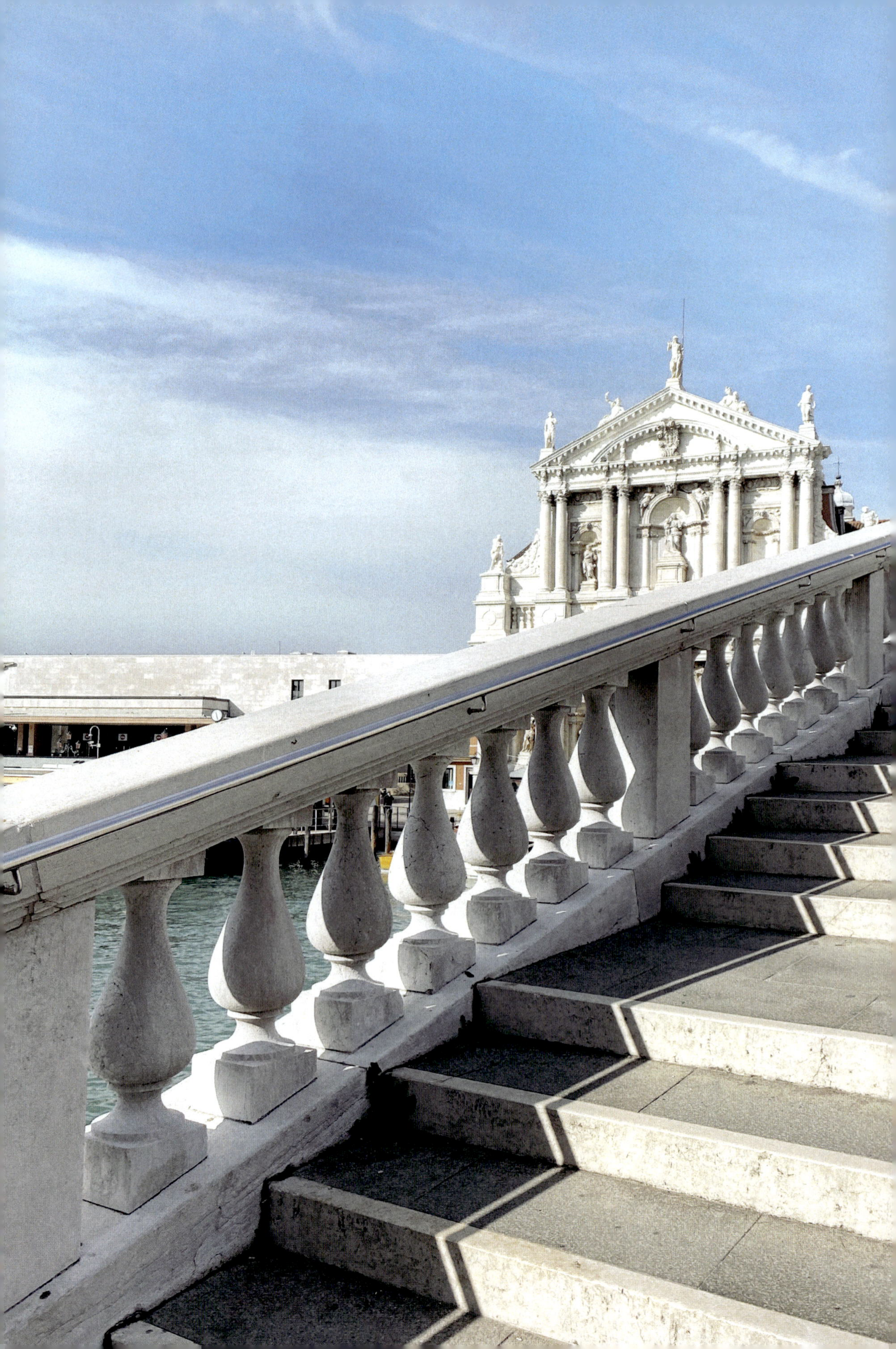

CANAL GRANDE BRIDGES

The bridges of the Canal Grande have their own character. The Ponte della Constituzione has a modern, streamlined design, introducing the 21st century to Venice, whereas the Ponte di Rialto takes us back to the Renaissance.

Ponte della Constituzione – Constitution Bridge

The bridge is also called the Ponte di Calatrava after the Spanish architect Santiago Calatrava, who designed and built it. The bridge was completed in 2008 and is the youngest of the Canal Grande bridges – a modern and transparent design where the water and horizon are visible through the material.

Ponte degli Scalzi – Bridge of the Barefoot

The bridge connects Santa Croce with Cannaregio and leads to the church Chiesa degli Scalzi (Chiesa di Santa Maria di Nazareth) – a Roman Catholic Carmelite Church. The Baroque-style church overlooks the canal and is decorated with saints sculptured by the artist Bernardo Falconi.

Ponte dell'Accademia – Accademia Bridge

It is the bridge for reaching the Accademia galleries. From this wooden bridge, there is a beautiful view over the Canal Grande towards the Venetian Lagoon on the horizon.

Ponte di Rialto – Rialto Bridge

It is the oldest of the Canal Grande bridges, with its iconic architecture. It is a masterpiece of bridges – world-famous for Venice.

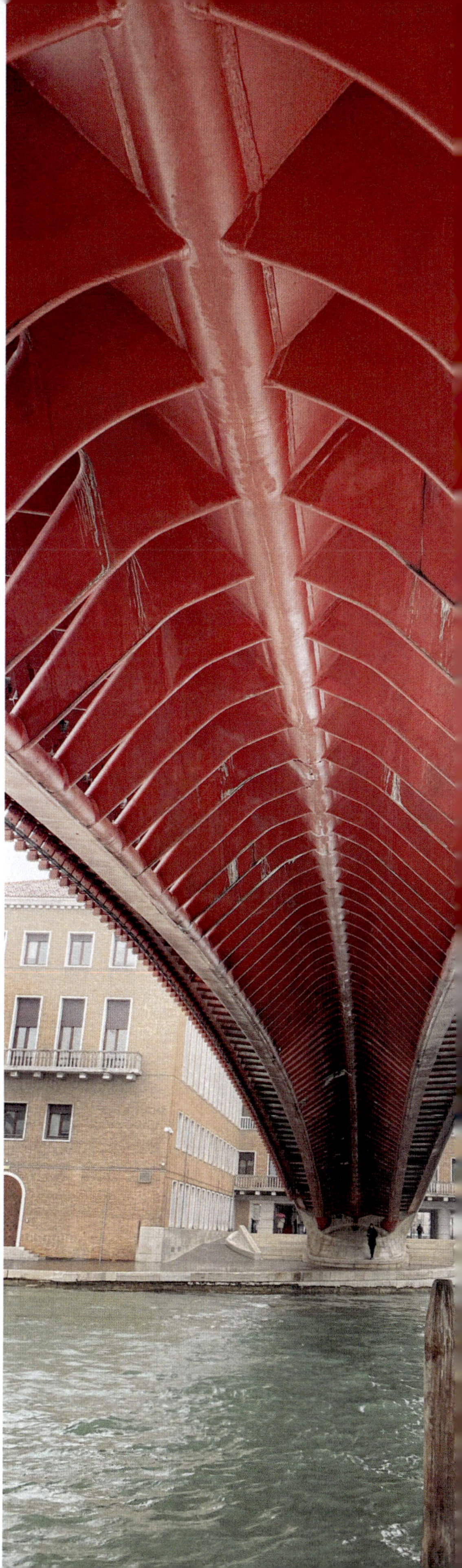

VIII

GALLERIE DEL–L'ACCADEMIA

BELLINI, BLUE AND RENAISSANCE ART

The Venetian art collection represents the Byzantine, Renaissance, and Baroque eras: the models, the paint, and the light – all exciting parts of the art process. The Renaissance work of Gianni Bellini's models came from patrician families in the city. Five hundred years later, their personalities come through in the paintings. The music-making angel in the San Giobbes Altarpiece feels youthful and contemporary when he looks up curiously from his playing. The blue colour with the exclusive ultramarine entered the art scene during the Renaissance, and the Gallerie shows many examples of divine blue dresses with the Virgin Mary as the leading lady.

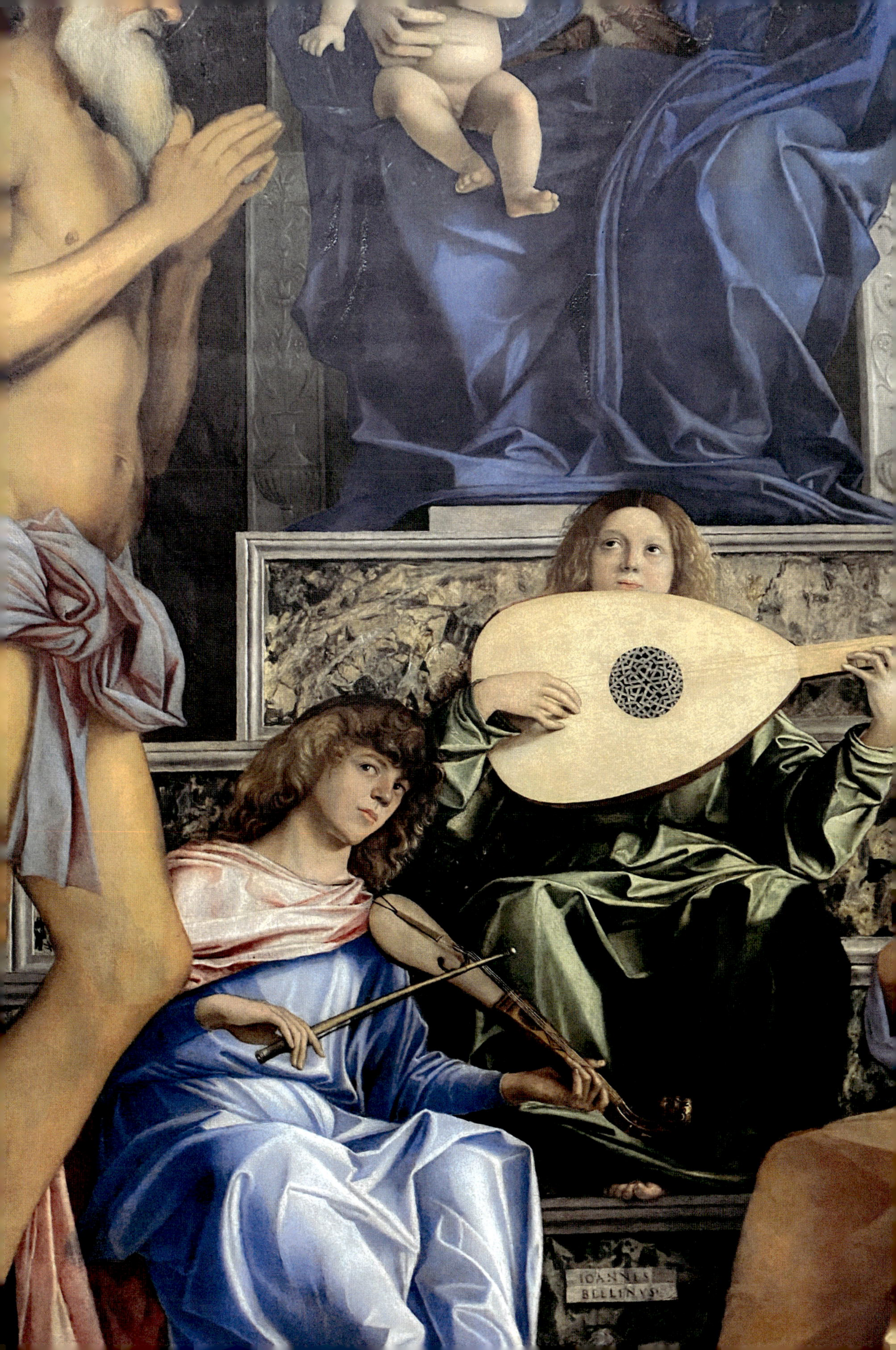
IOANNES
BELLINVS

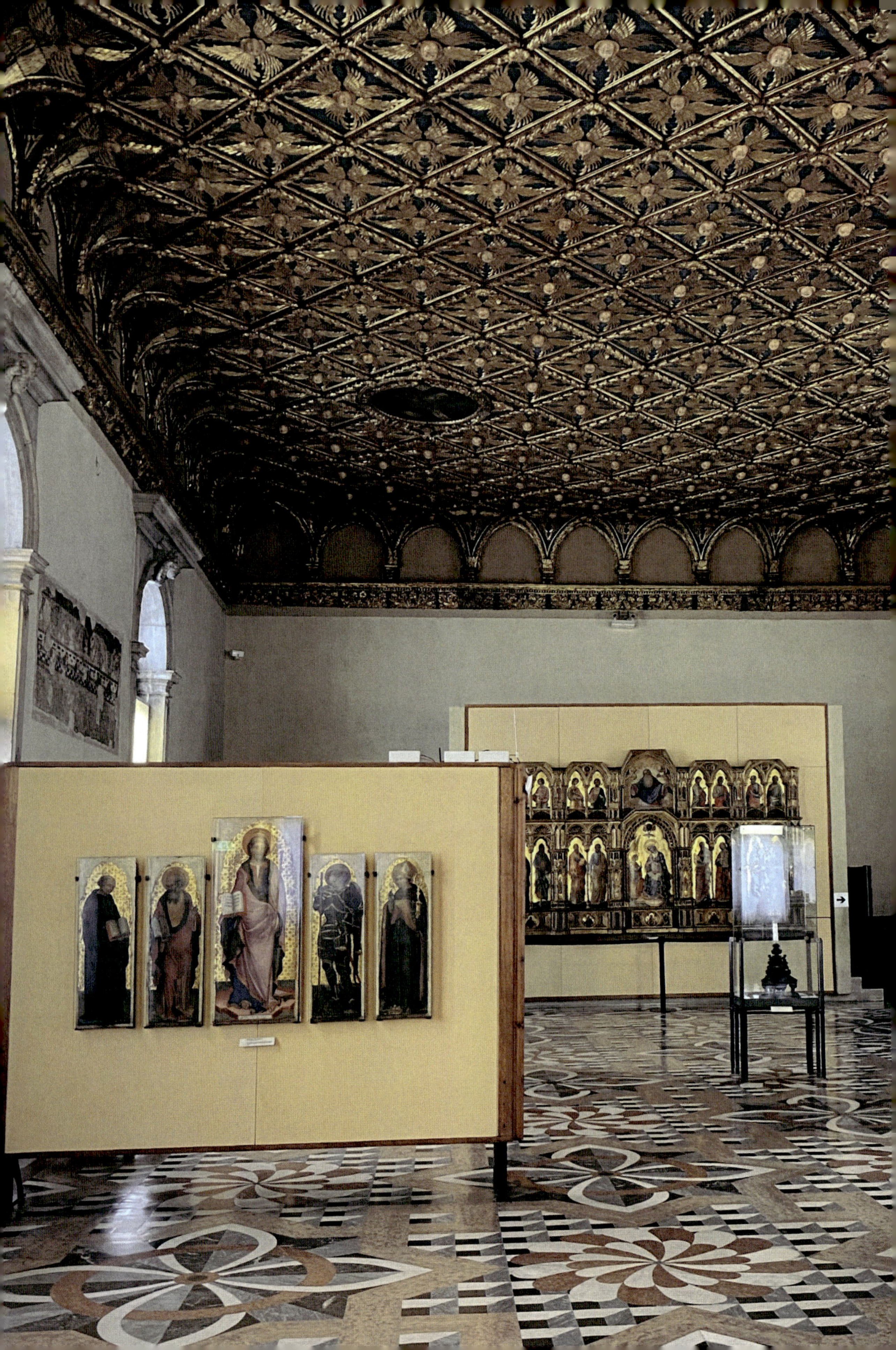

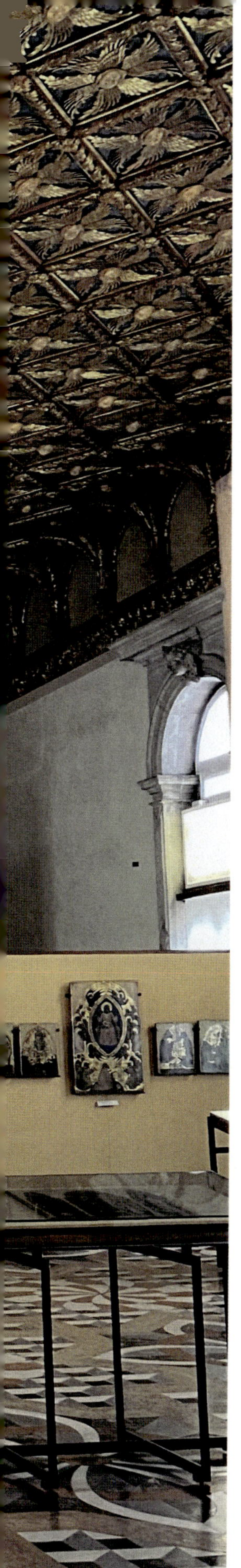

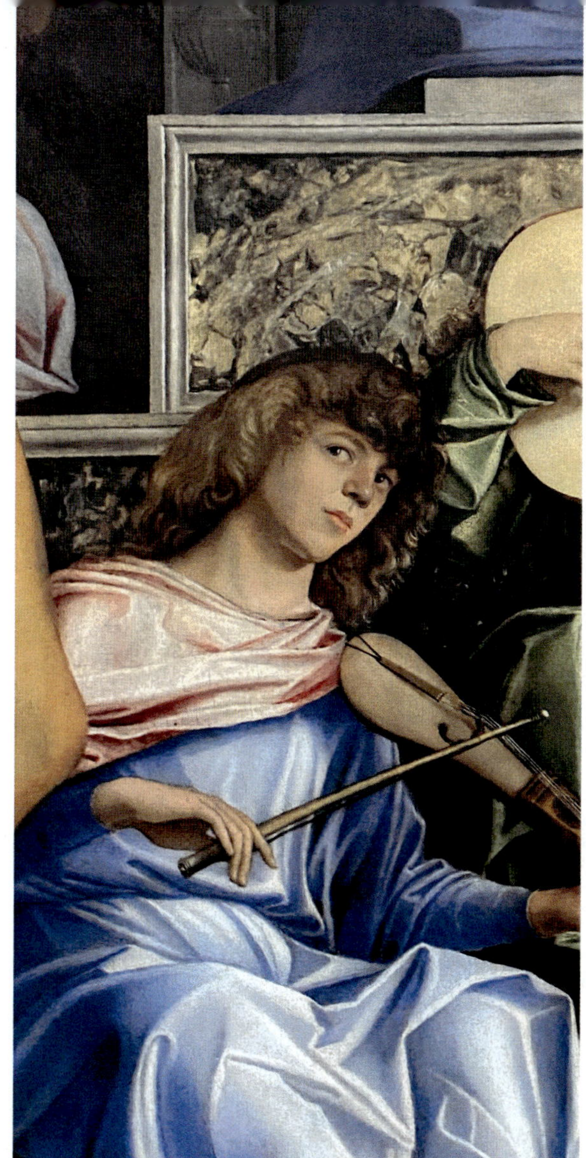

TIMELESS YOUTH – GIOVANNI BELLINI

The music-making angel in Giovanni Bellini's painting is timeless. The boy who once stood as a model for the image feels so present, contemporary, and retains a twinkle in his eye. He has not aged, even though 500 years have passed. He represents eternal youth. Bellini's San Giobbe Altarpiece is an early Renaissance and one of the Gallery's many valuable paintings.

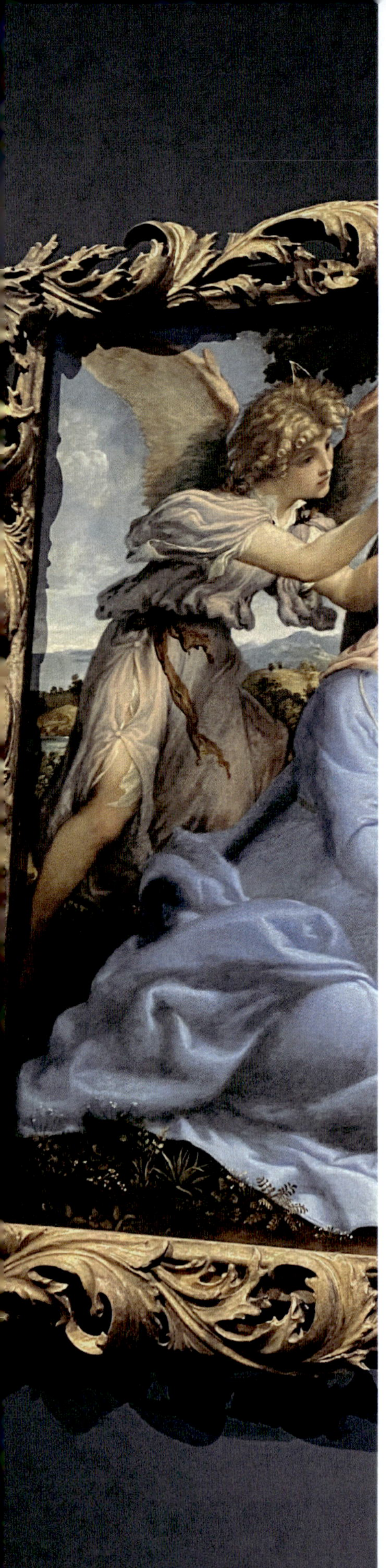

THE RENAISSANCE OF ULTRAMARINE

During the Renaissance, the colour blue became popular amongst Venetian artists, and the use of the pigment ultramarine represents the era. Ultramarine was derived from the expensive lapis lazuli gem found in Afghanistan. The high price of ultramarine did not stop the Venetian artists from using blue in different shades. The Virgin Mary was painted in a blue dress to express the divine, with various blue colours for different moods – from ultramarine to soft and light airy sky blue. The symbolism of colours was important during the Renaissance.

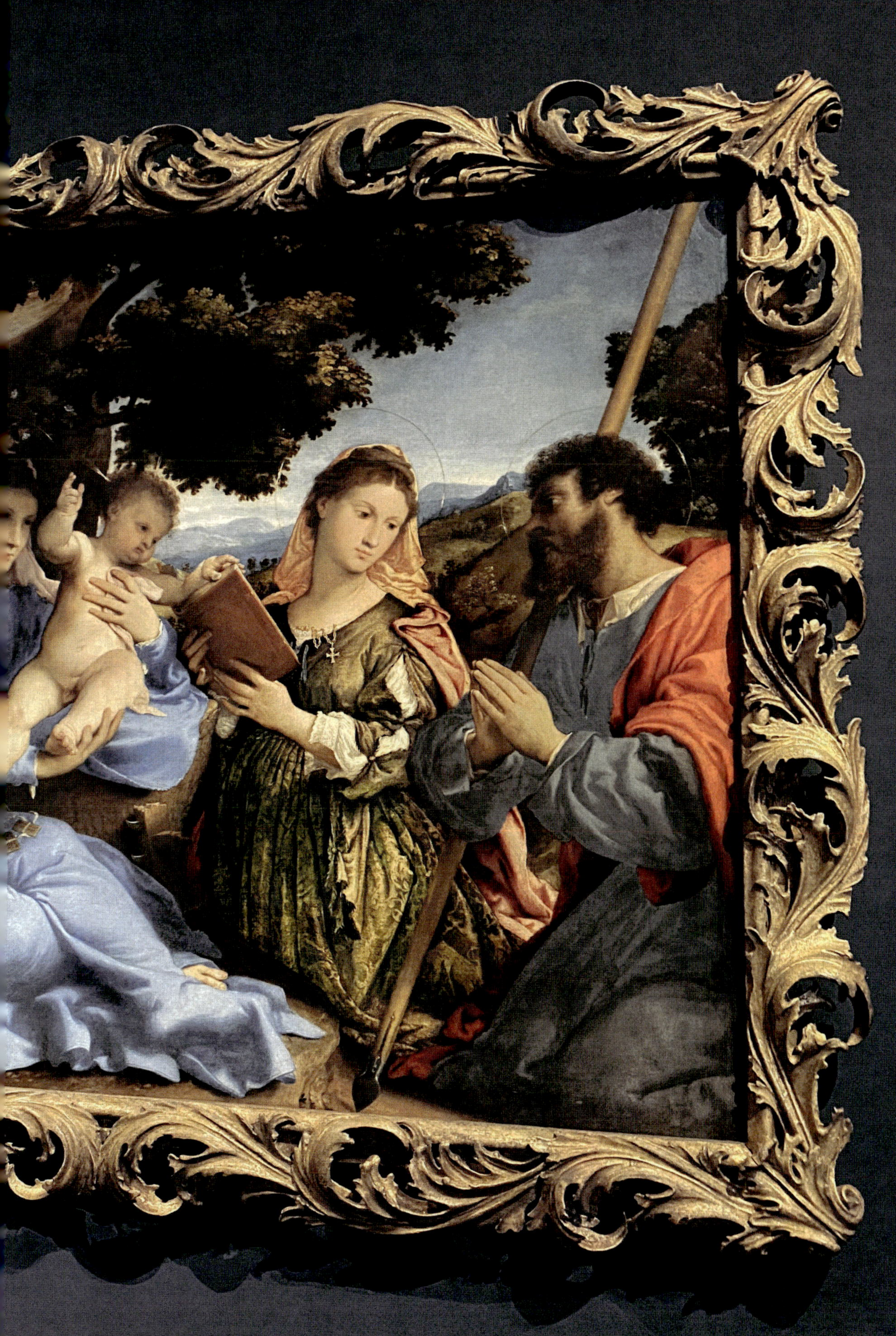

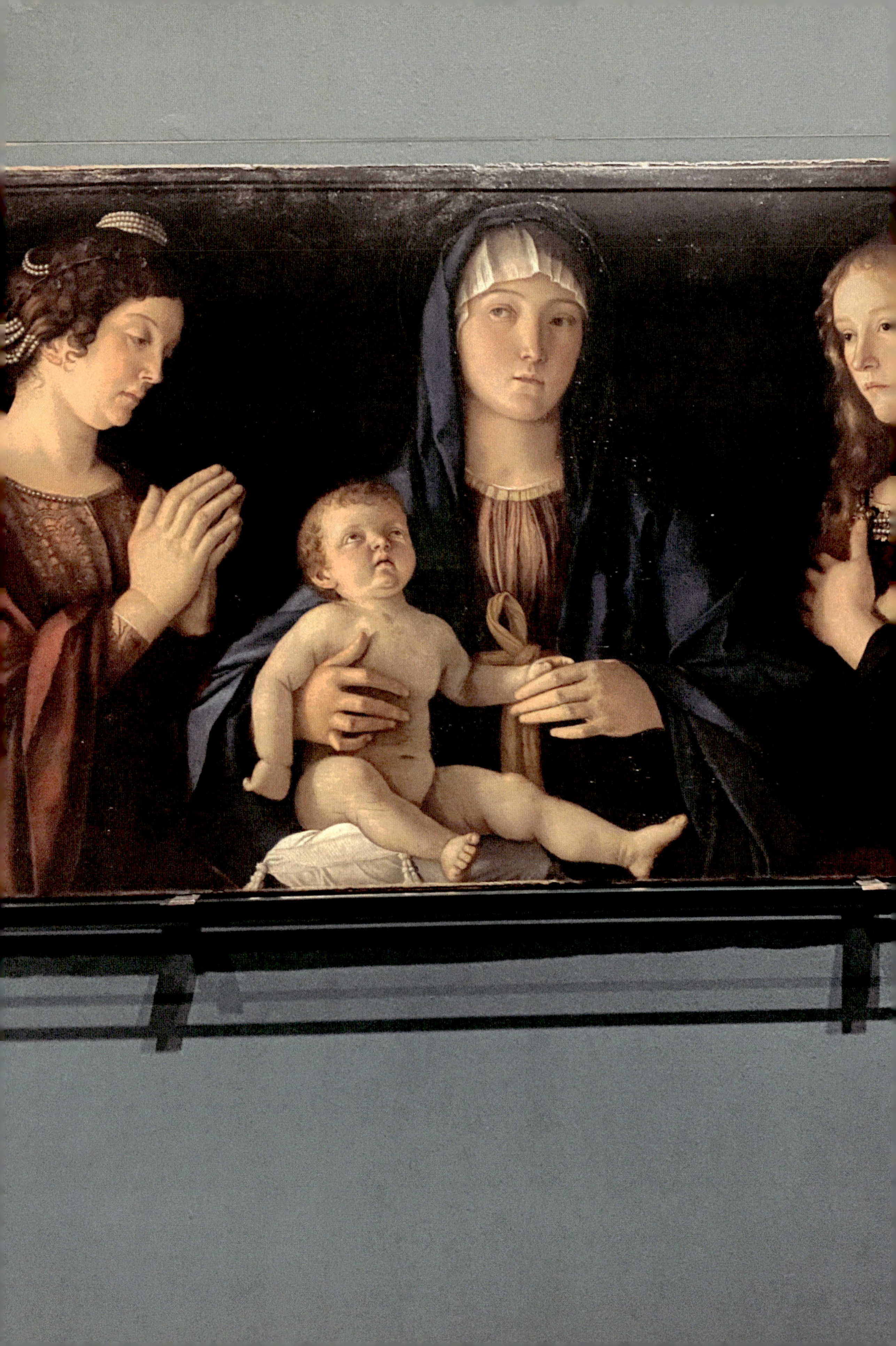

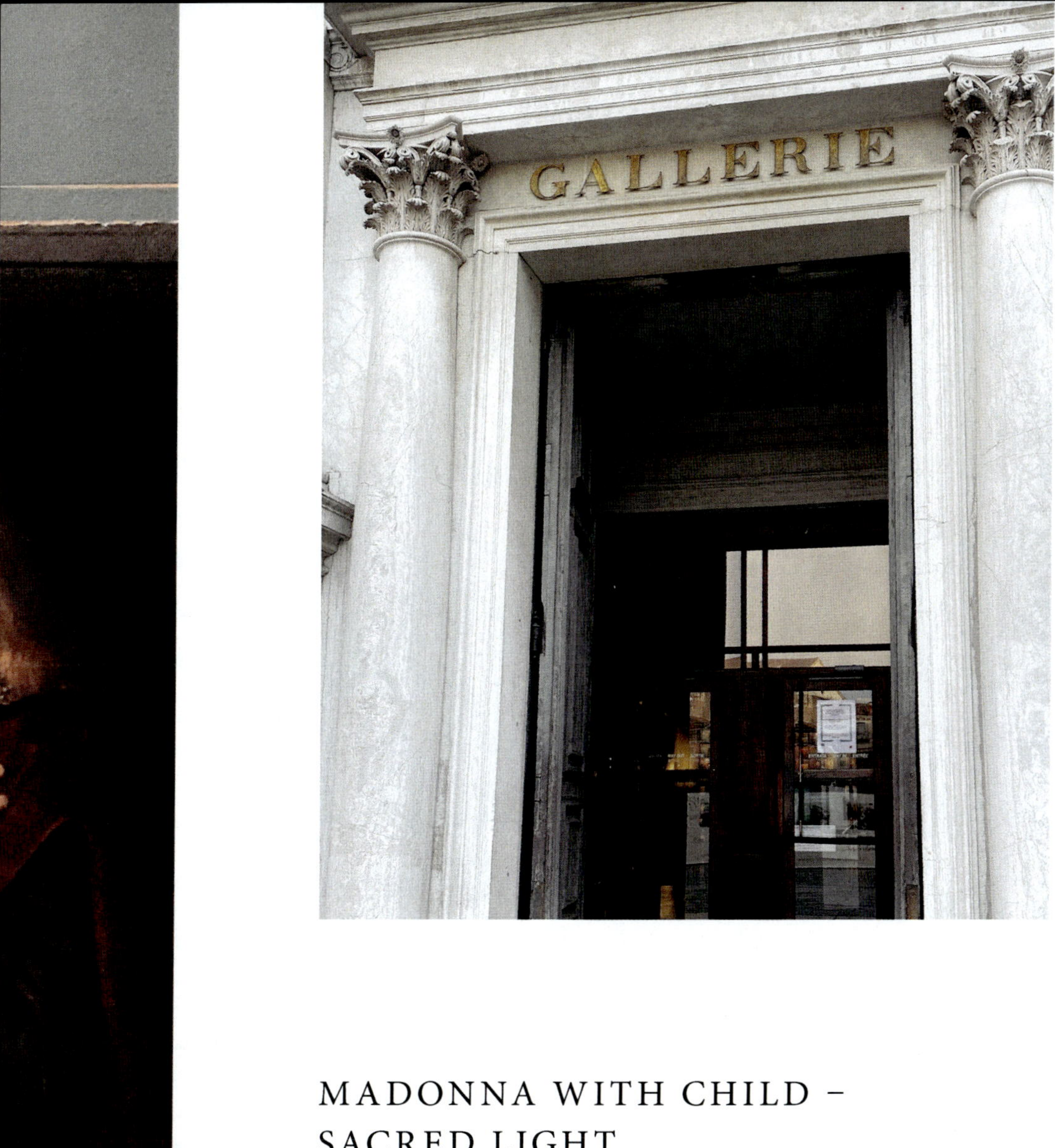

MADONNA WITH CHILD – SACRED LIGHT

There is a sacred light over the faces of the Virgin Mary with the Christ child. Saint Mary Magdalene and Saint Catherine of Alexandria stand on each side of her. All three women are in their thoughts. Giovanni Bellini is the painter behind this masterpiece, one of the Gallery's most famous paintings. The dark background is said to be influenced by Leonardo da Vinci, who was also active in Venice around 1500. The artists influenced each other, and different codes developed for the language of art. The Venetian patrician women who stood as models for Catherine and Mary Magdalene received eternal life through the painting.

IX

HOTEL DANIELI

A HOME FOR THE NOBILITY

Over the years, celebrities have passed through the main entrance and walked up the stairs under the magnificent Murano glass chandeliers. The Palazzo Dandolo has hosted important guests since the medieval ages. The view towards the Venetian Lagoon from the Palace is splendid. Authors, novelists, and poets like Marcel Proust, Charles Dickens, Wolfgang von Goethe, and Percy Shelley have all stayed here during visits to Venice. The Palazzo Dandolo, later turned into a hotel, was built in the 14th century by and for the noble Dandolo family. The family had four Doges elected to serve the Venetian Republic.

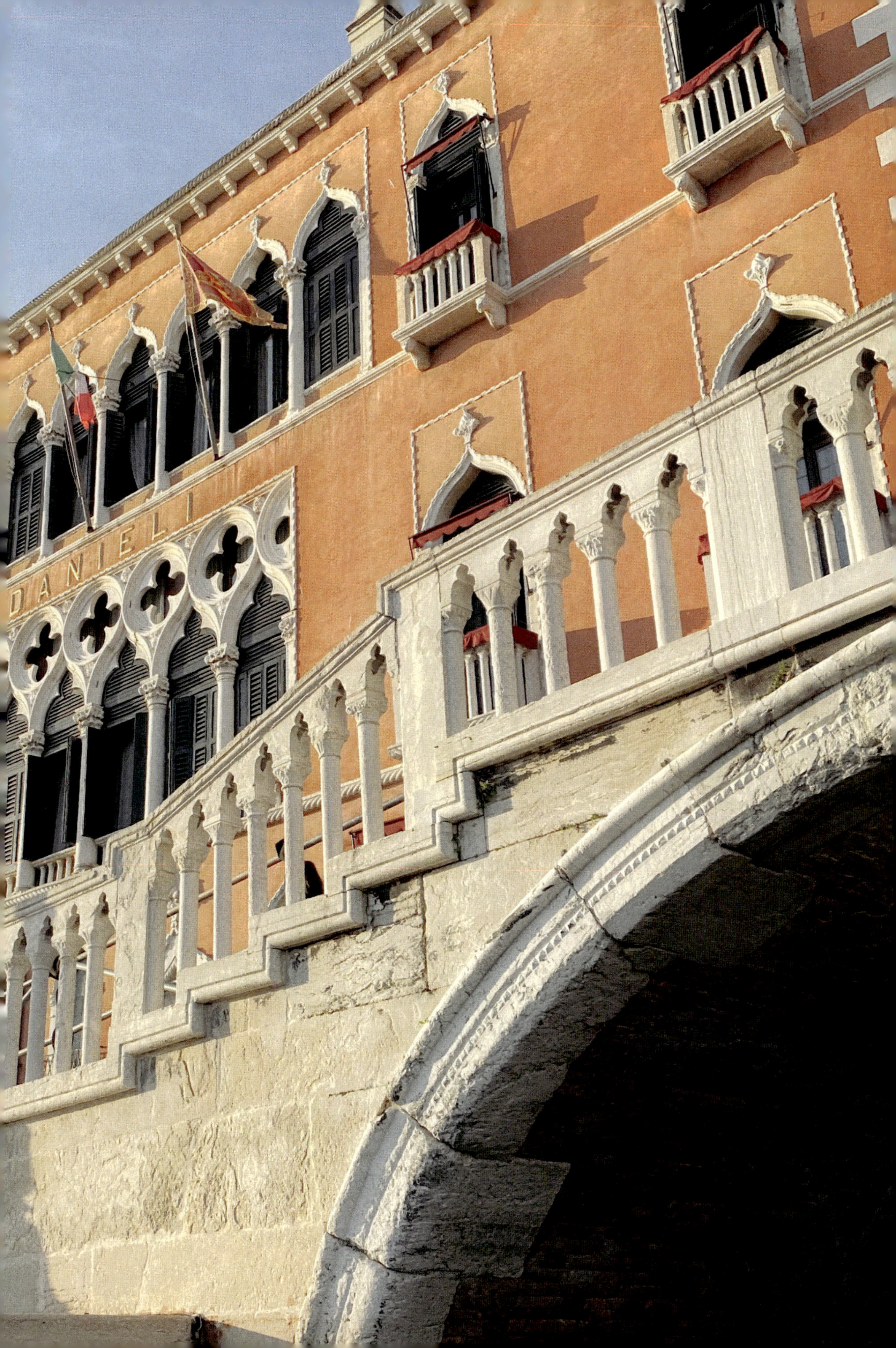
DANIELI

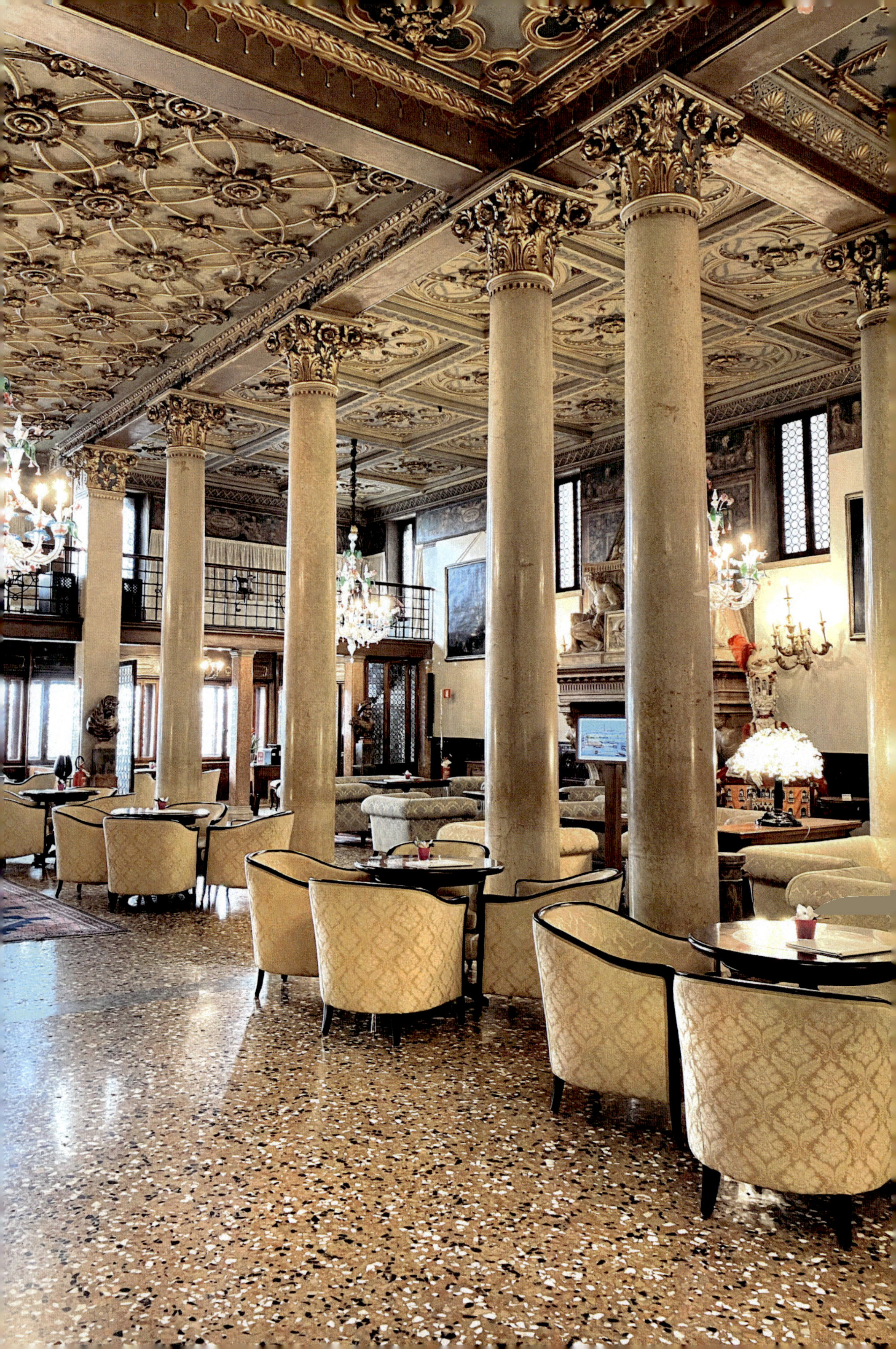

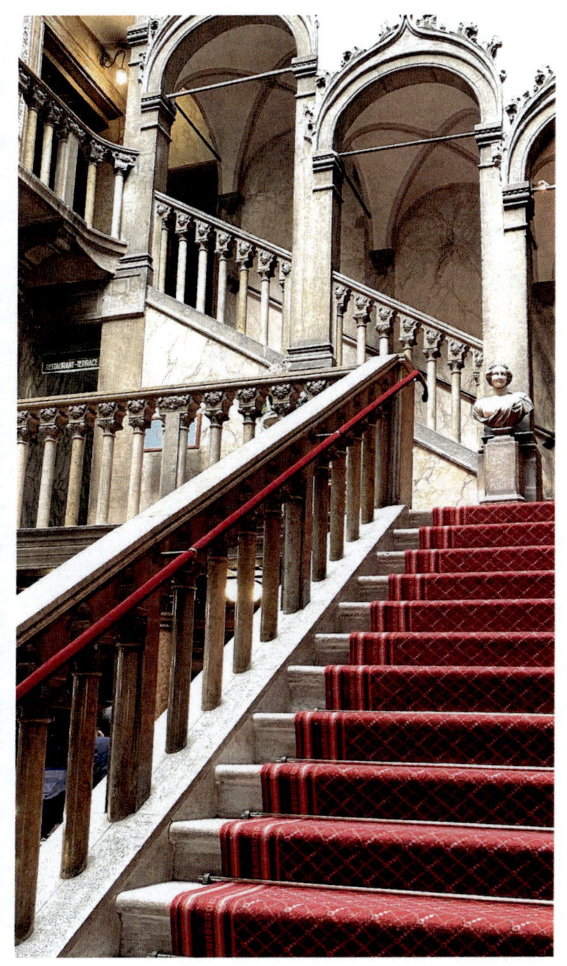

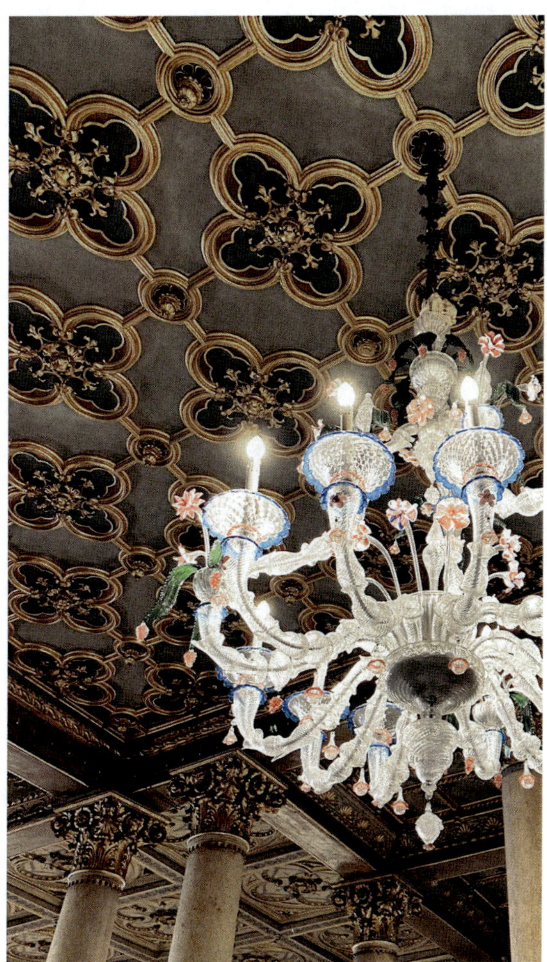

HOTEL DANIELI – GOETHE, DICKENS AND PROUST

The Palazzo Dandolo was built in the 14th century by the noble Dandolo family. Located in the Castello sestiere by the Venetian Lagoon. The original Palace has hosted important guests since the medieval ages. In 1822, the Palazzo Dandolo was turned into a Hotel, Hotel Danieli, named after the nickname "Danieli" of its owner, Giuseppe Dal Niel. Over the years, many celebrities have passed through the main entrance and walked up the red carpet.

The magnificent Murano glass chandeliers decorate the ceiling. The interior is lavish, filled with opulent furniture and golden details. Authors, novelists, and poets like Marcel Proust, Charles Dickens, Wolfgang von Goethe, and Percy Shelley have all stayed in the Palace during their stays in Venice.

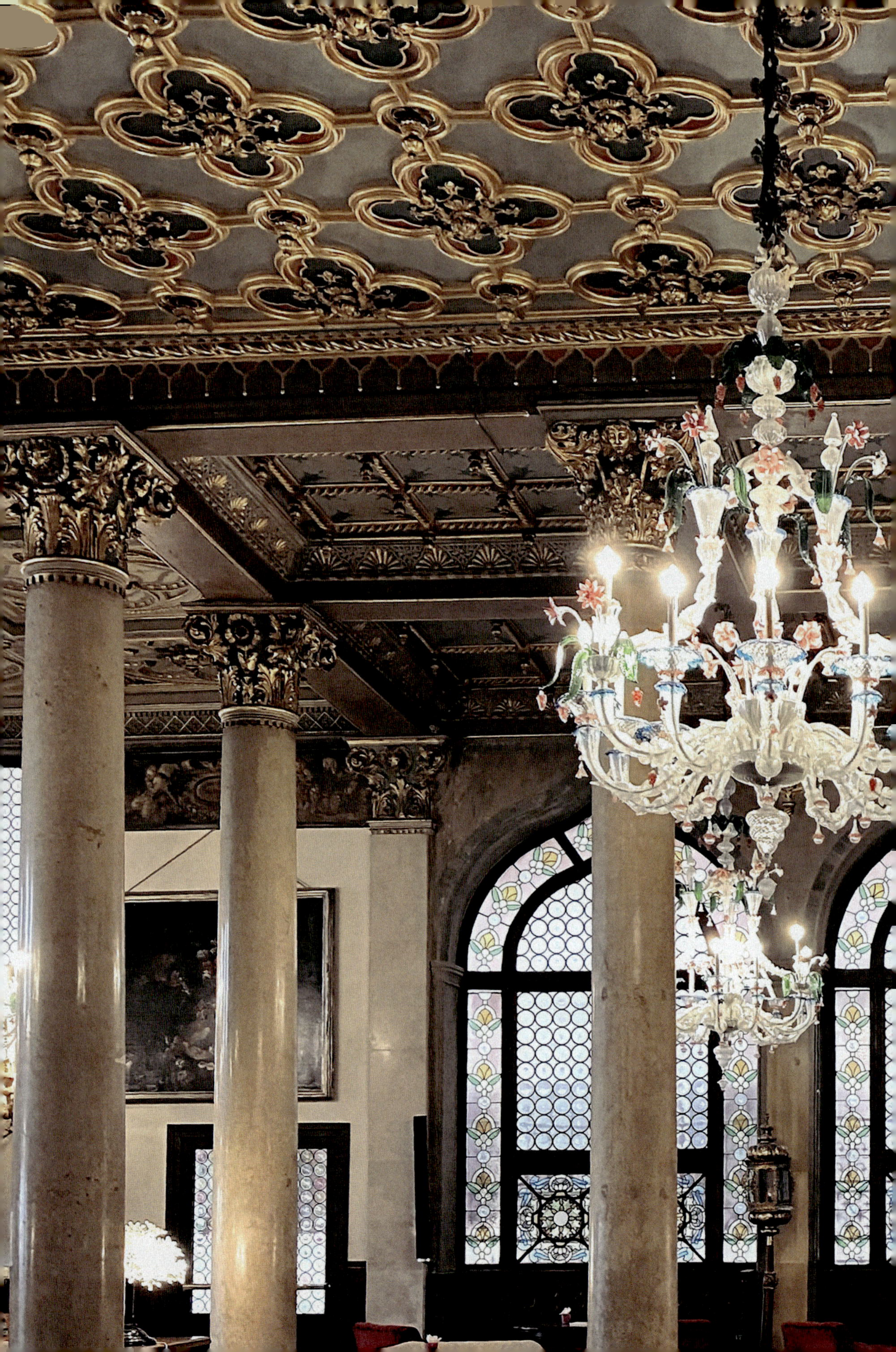

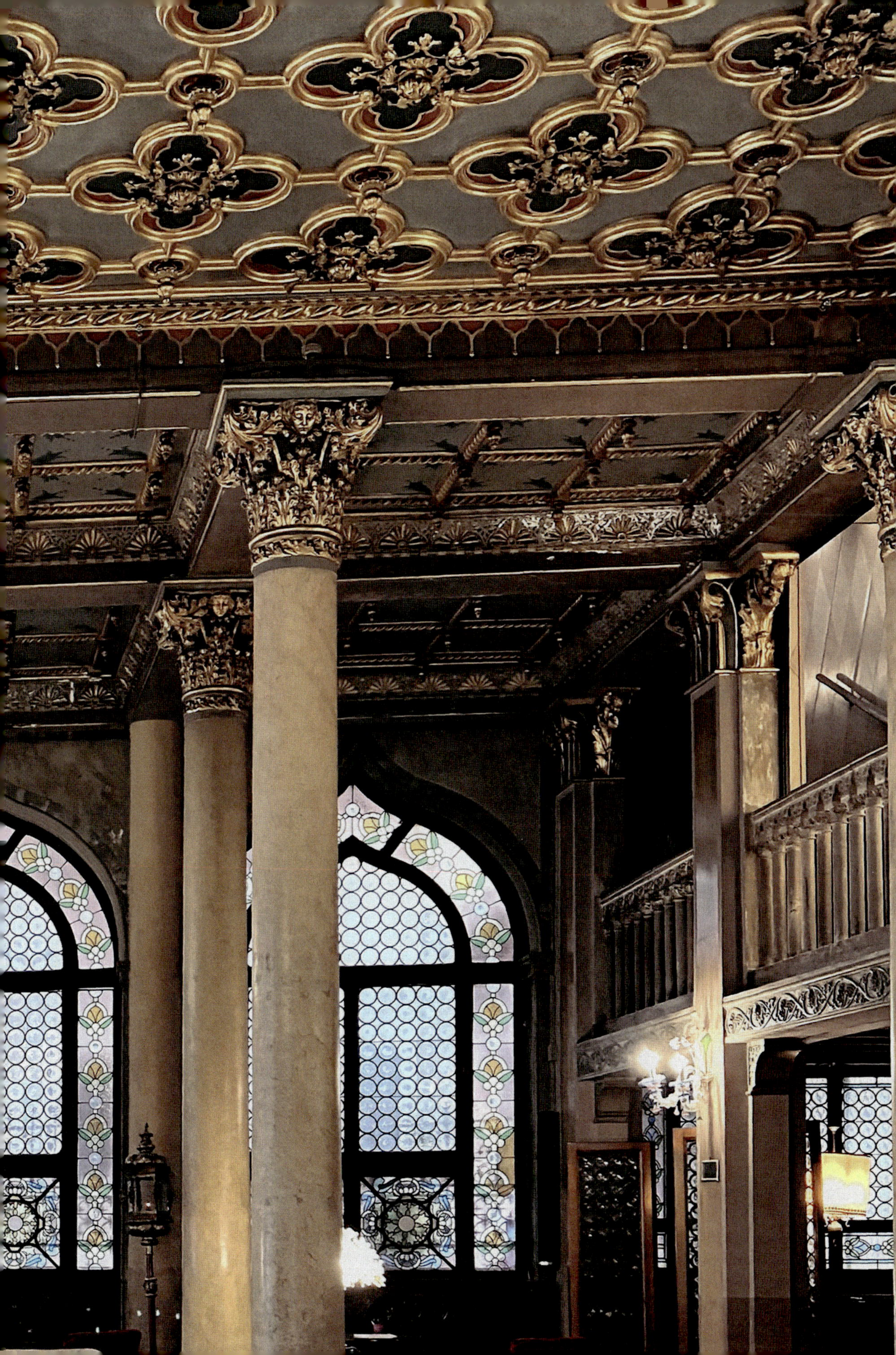

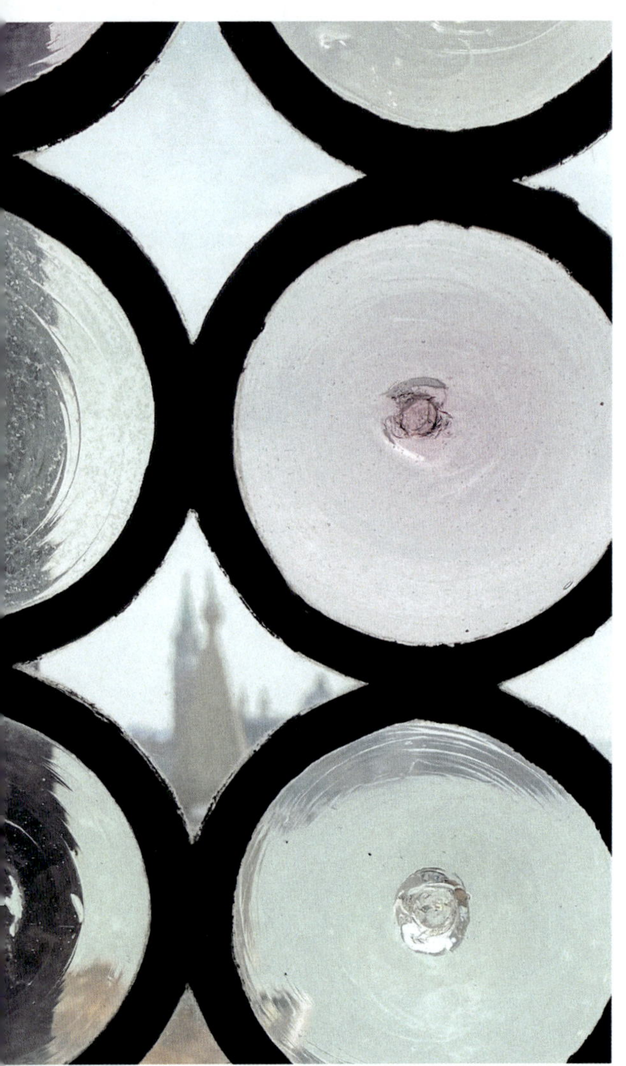

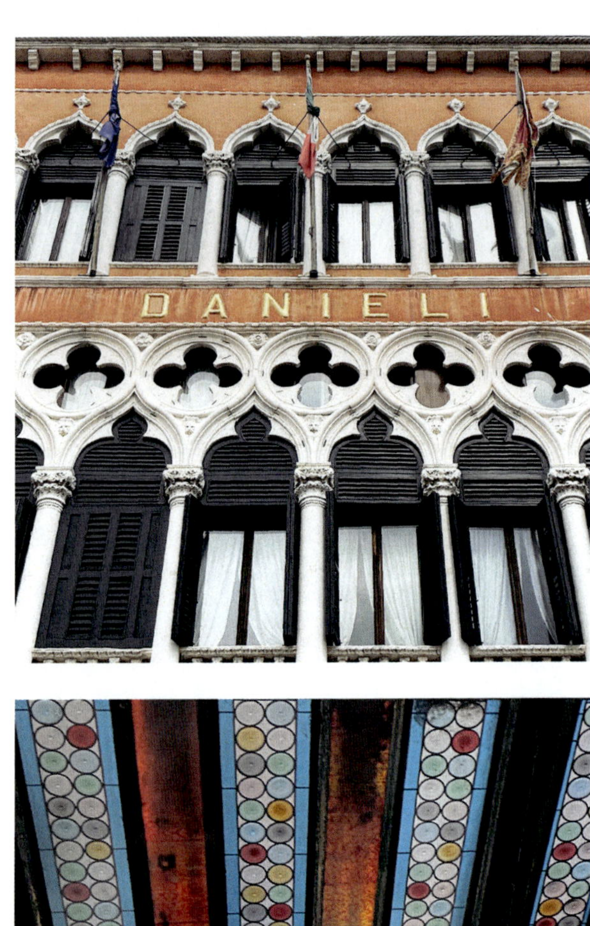

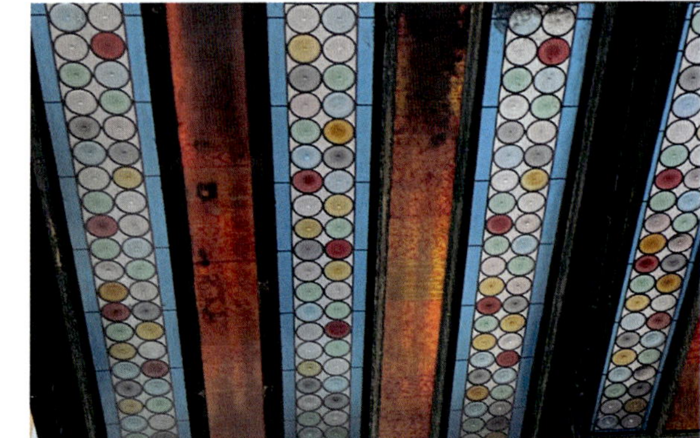

OPULENT MURANO GLASS – VENETIAN HERITAGE

Hotel Danieli has Venetian Murano glass in many shapes and forms – the entrance roof, the interior chandeliers, and the façade windows. Impressive Murano glass chandeliers also decorate the rooms. Venice has a long glass-making history connected to the Island of Murano, dating back to the High Middle Ages. Roman Empire knowledge blended with new knowledge from the Byzantine Empire and influences from the Orient. Typical is pastel-stain glass in pink, green, blue, and purple framed in circular shapes. The Murano glass chandelier is opulent and romantic, covered in glass with design elements of coloured flowers.

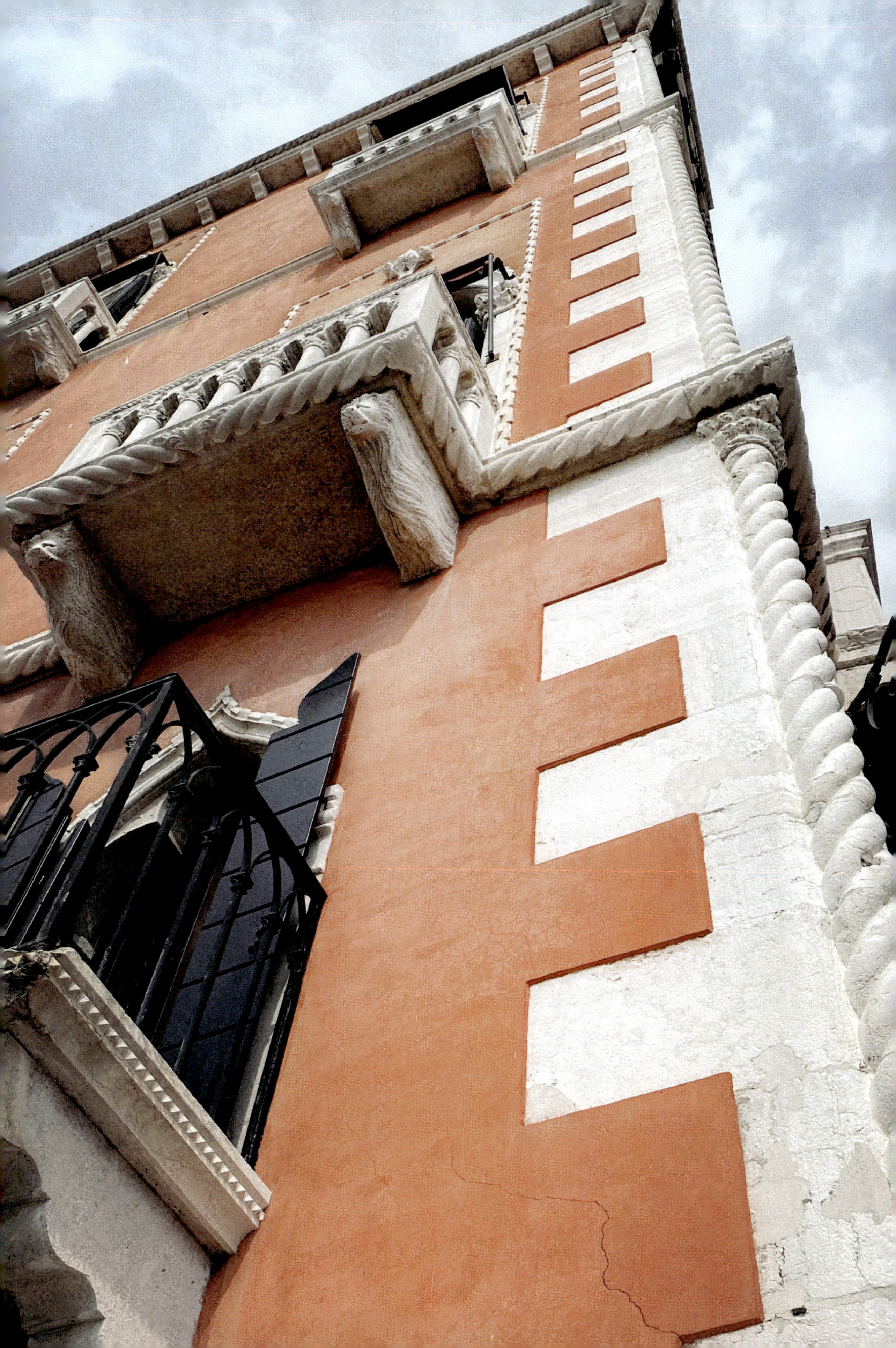

X

ADRIATIC SEA WATERFRONT

THE VENETIAN LAGOON

Venice has an impressive waterfront by the Lagoon of the Adriatic Sea. The stylish Basilica di San Giorgio Maggiore, by the architect Andrea Palladio, is a true iconic landmark in the Venice Lagoon and can be viewed from the waterfront. The gondolas lie tied and bob in the water, waiting to enter the canals. Napoleon's Royal Gardens offers a green retreat from the bustling city behind its beautiful black iron fences. In the afternoon, the Riva degli Schiavoni is soaked in sunshine. Over the centuries, people have enjoyed a pleasant stroll along this adorable seafront promenade, passing by the Doge's Palace, Hotel Danieli, and other prominent Palaces.

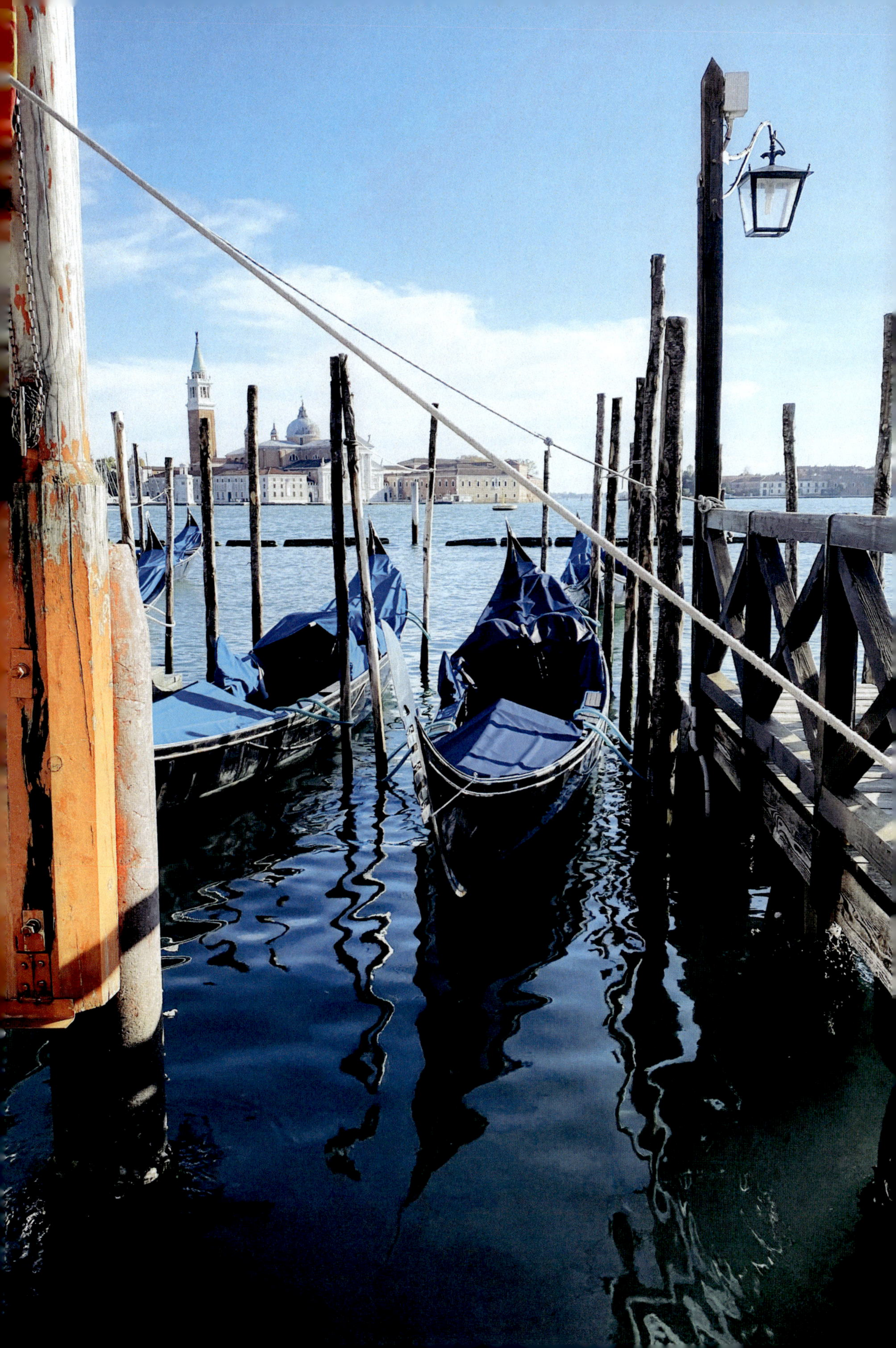

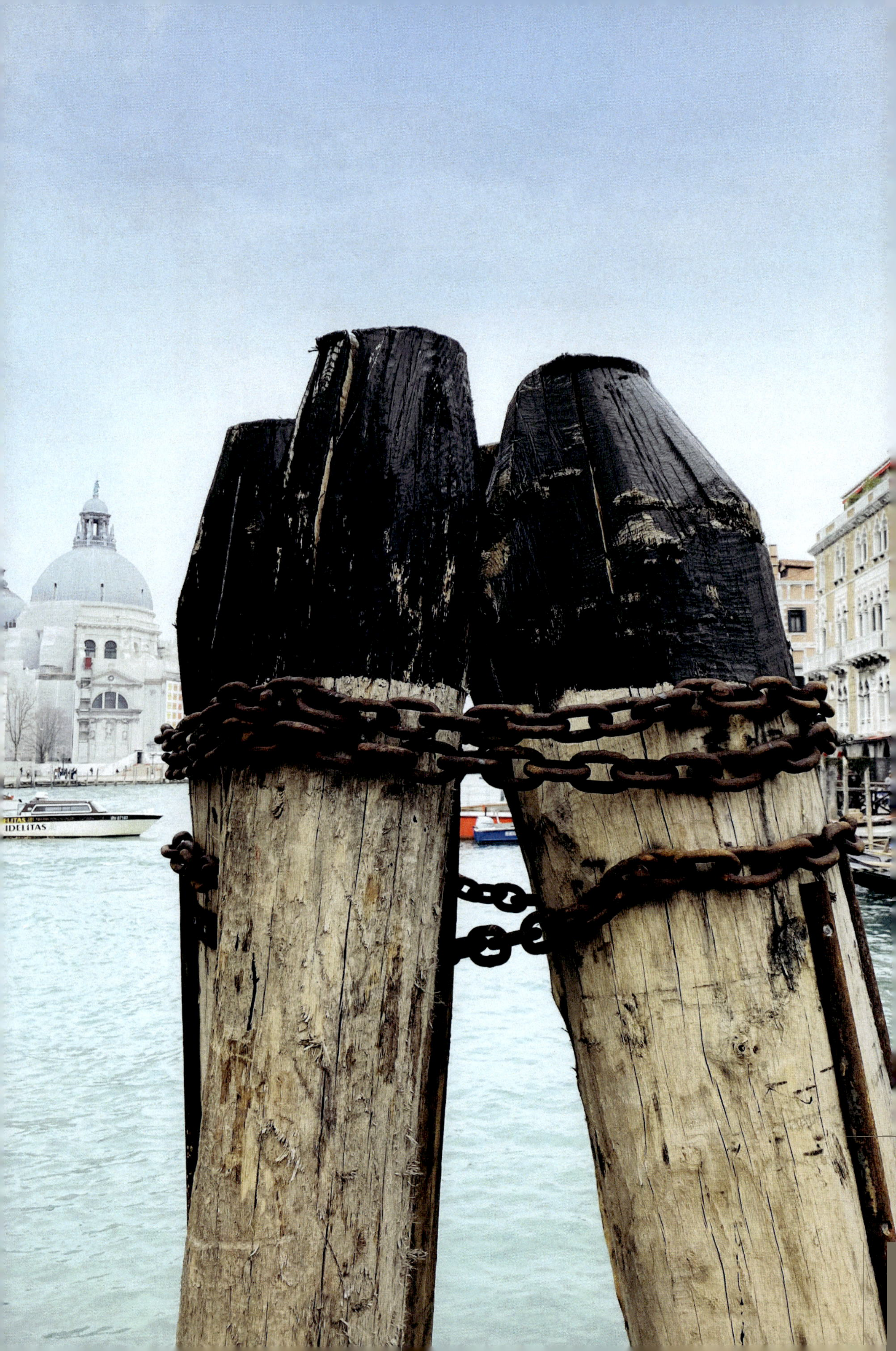

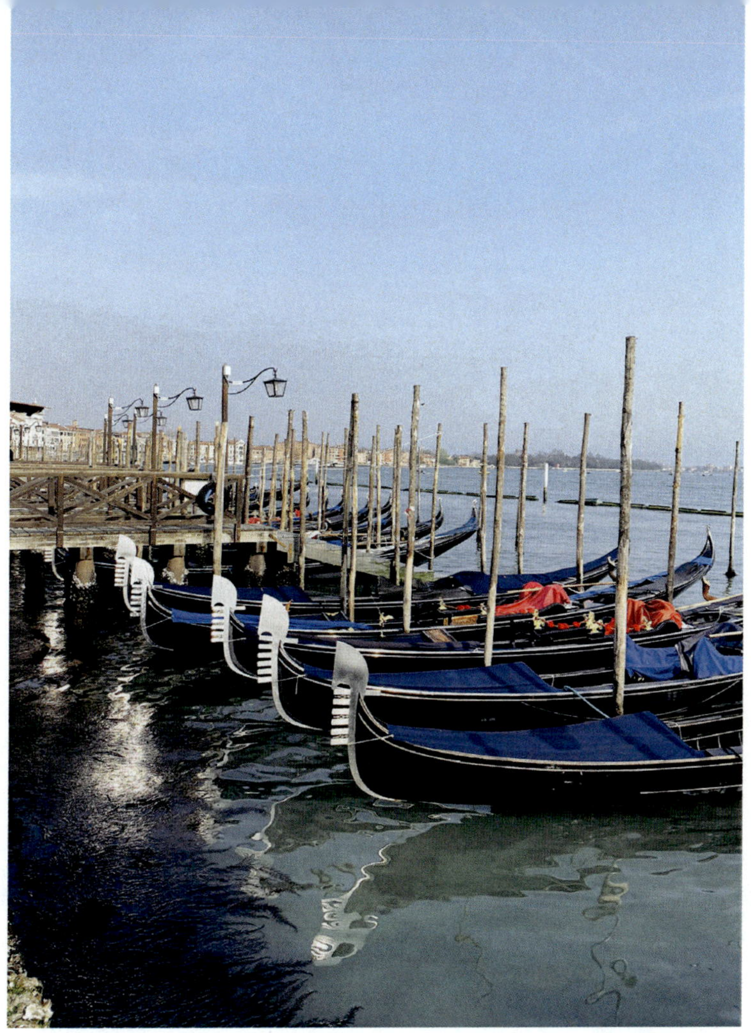

FOUNDATION OF VENICE

Venice is a city built on marshy small islands and wooden platforms with wooden stakes driven into the ground. The wooden stakes of Venice are an essential part of its identity and foundation. Along the waterfront to the Adriatic Lagoon, the gondolas are tied to the wooden stakes and placed in a perfect lineup.

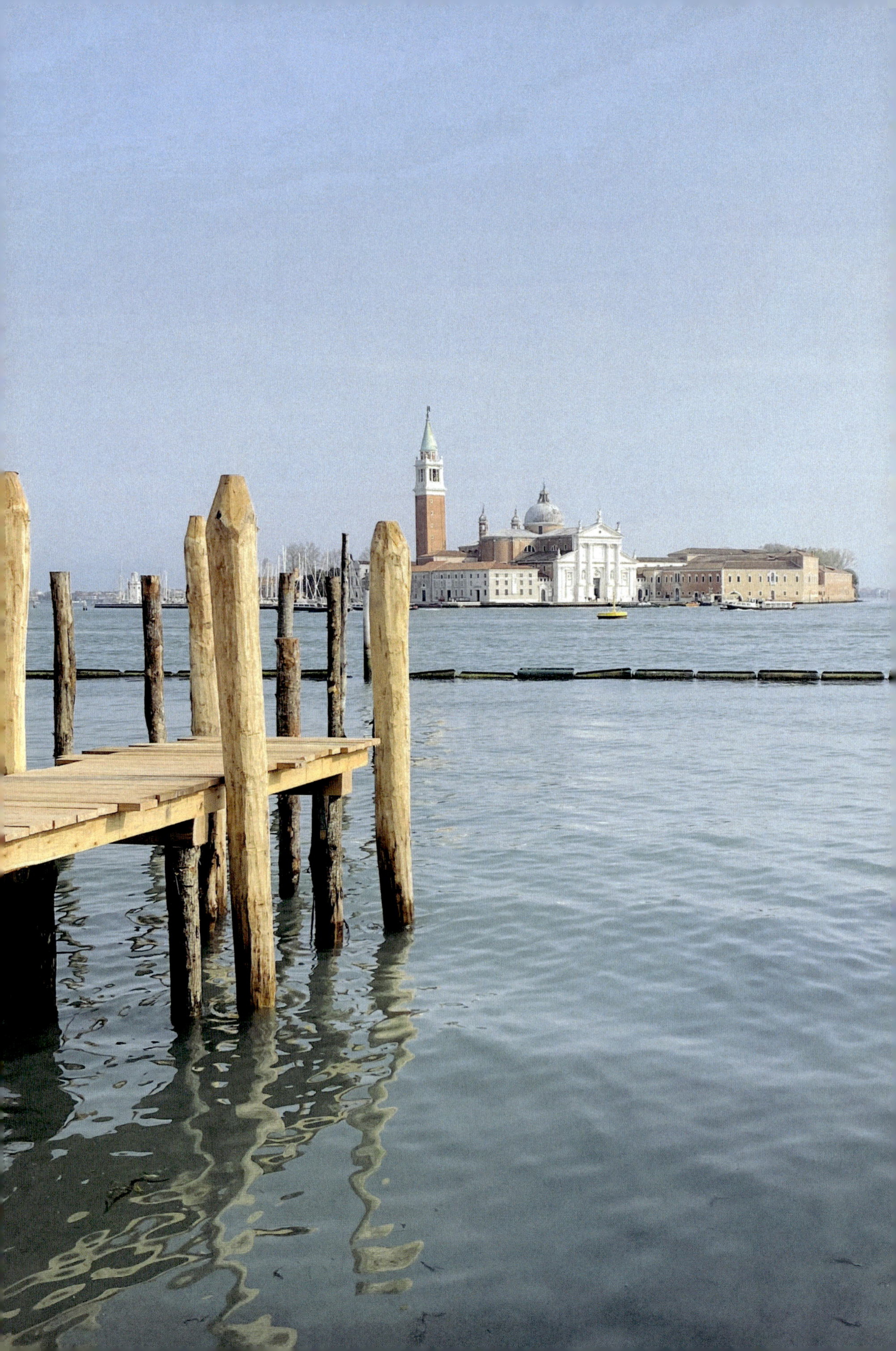

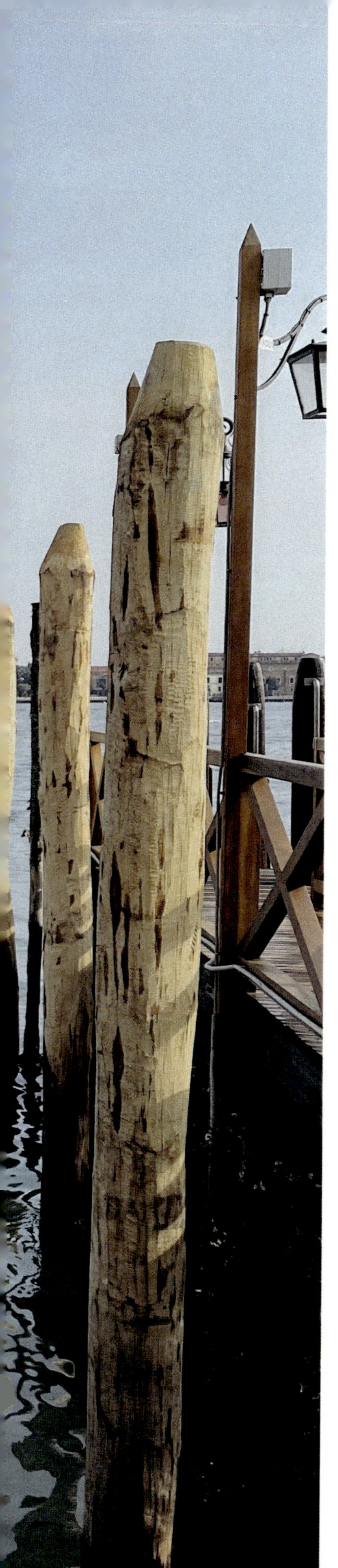

BASILICA DI SAN GIORGIO MAGGIORE BY PALLADIO

The stylish Benedictine church was designed by the Renaissance architect Andrea Palladio and built on the island named San Giorgio Maggiore. The white marble façade is like a Roman temple with its perfect symmetry.

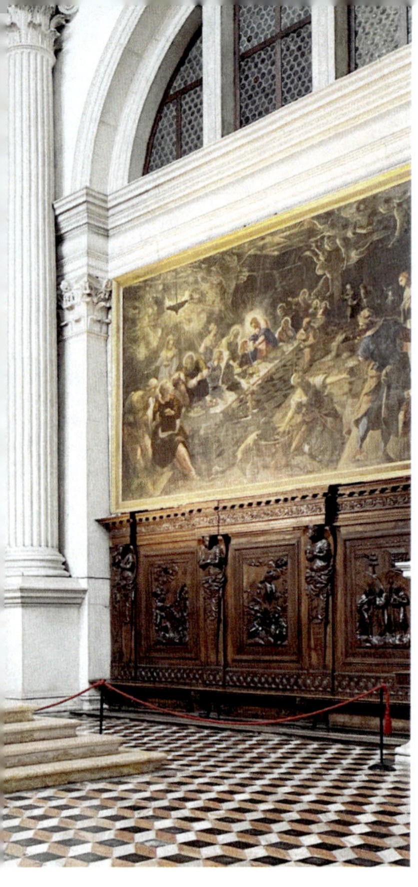

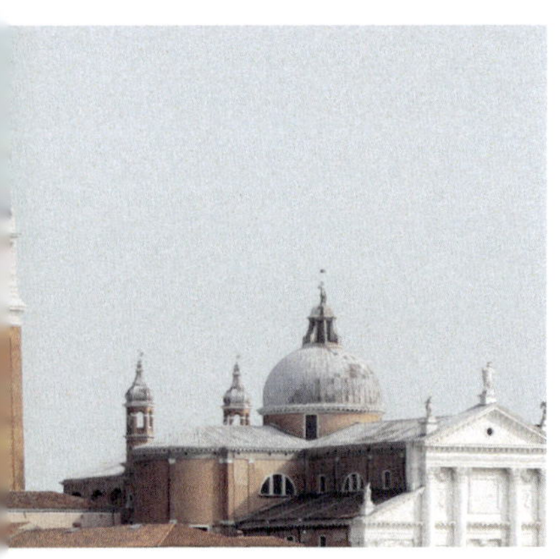

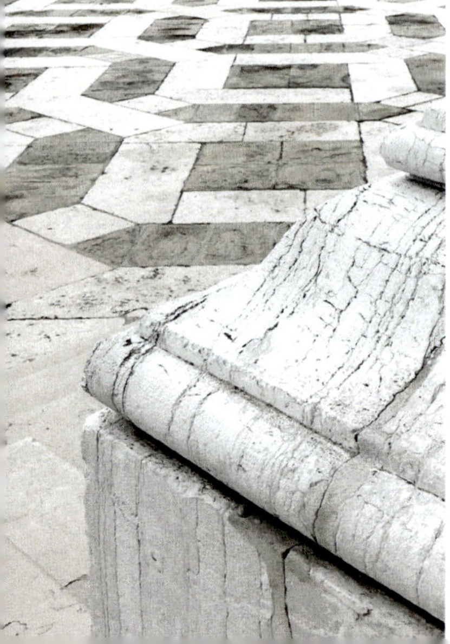

A SHIELD FOR PEACE AND CHRISTIANITY

At the front façade above the door, a coat of arms with soft pastel colours in green, blue, and brown guards the entrance. The coat of arms is designed with symbolic elements including the Pope's triple tiara, the two crossed keys of St. Peter, and a cross bottony with PAX (Peace).

The church interior of the Basilica di San Giorgio Maggiore is light white, with just a few impressive large paintings. One is "Last Supper" by the Renaissance artist Jacopo Tintoretto.

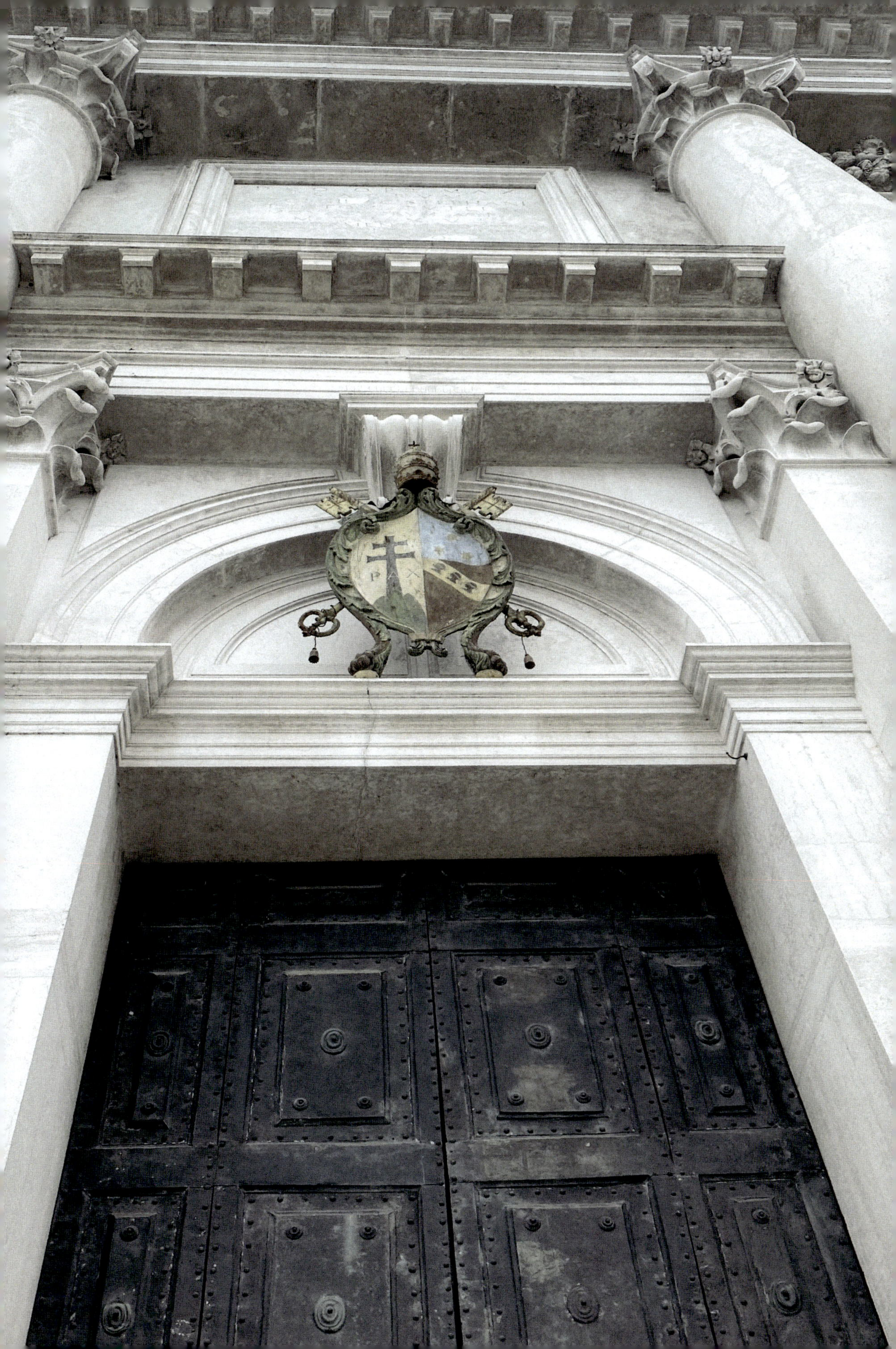
PAX

GIARDINI REALI – NAPOLEON'S GREEN LEGACY

The Royal Gardens (Giardini Reali), also called Napoleon's Gardens, is a green retreat near the waterfront. Napoleon wanted to create a prominent royal garden in Paris's style. The gardens have a great location facing the Venetian Lagoon and Adriatic waterfront, just behind Piazza San Marco. Here, you can find a calm space behind the beautifully designed iron fences, providing a perfect break from the intensity of the city.

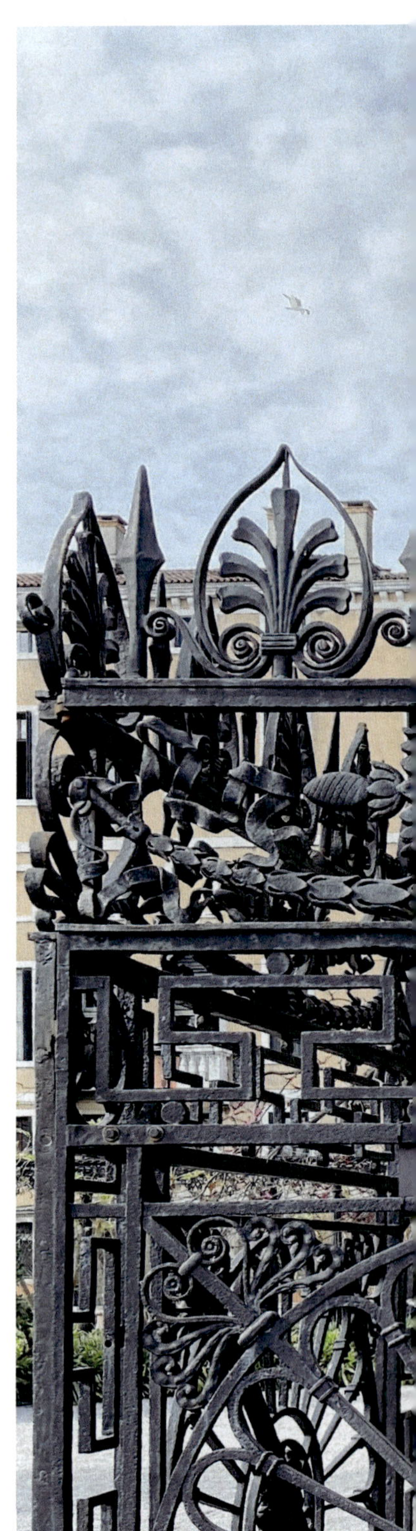

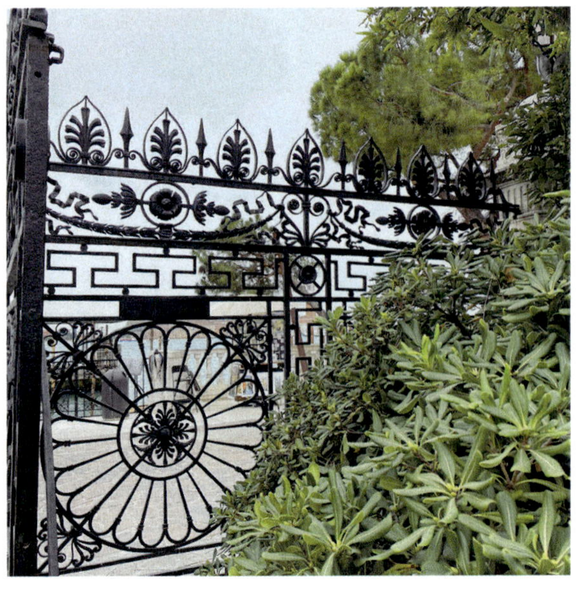

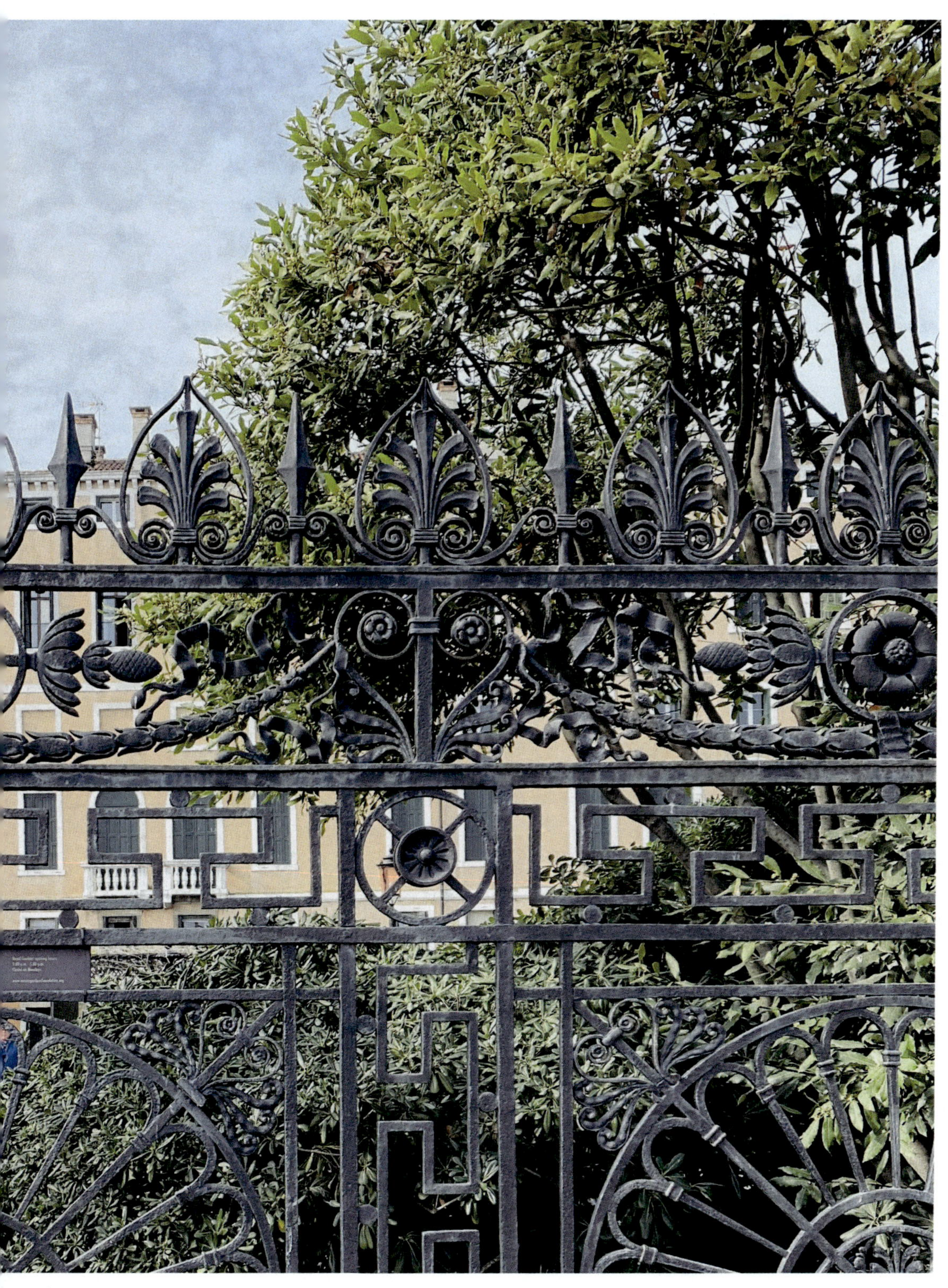

RIVA DEGLI SCHIAVONI – SOAKED IN SUNSHINE

In the afternoon, the waterfront area, Riva degli Schiavoni, is soaked in sunshine. Over centuries, the Venetians have strolled along this adorable seafront promenade, passing by the Doge's Palace and the prominent Palaces, with the skyline of the magnificent, baroque-style church Santa Maria della Salute. Before it turns dark, we give a last Salute to this beautiful city with its endless and timeless beauty and burning red sky.

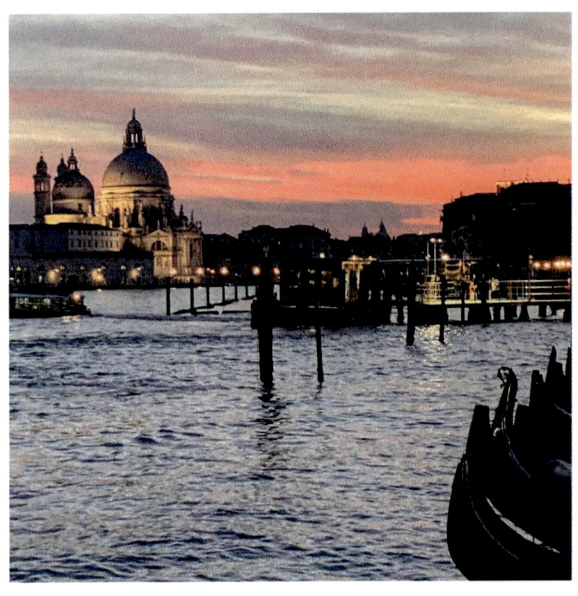

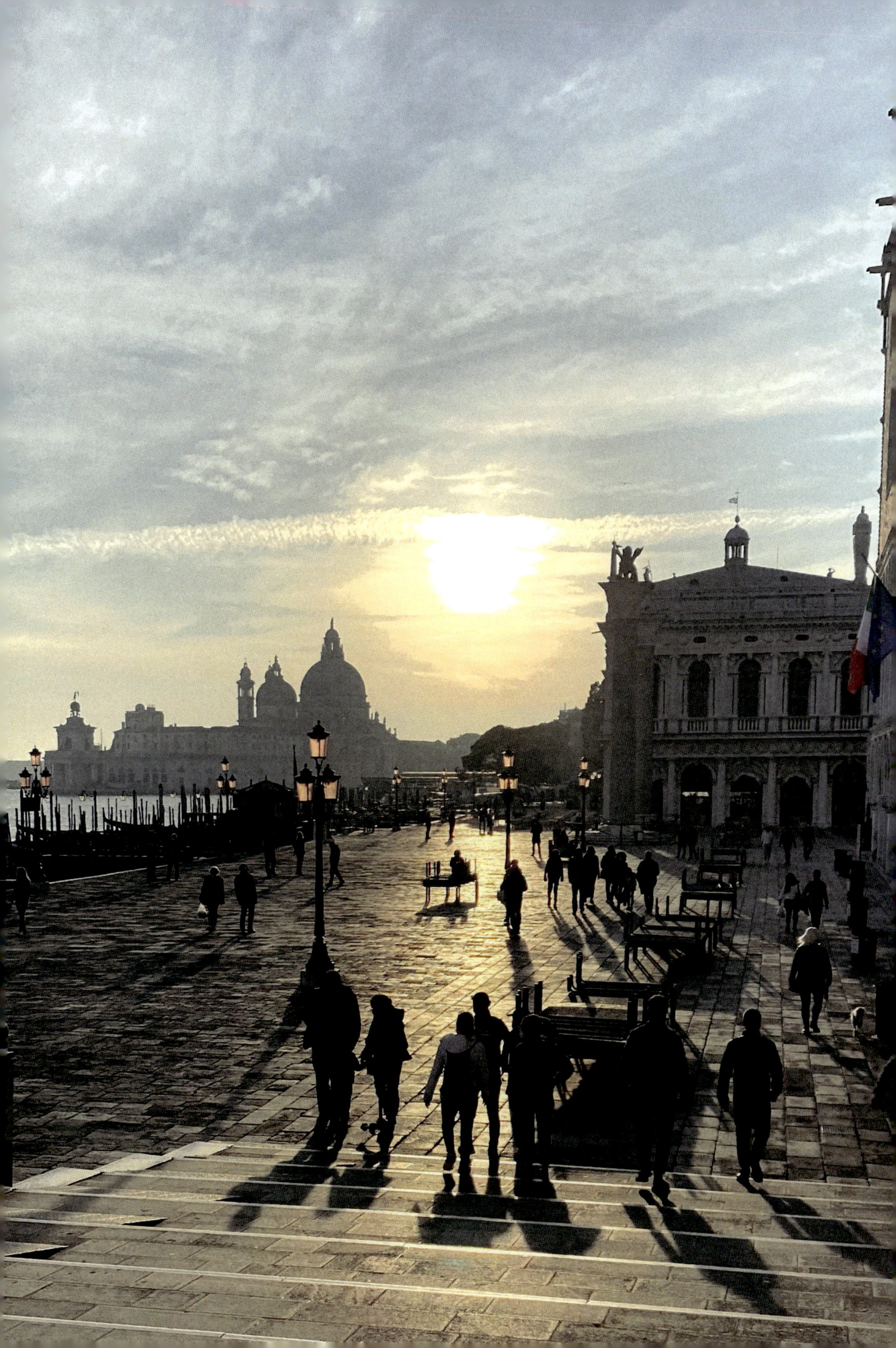

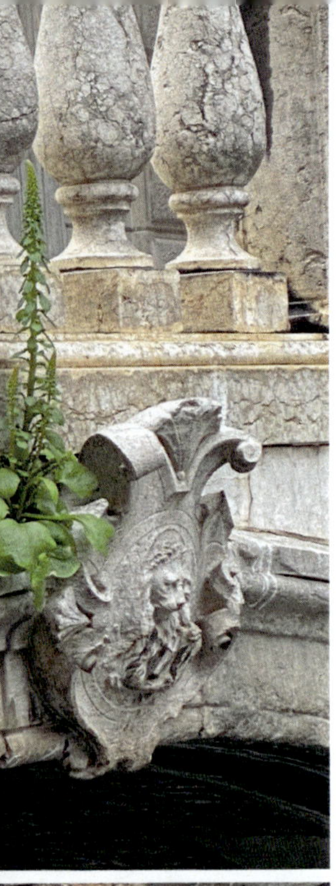

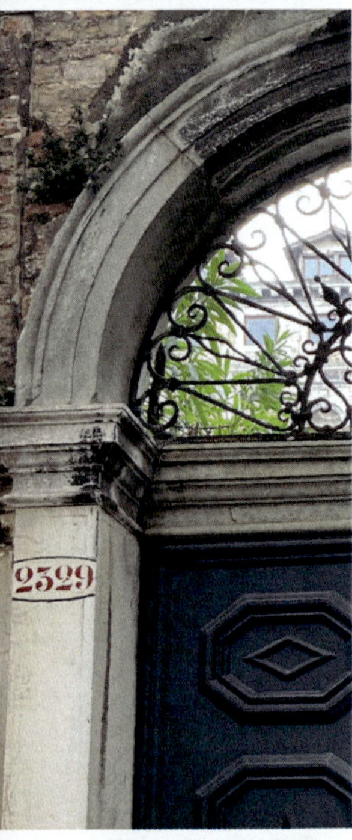

SOURCES AND FURTHER READING

BOOKS, ARTICLES, CREDITS AND WEBSITES

VENICE LEGACY

A History of Venice: Queen of the Seas, Professor Thomas F. Madden, 2010

Doge Palace Venice, Consorzio Museum, 2019

Eyewitness Travel Guides Italy, 2004

Italy Magazine, Inside the Prison of Venice Republic

The Guardian, Patriarchy on the Canal, 2017

The New York Times, Flooding of Venice, 2019

New York Times, Goethe's Italian Journey, 1986

Oddsalon.com, Giacomo Casanova breaks out of Prison, 2016

The Paris Review, True Blue, 2015

The Venetians – A New History: From Marco Polo to Casanova
Paul Strathern, 2014

Venice, Jan Morris, 2004

Worldhistory.org, The Hippodrome of Constantinople, 2017

CREDITS MASTERPIECES

Palazzo Ducale

Il Paradiso, Tintoretto, 1588-1594

Winged Lion of Saint Mark, Vittore Carpaccio, 1516

Gallerie dell'Accademia

San Giobbe Altarpiece, Giovanni Bellini, 1487

Madonna and Child with Saint Catherine and Thomas, Lorenzo Lotto, 1526-28, on loan from Kunsthistorisches Museum, Vienna

Madonna with Child with Saint Catherine of Alexandria and Mary Magdalene, Giovanni Bellini, 1490

Basilica di San Giorgio Maggiore

Last Supper, Tintoretto, 1592-1594

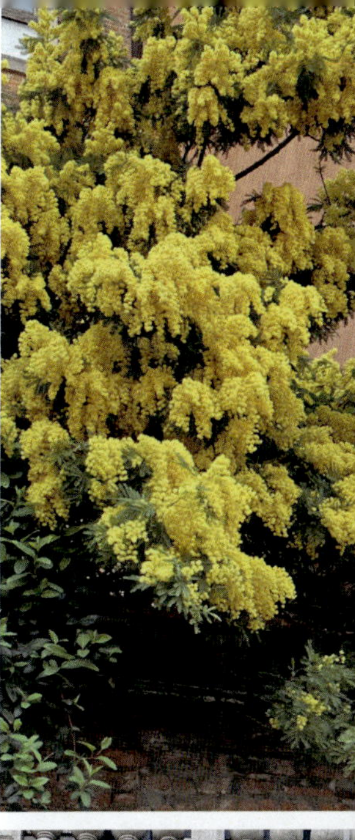

CANALS, BRIDGES, AND GONDOLAS

Citywonders.com

Deepinvenice.com

Explore-italian-culture.com

Gondola-rides-venice.com

Photowalkinvenice.com

Rowvenice.com

Study.com

Veniceinsiderguide.com

Thetravelinpink.com

Visitvenezia.eu

TRAVEL AND OTHER STORIES

Caffevenetico.it

Four-magazine.com, Palatial Paradise Hotel Danieli, 2020

Venice-guide.info

Venetosecrets.com

ART, SCULPTURE AND ARCHITECTURE

Allaboutvenice.com

Architecturaldigest.com

Artsandculture.google.com

Atlasobscura.com

Basilicasanmarco.it

Gallerieaccademia.it

Glassofvenice.com

Imperialporphyry.com

Palazzoducale.visitmuve.it

Savevenice.org

Romeandart.eu

Venecisima.com

Venetoinside.com

FACTS

Britannica.com

Wikipedia.com

Worldhistory.org

Researchgate.net

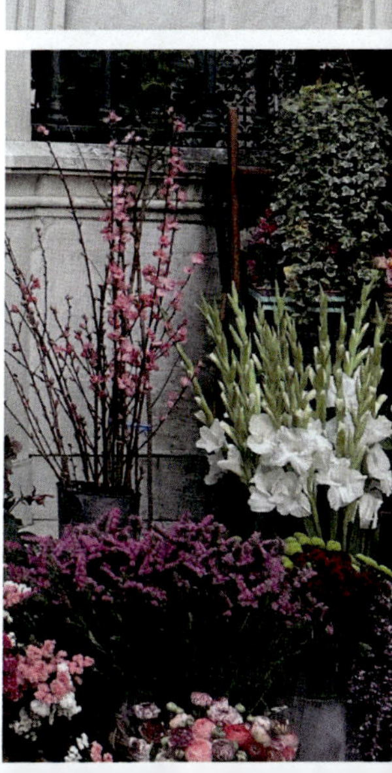

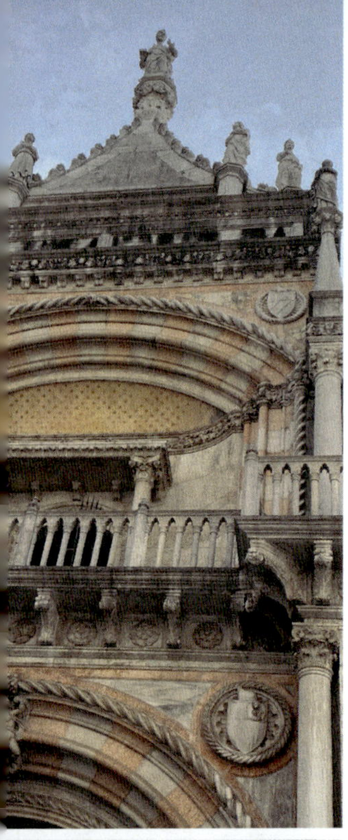

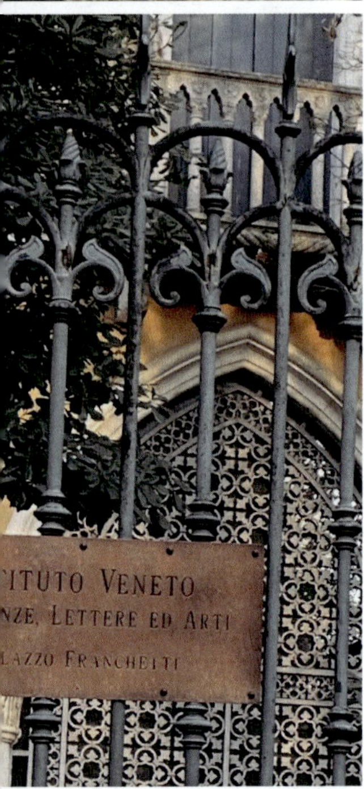

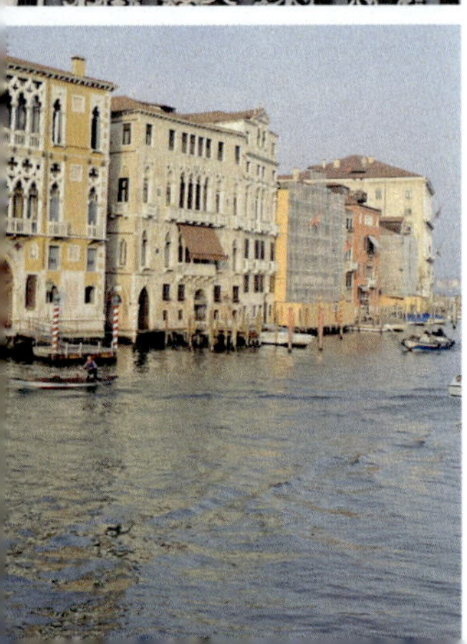

ACKNOWLEDGEMENTS

Thanks to all the friendly Venetians who have shared their knowledge, stories, and passion while working on this book and for being so warm-hearted in every possible way. A special thanks to the gondolier, Nicola, who steered his gondola through the canals as I did the photography work for the book. Thanks also to my lovely family, fantastic Adentity colleagues, and friends for your encouragement and support and for making this book possible.

INFORMATION

First published: June, 2024

Original title: Venice – Impressions of Timeless Beauty

Language: English

Publisher: Adentity, Sweden

Photography & Text: Lina Nicander

Layout: Sophia Wahlgren

ISBN CODE 978-91-527-9997-0

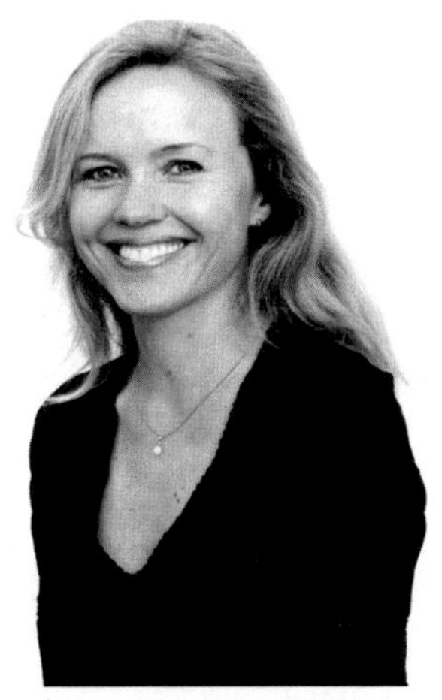

Photo: Fredrik Birkler

ABOUT LINA NICANDER

Lina Nicander is a passionate traveller with a great interest in languages, culture, art, architecture, nature, and history. She has a great love for photography and sharing knowledge, experiences, and stories. She is the founder and co-partner of a successful marketing and communications agency in Sweden. In 2018, Lina published her first book about Sri Lanka, "Explore the Beauty of Sri Lanka". The work with her second book "Venice – Impressions of Timeless Beauty" is a continuation of her endeavour – Photography, stories with a holistic perspective on history, architecture, art, and craft where beauty and timelessness are in focus. Italy has a special place in her heart, expressed in this book.

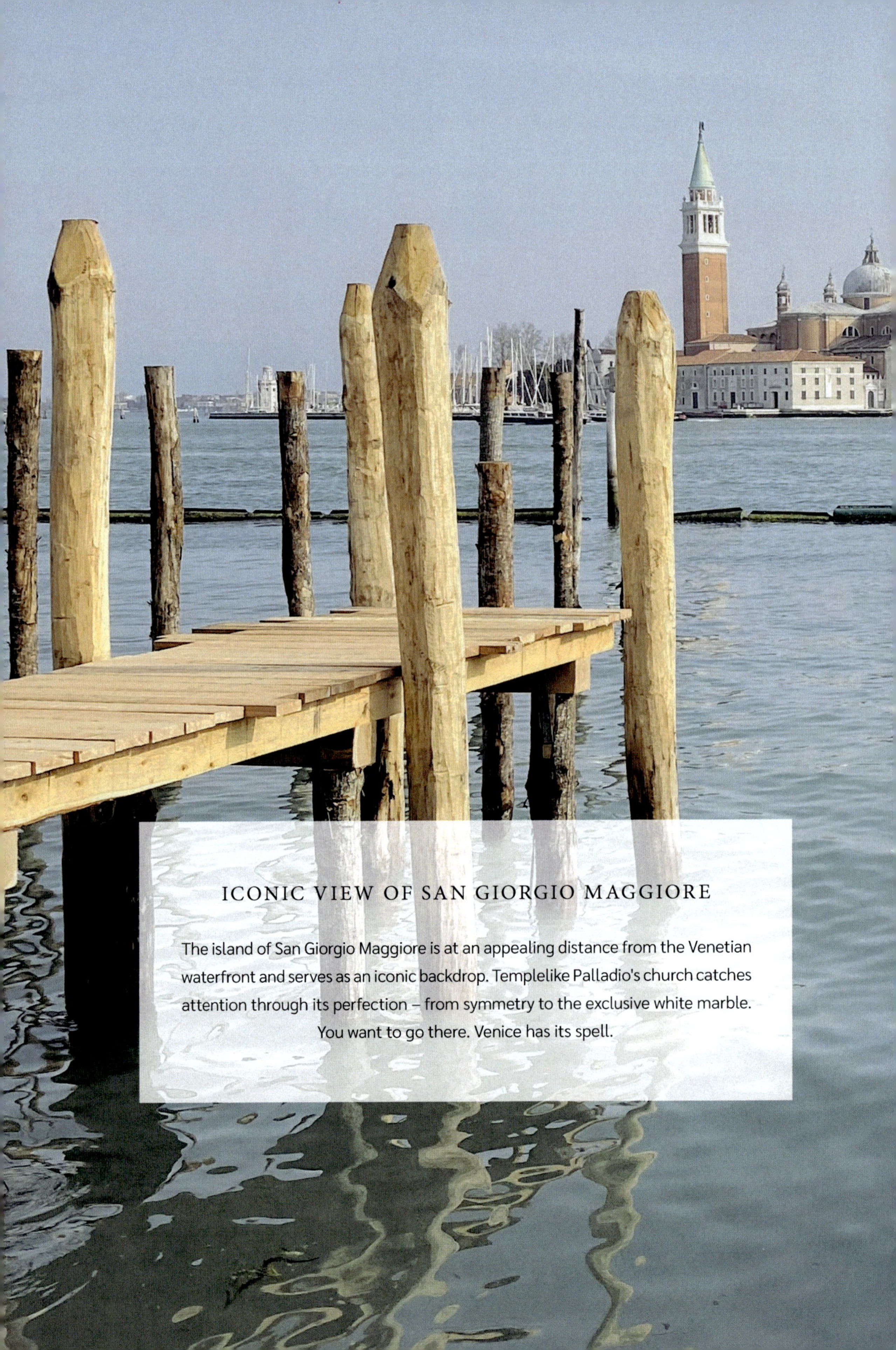

ICONIC VIEW OF SAN GIORGIO MAGGIORE

The island of San Giorgio Maggiore is at an appealing distance from the Venetian waterfront and serves as an iconic backdrop. Templelike Palladio's church catches attention through its perfection – from symmetry to the exclusive white marble. You want to go there. Venice has its spell.

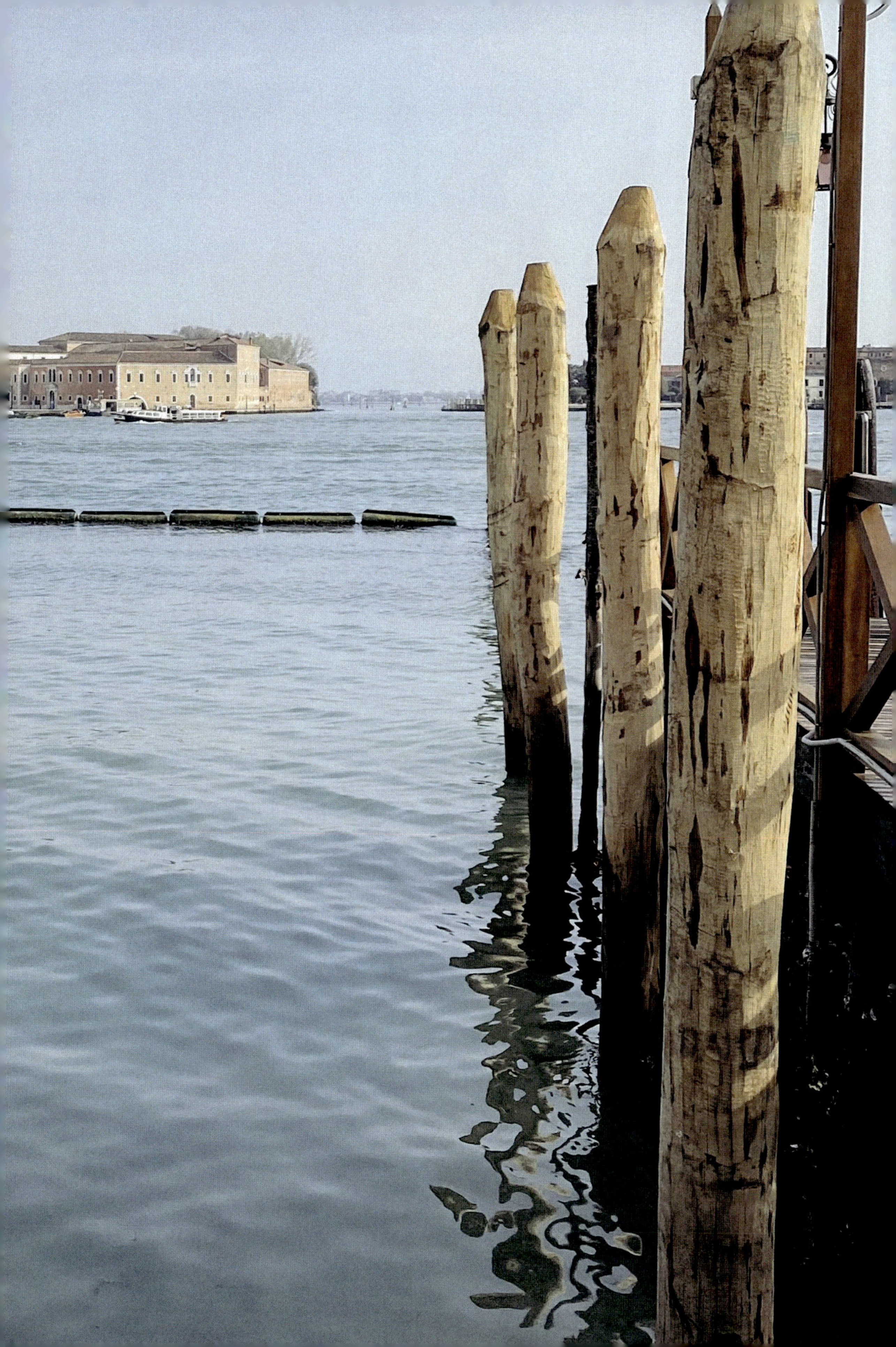

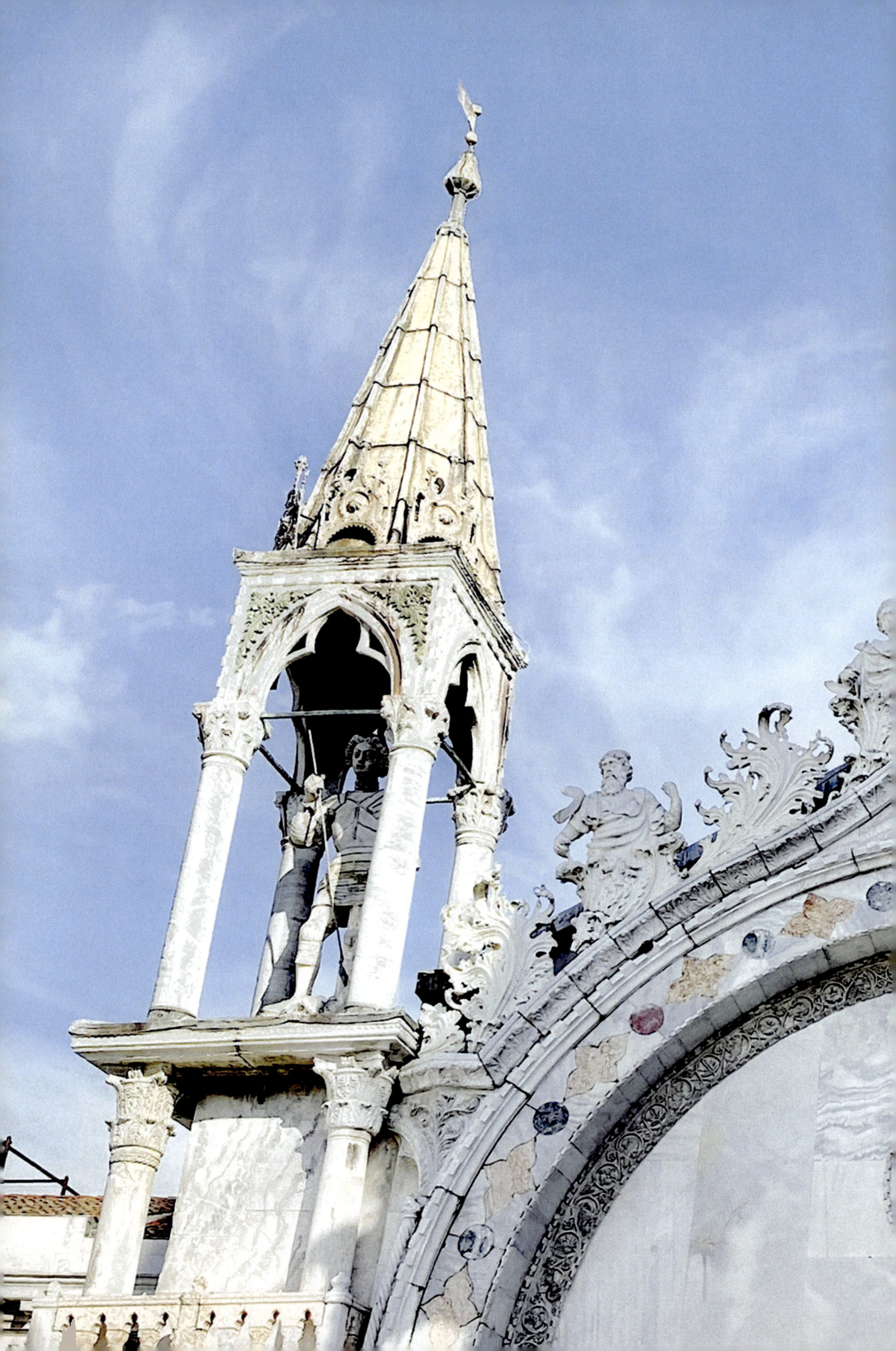

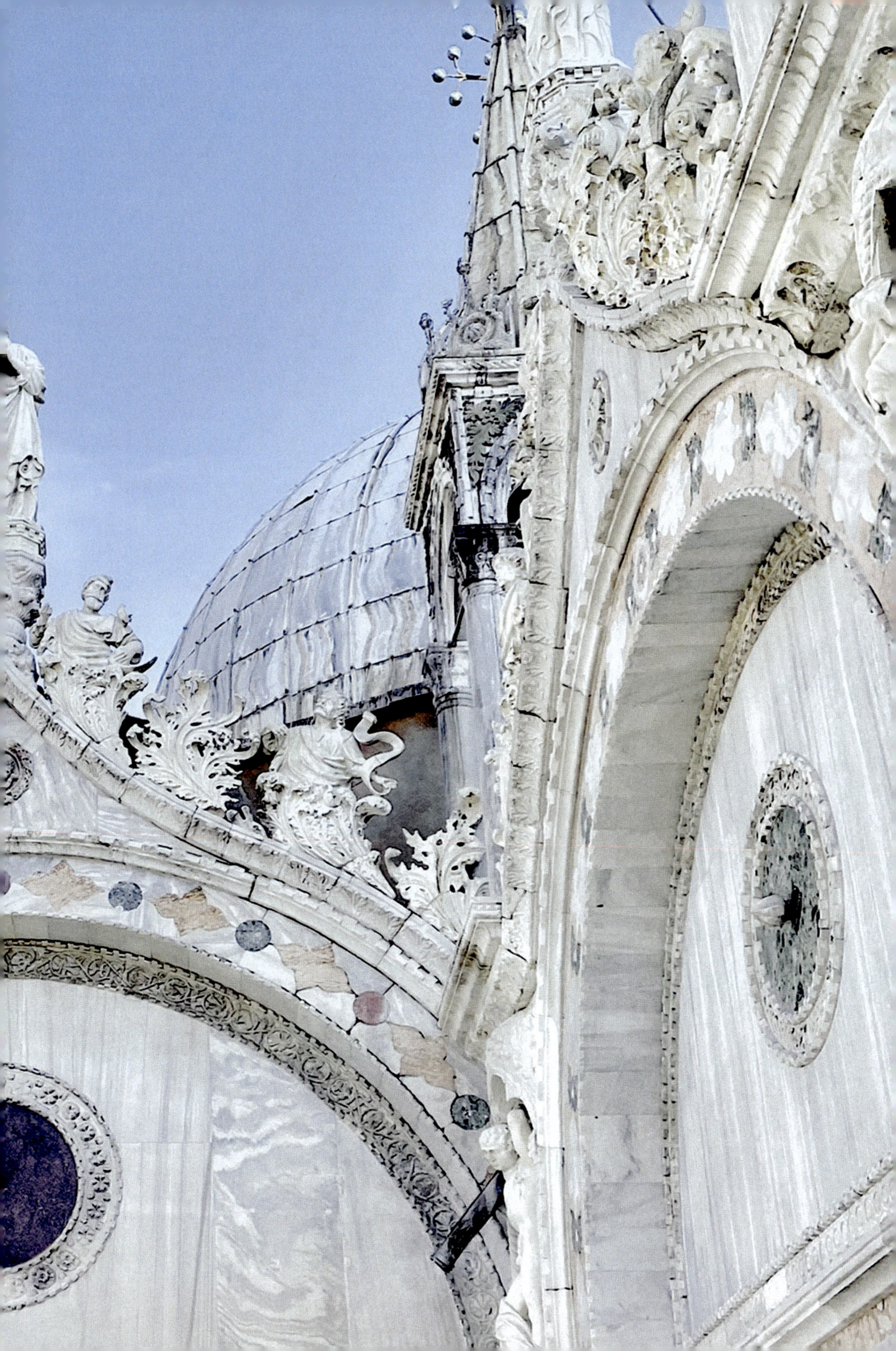

Made in the USA
Columbia, SC
12 February 2025

fddc8b7d-c809-4830-bf1e-c24e93637349R02